In memory
and to the u
of Whitley P4986
shot down 17. August 1940

Ute   bi Edgard

THE
WHITLEY BOYS

*The story of
No. 4 (Bomber) Group's operations
in the first year of WWII*

G. L. 'Larry' Donnelly DFM

AIR RESEARCH PUBLICATIONS

First published 1991.
This edition published 1998
by Air Research Publications
PO Box 223, Walton on Thames
Surrey, KT12 3YQ.
England.

Consultant editor John Foreman.

Printed by Interprint,
Malta.

ISBN 1 871187 36 2

Dedication

To the other 'Few', the bomber crews of 1939/40 including the 'Tradesmen' aircrew, especially those who made the supreme sacrifice.

Contents

Bibliography

The Royal Air Force 1939-1945, Vol.1 The Fight Against Odds.
D Richards HMSO.
The Whitley File. Air Britain (Historians) Ltd.
Bomber Squadrons of the RAF. P Noyes. Macdonald & James
Bomber Command. HMSO 1941.
Bomber Command. M Hastings. Michael Joseph.
Bomber Offensive. Marshal of the RAF Sir Arthur Harris.
Greenhill Books.
The Strategic Air Offensive Against Germany 1939-1945.
Sir Charles Webster & Dr Noble Frankland. HMSO 1961.
Before the Storm. R Jackson. Arthur Barker Ltd.
Out of the Blue. Laddie Lucas. Hutchinson & Co.
Pathfinder. AVM D C T Bennett CB CBE DSO
Frederick Muller Ltd.
Norway 1940. Bernard Ash. Cassell.
Only Owls and Bloody Fools Fly at Night.
Gp Cpt T Sawyer. Kimber.
The Bomber Command War Diaries.
M Middlebrook & C Everitt. Viking.
The Merlin at War. I Lloyd. McMillan.
The WWII Fact Book. C Campbell. Mcdonald.
2 Group. M J Bowyer. Faber and Faber.
The 'Phoney War' on the Home Front. E S Turner. Joseph.
Public Record Office Files:
AIR25/93,96,98.AIR27/141,147,491,495,498,543,
546,548,655,659A&B,807,812.AIR22/311,312.
AIR10/2096. AIR35/349. AVIA15/150.
RAF Air Publications:
AP.982 Wireless Operator's 'X' Code Book.
AP.1186 RAF Signals Vols. I & III.
AP.1695D. RAF Armaments Vol. I.
AP.1522. Whitley V. Pilots' Notes.
AP.2276. RAF SignalsVol. I.
AHB Monograph. Armament.
Weather Charts from the National Meteorological Archive,
Bracknell.

Foreword

By

Group Captain T. G. 'Hamish' Mahaddie DSO, DFC, AFC & Bar, CzMC, FrAeS, RAF (Retd.)

I admit to a deal of embarrassment in being invited to write a foreword to my Oppo Larry Donnelly's tome, The Whitley Boys, as I am sure that there are better candidates among the Whitley survivors still at large. Certainly those who have now left us would, I am sure, have taken much pride and a measure of nostalgia in recalling those early days and nights of WWII that were so eventful. I recall my first Whitley sortie which involved crews from my squadron, No. 77, and from No. 102 Squadron both of which were based at Driffield. It was to take a load of propaganda leaflets to the Ruhr via Kiel, just a quiet cross-country exercise, no Flak or fighters and oddly enough only two searchlights which seemed to be denoting the northern and southern boundaries of the Ruhr. The bundles of leaflets were stowed in large paper parcels that were to be 'decanted' by the second pilot, a famous 4 Group character called Spike Edmonds, and the W/T operator. As Larry describes here the bundles had to be untied and released down the flare chute, but our wireless operator got fed up with cutting the strings and taking off elastic bands and pushed the bundles down the chute intact. Spike remonstrated with him and reminded him very crossly that he must cut the string, otherwise some ****** squarehead might be hurt if one fell on his head!

After dropping the leaflets we set course for home, but inadvertently strayed over neutral Belgium whose authorities resented our intrusion of their airspace and sent up fighters to 'invite' us to land. How we managed to extricate ourselves from that situation is also described within these pages.

The Phoney War gave 4 Group much time for training in actual war conditions and the group was well represented on what is acclaimed as the first night-bombing sortie of the war, namely the bombing of the German seaplane base of Hornum on the island of Sylt on March 19th/20th, 1940. It took the Butt Report of late 1941 to focus attention on just how badly the bomber offensive could be measured in terms of damage to the Third Reich. The army and navy were swift to clamour for the liquidation of Bomber Command, but help was at hand. Early in 1942 Sir Arthur Harris left the Air Ministry and became Commander-in-Chief Bomber Command.

Possibly the biggest single factor to redress the situation was Harris's Thousand Plan, when he devised a scheme to put 1,000 bombers over a large German target in less than one hour. It was put into practice at the end of May, 1942, resulting in the devastation of Cologne and a reprieve for the Bomber Offensive.

Shortly after the success of the Cologne raid, Harris was ordered by the Air Ministry to form a target finding and marking force called the Path Finder Force. Despite his fierce opposition to what Harris called a *Corps Elite*, the Air Ministry insisted that the Path Finders were essential to spearhead the force of 3,500 bombers envisaged for the offensive and he was over ruled. Kindly note, dear reader, that whilst the Chiefs of Air Staff Committee set aside some 3,500 bombers for the task of neutralising the Third Reich's capacity to continue the war, on the last day of hostilities the Command's first line strength was still less than half of the envisaged figure. In my opinion had Harris possessed the full complement of aircraft required for the task, he would have completed it earlier.

I commend you to this book, describing as it does 4 Group's operations during 1939 and 1940 as experienced by the tradesmen aircrew. It will prove a well researched contribution to the history of the bombing war. It is worth recalling that 4 Group was a nursery for many of the great master bombers who were able to develop the Harris Offensive as it improved year on year until final victory. I name but a few of those outstanding characters; Len Cheshire, Willie Tait, Jimmy Marks, Don Bennett, Johnny Fauquier and 'Moose' Fulton among a host of others of that ilk.

'Hamish' Mahaddie

Introduction

During the 1930s, Hitler's rise to power in Germany and his policy of rearmament were ominous indications of the possibility of war. As a consequence of this, the British Government gave priority to the expansion and rearming of the armed forces with the Royal Navy receiving first priority and the Air Home Defence Force, second. Third priority was given to any offensive action which might be taken, resulting in the formation of RAF Bomber Command on 14th July, 1936, with its Headquarters at RAF Uxbridge. It initially controlled four groups; Nos. 1, 2, 3 and 6, the latter an auxiliary group. No. 4 Group was added on 1st April, 1937, with Air Commodore T. A. Harris (as he then was) as its first Air Officer Commanding. During World War Two, 'Bomber' Harris was to become the Command's most famous Commander-in-Chief. A further group, No. 5, was added on 1st September, 1937, with Air Commodore W. B. Calloway as Air Officer Commanding.

The Air Ministry during this time was giving priority to the design and production of heavy bombers. The requirements for these were maximum range and bomb load with a crew compliment of two pilots, two air gunners and one wireless operator. This resulted in the acceptance of the Wellington, Whitley and Hampden twin-engine 'heavy' bombers with which No. 3 (Wellington), No. 4 (Whitley) and No. 5 (Hampden) Groups were equipped.

The Whitley Mk. 1, a mid-wing monoplane powered by two Armstrong Siddeley Tiger IX engines, first entered service at the beginning of March, 1937, No. 10 Squadron being the first 4 Group unit to be equipped with this aircraft. Re- equipment of the other squadrons in the group followed in due course.

The Whitley was the first RAF heavy bomber to have a retractable undercarriage, turreted defensive armament and be designed purely for night operations. Replacing the Handley-Page Heyford biplane, its load carrying capacity, performance and sturdy construction were improvements on its predecessors. Development continued and new versions of the Whitley with improved power plants, bomb carrying capacity and defensive armament entered service. However, at the outbreak of WWII in September, 1939, a good proportion of 4 Group's squadrons were still equipped with the Tiger engined versions, which in the opinion of the former Armstrong Whitworth chief test pilot fell short of the requirements for efficient long range bomber operations in adverse weather conditions. He commented,

"I don't think the Air Ministry fully appreciated when the Whitley was designed, what a bomber crew would need in the way of comfort and space on long range missions. There were too many sharp corners which had to be padded and heating was almost non-existent until the Rolls-Royce Merlin engines were fitted, after which there was some improvement."

All the troubles on the Whitley Mks. I, II and III were due to the Tiger engines which were unreliable. My log book told a real tale of woe with engine failures on test after test. I was therefore delighted when I heard the news early in 1938 that it had been decided to fit Merlins."*

The first Merlin engined Whitley, the Mk. IV, entered service in May 1939, when once again No. 10 Squadron at Dishforth were the first 4 Group unit to receive them. The Mk. IV proved to be more reliable with regard to the engines, but it still lacked suitable defensive armament. Like the Mk. III it only had a single Vickers Gas Operated machine gun, known as the VGO, in a power operated front turret, twin Browning .303s in a power operated mid-under turret and a single VGO in a manually operated tail turret. Defensive armament was slightly improved with the introduction of the Mk. V, which was equipped with four Brownings in a power operated tail turret. The mid-under turret was then deleted. No. 77 Squadron at RAF Driffield received the first Mk. Vs on 27th September, 1939, but the rest of the group did not complete the conversion to Mk. Vs until May, 1940.

Despite its improvements the Mk. V had its short comings and its cruising speed was still only 135-140 mph, if you were lucky! It enjoyed the affection of most crews who overlooked its drawbacks and appreciated the handling qualities and sturdy construction which enabled it to absorb considerable punishment. A fitting comment was;

"She may be slow and ugly, but thank God she's built like a brick out-house!"

Air-vice Marshal D. T. C. Bennett, CB, CBE, DSO, recalling the Whitley in his memoirs stated,

"This very good work horse did a job quite as well as the more famous Wellington".**

The expansion of the RAF which lead to the creation of Bomber Command also included a requirement for an additional 2,500 pilots,

*The Whitley File, Air Britain (Historians) Ltd.
**Pathfinder, Air-Vice Marshal D. T. C. Bennett. Goodall Publications Ltd.

Forerunner of the Whitley, the Armstrong Whitworth A.W.23, K3585. (Chaz Bowyer).

The Whitley Mk.I prototype, K4586, which made its first flight on March 17th, 1936. (Chaz Bowyer).

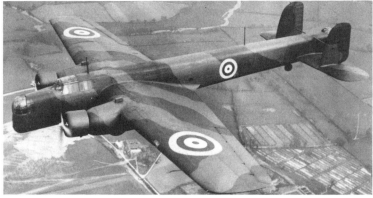

Whitley Mk.I, K7191, seen here in pre-war colours, served with No.10 Squadron before the war and went on to No.166 Squadron and No. 7 BGS. (Chaz Bowyer).

2,069 air-observers, 3,867 wireless operator/air gunners (WOP/AGs) and 554 air-gunners. These WOP/AGs and gunners were to be employed as full time aircrew, a change from the existing policy of employing ground crew tradesmen in a part time aircrew capacity, which was now considered to be impractical. It was therefore decided, in 1938, that in future WOP/AGs should be drawn from the ranks of boy entrant wireless operators and they should be employed continuously on aircrew duties. After three years as WOP/AG, 25% would be selected as Air Observers.* However, before this plan could be implemented it was overtaken by the outbreak of WWII. The existing tradesmen aircrew were incorporated as full time aircrew members, continuing in their lowly rank and status. For their extra duties they were paid the munificent sum of one shilling and sixpence (7.5p) per day 'flying pay' bonus in addition to their trade pay. It was not until 27th May, 1940, that their status was improved and it was decreed that the lowest aircrew rank would be that of sergeant. All the surviving operational tradesmen were promoted and from this date all WOP/AGs and gunners were given the rank of sergeant on successful completion of their training.

This is the narrative record of 4 Group Whitley bomber operations during the first year of WWII as recalled by one of the afore mentioned tradesmen aircrew. It covers the months of the so-called 'Phoney War' when Whitley crews carried out 'Bumph' (leaflet) raids and reconnaissance over Germany, Austria, Poland, and Czechoslovakia as well as offensive 'sweeps' over the North Sea and security patrols over the German mine-laying seaplane bases During this time crews had to contend with the German anti aircraft defences as well as the hazardous flying conditions of the atrocious winter of 1939/40.

When Germany invaded Norway and Denmark the Whitley crews took part in bombing raids against German shipping and occupied airfields. These were followed by attacks on German troops and road/rail communications during the invasion of France and the Low Countries. After the evacuation of the remnants of the British Expeditionary Force from Dunkirk and the fall of France the Whitley squadrons, along with their Wellington and Hampden counterparts, commenced the strategic night bombing against Germany. The shipping and material which Hitler was assembling in the occupied ports for the projected invasion of Britain also became targets. Night

*RAF Signals, Vol.III.

after night the aircraft of this small force ranged far and wide over Germany and Occupied Europe, flying in all weather conditions to carry out attacks against heavily defended targets.

Post-war historians have referred to these attacks as nuisance raids which seldom caused much damage, but they cannot deny the profound effects the raids had on the moral of the apprehensive population of Britain. It was the lessons learnt by the crews involved in operations over Germany during the first year of the war which resulted in Bomber Command becoming such a mighty force later. The contribution of the Whitley squadrons of 4 Group was considerable. Before the end of the first week of the war all five operational squadrons of the group had carried out raids over Germany, the first of the bomber groups to do so, and during the first year they achieved other notable 'Firsts':-

3rd-4th September, 1939. First RAF aircraft to fly over the German mainland.

1st-2nd October, 1939. First RAF aircraft to fly over Berlin.

12th-13th January, 1940. First RAF aircraft to fly over Occupied Czechoslovakia and Austria.

7th-8th March, 1940. First RAF aircraft to fly over Occupied Poland.

19th-20th March, 1940. First RAF bombing attack against a German land target.*

11th-12th June, 1940. First RAF bombing attack against an Italian target.

25th-26th August 1940. First RAF bombing attack against Berlin.**

*This raid was shared with Hampdens of 5 Group.
**This raid included Hampdens of 5 Group and Wellingtons of 3 Group.

13

Acknowledgements

My sincere thanks are due to the following: Norman Franks, my guide and mentor, for his invaluable assistance. My Whitley contemporaries, Group Captain 'Hamish' Mahaddie for his foreword, Squadron Leader J. Verran of No. 102 Squadron and Pilot Officer Harry Welte of No. 58 Squadron. Squadron Leader R. Chance and Flight Lieutenant M. Lucas of No. 77 Squadron for their accounts. Squadron Leader J. G. Cairns, Flight Lieutenant M. Niman and Flying Officer G. F. Dove of No. 10 Squadron for their photographs and experiences. Chaz Bowyer for the use of his photographs. Mr G. Day of the Air Historical Branch for guiding my research into the Bomber Command 'loss' cards. The staff of the Public Record Office, Kew, and the photographic department of the RAF Museum, Hendon. Misses Greta and Mariann Fleischman for their translating. Herr Werner Eckel for his account of the 'Tomlin' incident and my dear wife for her tolerance and understanding while I lived in the past, writing *The Whitley Boys*.

14

Chapter One

Tradesmen Aircrew

As far back as I can remember I have had an abiding interest in aeroplanes and anything to do with flying. When I was a schoolboy in the early thirties the aeroplane was still something of a novelty and whenever one flew over our remote part of the country I would watch until it disappeared from sight. If, by chance, it was from the nearest RAF station, some 40 miles away, and performed aerobatics my imagination and fantasies ran riot.

Most of my meagre pocket money was spent on aero-modelling kits and books relating to flying. I was an ardent fan of W. C. Johns' immortal Biggles and I avidly read books describing the exploits of the WWI aces, Mannock, Bishop, Collishaw, McCudden, Ball, Guynemer, Fonck, Boelke, Immelmann and Richthofen. All this stimulated my imagination and desire to fly.

At this time the only opportunity for anyone other than the wealthy section of our society to learn to fly, or fly in any capacity, was to join the Royal Air Force, but recruitment was very selective. However, in 1936 Hitler's aggressive activities in Europe resulted in the decision to increase the strength of our armed forces, particularly the RAF, thus enhancing the opportunities for the air-minded youngsters like myself. So, shortly after leaving school and unbeknown to my parents, I presented myself at the nearest RAF recruiting office, offering my services and requesting to be trained as a pilot. I was lucky that the recruiting sergeant treated my request with amused tolerance. Instead of throwing me out and telling me to come back when I had grown up, he tactfully explained that I was far too young and didn't have the necessary qualifications. He did explain that if I enlisted as an airman there would be other opportunities to fly, for instance, as a wireless-operator or air-gunner. Also as a tradesman, after I had served for two years and/or reached Leading Aircraftsman status, I would have the opportunity to apply to re-muster as sergeant pilot or air observer.

Armed with all the printed recruiting propaganda I could carry, I returned home. At what I considered an opportune moment I asked my parents for their permission to enlist, which the recruiting sergeant had informed me was a requirement because I was under age. To my intense disappointment they refused, saying that I was far too young to embark on such a venture. They did offer a glimmer of hope by telling me that they would reconsider if I was of the same mind when I was older. Not to be put off I enlisted the support of an ally in the shape of my uncle, who had previously been a ship's wireless operator and who was now employed by the RAF in a civilian capacity at RAF Cranwell. His job was to instruct young would-be wireless operators in sending and receiving Morse Code. He knew of my intense interest in aviation and the RAF and at my request promised to talk to my parents and convince them that life in the RAF would be just the thing for a keen young lad. He also advised me that if I decided to become a wireless operator it would be a good idea to do some preparation before attempting to enlist. He loaned me his copy of the Admiralty Handbook on Electrics and Wireless Telegraphy, and I set about assimilating its mysteries. I saved my pocket money and purchased a Morse key and battery operated buzzer with which I attempted to master the art of sending and receiving the Morse Code.

During the months that followed the incessant rasp of the Morse buzzer must have driven my parents to distraction, but it eventually had the desired effect. I think they reached the conclusion that my intentions were serious and not just a passing phase. The reassurance of my uncle, who promised to keep an eye on me if I went to Cranwell, had a further influence and so my parents gave their permission for me to join the RAF. Highly elated I submitted my application and in time, after successfully passing the entrance and medical examinations, I was accepted by the RAF and sent to Cranwell to be trained as a wireless operator.

I took to service life like a duck to water, even the square bashing, rifle drill and strict discipline did not deter me. In charge of all the recruits was 'Mister' Billings, the station warrant officer, whose stentorian bellow of 'Boy' or 'Airman', petrified everyone within earshot. The facilities provided and the opportunities to indulge in the numerous sporting activities far outweighed anything previously available to me in civilian life and more than compensated for any of the more irksome parts of our training.

My pre-enlistment homework with the Admiralty Handbook and the Morse buzzer paid dividends and I was able to progress through the technical training, but of course for me the highlight was flying. My enthusiasm to get airborne as soon as I could resulted in my first run in with authority. It happened shortly after I arrived at Cranwell.

Each Saturday morning we participated in the station colour-hoisting parade, when we were inspected and marched past the commanding officer, a painless procedure which everyone accepted as a matter of course, it was the aftermath which was the bind. After being marched back to the domestic area we were detailed to carry out fatigues for the rest of the morning. This was looked upon by the powers that be as an essential part of our character building process.

After two such Saturday mornings my enthusiasm for cleaning the ablutions and washing greasy pans in the cook-house waned, so after the next parade I skived off and went to the aerodrome to watch the flying and hopefully scrounge a flight. There was not much flying activity, but after pestering one of the ground crew working on the parked machines he told me that the D. H. Rapide he was working on would soon go on an air test and pointed out the pilot who would be flying it. Luckily for me he was a sergeant pilot, for I would not have had the nerve to approach an officer, and I asked him if I could go on the air test. To my pleasure and surprise he told me to get my name put in the flight authorisation book and join the other two tradesmen who were to accompany him. I did as bid and eventually climbed aboard where I took my place in one of the canvas seats in the fuselage. Soon the engines started and it was not long before we were taxiing out to take off. When the time came for take off I hung onto my seat for all I was worth. Being my very first flight my excitement was tinged with a certain amount of apprehension, but as the D. H. left the ground and climbed away my trepidation subsided and I settled down to enjoy my first sortie into the wide blue yonder. It exceeded all my expectations and even though the flying conditions were slightly turbulent I am glad to say that I did not feel any inclination to get rid of my breakfast. The flight only lasted 45 minutes, but it had really whetted my appetite and I was sorry when we landed and taxied back to the parking area. Thanking my pilot, I made my way back to join the others who were returning from their fatigues. They told me that my absence had been noticed by the discipline corporal. When he confronted me and asked where I had been, I proudly admitted that I had been flying. He nearly blew a gasket. "Flying!" he bellowed, "you're on a Fizzer!* Your feet won't touch the deck until you see the CO!" The tragic outcome was seven day's Jankers, which meant being confined to camp and having to report to the guardroom every morning, noon and night for seven

* Form 252 - Charge Sheet.

days. I had to wear full webbing equipment and back packs and the SPs. subjected me to rigorous inspections. In the evening this was followed by a session on fatigues. However, I considered this was a small price to pay for my introduction to flying.

My first official flight took place two weeks later when all the members of our course were marched to the South 'Drome where we boarded a twin engined Vickers Valentia biplane bomber / transport aircraft for what was described as an air experience flight. Just before the aircraft taxied out one of the ground crew airmen brought in a large steel bucket which he fixed to the floor in the centre of the fuselage. There was no mistaking its purpose, especially when he announced with a leer, "Have a good trip Sprogs, but remember who ever uses it cleans it." Having been blooded by my previous flight in the Rapide I had no qualms and although the old Valentia was slow and lumbering I enjoyed the short time we were airborne. I was convinced that I was in my element. However, not so some of my less fortunate companions, who had recourse to the bucket and paid the penalty when we landed.

After that initial taste of the air we had to wait until we reached the final phase of our training for our next flying session. It was worth waiting for because instead of the Valentia we flew in single-engine Wapiti bi-planes. In our estimation they were our idea of 'real' aeroplanes. This final part of our training was to give us practice in air-to-ground W/T communication. For each flight we were kitted out with Sidcot flying suits, leather flying helmets, goggles, parachutes and harness - we were real aviators at last. Before our first flight we were briefed by a grizzled old flight sergeant, wearing the old wireless-operator's 'Sparks' badge and the air-gunner's 'winged bullet'. After covering the tasks we were to carry out and the flight safety procedures he ended his talk by sadistically offering the advice, "If any of you lads think you'll be air sick, eat strawberry jam before you go."

My first flight in the Wapiti was memorable. Attired in an oversized Sidcot and an over-tight parachute harness I was assisted into the open rear cockpit by one of the ground crew who told me not to forget to attach the Monkey Chain. This was a webbing strap attached to the floor which clipped onto a metal loop on the parachute harness between your legs - the only means of preventing you from inadvertently falling out of the aircraft.

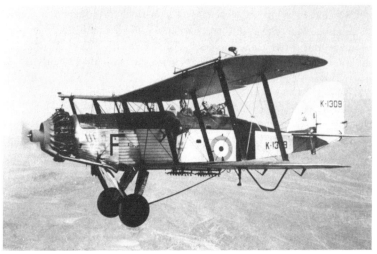

The Westland Wapiti, similar to the one I made my first 'real' flight in from Cranwell. (Chaz Bowyer)

Once safely on board I stowed my 'chute and connected my helmet lead to the W/T set. the pilot gave a thumbs up sign, turned the aircraft into wind and opened the throttle. The Wapiti gathered speed and before I knew it we were airborne, climbing away from the aerodrome and heading over the fields of Lincolnshire for the east coast. The weather was good with only one or two fluffy fair weather cumulus and the visibility was excellent. Just the conditions for indoctrination into the real joy of flying. Standing in the open cockpit with the slip-stream whistling around me as we flew over the patchwork pattern of fields created a euphoria which was to hook me on flying for the rest of my days. However, it wasn't all kicks and thrills. I had a job to do, so reeling out the trailing aerial I got cracking. I found that tuning and operating the W/T equipment in the air had its difficulties. Although the weather was good there was a certain amount of turbulence which didn't help when it came to changing the transmitter coils, but I managed to carry out my scheduled exercise as briefed. On the way back the pilot carried out a few turns and gentle zooms, I suppose to relieve the boredom of having to fly straight and level while we key-bashers did our stuff. Although it was not authorised, some of us were later initiated into the thrills of aerobatics by some of the would-be 'aces'.

It was not long before we reached the airfield and joined the circuit for landing. Standing in the rear cockpit I had a grandstand view as we came in on our final approach. The initial descent was gradual, but as we got near the ground it seemed to rush up towards us. I braced myself for the crunch, but the pilot skilfully rounded out and the aircraft floated gently to the ground. On completion of the short, but bumpy landing run we taxied back to the parking area where we were marshalled to a halt by the ground crew. I released my monkey chain and climbed out of the rear cockpit, highly elated at having completed my first real flight. The flight rigger then came rushing up to me and asked menacingly, "You haven't been sick have you?" I was pleased to reassure him that I hadn't and just for his information I had chosen to ignore the Chiefy's advice re strawberry jam.

Over the next weeks we continued with the training flights during which the W/T exercises got progressively more complicated to test our proficiency. We were lucky with the weather and we were able to complete the full schedule without delay. Every flight was, for me, an adventure which further convinced me that I had found my true vocation.

Just before we completed the course we were given a choice of postings and asked to select three RAF stations in order of preference. Most of us chose the bases nearest our homes, despite the advice from a cynical orderly room clerk that if we wished to get near home we should select the three stations furthest away. My main concern was that I should be posted to a squadron where I would have the opportunity to fly. At that time, there was a possibility of being posted to a W/T ground station (perish the thought) because wireless operators were still looked upon primarily as tradesmen and only as part-time flyers. However, it turned out as I wished. I was posted to a squadron and as a bonus it was based not too far from my home.

On a sunny afternoon in the beginning of May, 1939, three RAF airmen dressed in their best blue, wearing webbing equipment, full packs and carrying heavy kit bags alighted from a train at Thirsk Station. The three of us, Joe Fahy, Tam Mathews and myself, newly qualified Aircraftsmen Wireless Operators all, were on our way to join No. 10 Whitley Bomber Squadron at RAF Dishforth, Yorkshire.

Joe, Tam and myself, looking like three large blue snails with our houses on our backs, passed through the station exit. Outside was an

RAF three-ton truck being loaded with packages by the driver and his mate. The driver paused in his labours, "You must be the new postings," he said. After we had answered in the affirmative he continued, "Dump your kit bags inside, then give us a hand with this lot and we'll be off." We soon had the job completed and piled on board among the packages. The journey to RAF Dishforth was short and hectic. The MT. driver was obviously a speed merchant who drove with his foot clamping the accelerator to the floorboards. As we sped around the bends in the narrow country roads we were thrown around in the back of the truck like peas in a bucket, but luckily the trip was not too long and we arrived at the guard room at Dishforth without mishap.

After disembarking and collecting our kit bags we reported to the Service Policeman (SP) on duty and gave him our movement orders which he perused. Then he told us to standby while he arranged for us to be escorted to the No.10 Squadron barrack block. It was not long before the orderly corporal appeared and at his bidding we picked up our kit bags and followed. In answer to our query, "What's it like here corporal?" He answered non-committedly, "It could be worse." Having just escaped from the rigid discipline of Cranwell, where tea buckets had to be burnished to a mirror finish and the SPs. inspected even the back of your cap badge before allowing you to leave camp, we knew he was right.

We soon reached a 'T'-shaped two-storey red brick barrack block which over looked the parade square and the corporal said, "This is it." Following him through the entrance we climbed the stairs to the first floor where he opened the door to one of the dormitories. As it was still mid-afternoon it was deserted, the occupants being at work. The room contained 24 beds, some of them made up for day use (folded half length with the three biscuit mattresses swathed in blankets and arranged to form a chair). On one side of each bed was a green painted steel locker which served as a wardrobe and on the other a plain scrubbed wooden bedside locker. Some of the beds were spare, so the corporal told Tam and I to take our pick, which we did. I selected one of the three at the end of the room. Joe was taken to the dormitory facing, where he was also allocated a bed. After dumping our kit bags and packs we were taken to the bedding store where we were issued with blankets and sheets. The corporal then left us and we staggered with our loads back to the barrack block.

It did not take long to unpack our kit bags and stow our belongings in our lockers. As it was now about 5 o'clock the room's other occupants were beginning to return from the hangars. They grabbed their towels from their bed side lockers and clattered off to the ablutions for a quick clean up before tea. From their accents most of them seemed to be from the northern counties. As newcomers and obvious Sprogs, Tam and I were for the most part ignored, but the airman occupying the bed-space nearest mine said, "Come on, grab your mug and irons, you've got to be quick off the mark if you want to be fed here." I obediently did as he proposed and followed him, being joined by Joe and Tam on the way. We left the barrack block and walked around the parade square to join the throng of airmen entering the cook-house. After eventually collecting our food from the servery we seated ourselves at one of the long tables which was occupied by some of the men in our room and tucked in, keeping quiet, but listening with interest to their shop talk. Some of them wore Good Conduct Stripes (having served at least three years - it was said the award was given for three years of undetected crime!) and, even more impressive to we Sprogs, one or two wore medal ribbons denoting service overseas. Others wore the air-gunners flying badge, the coveted winged bullet, I looked on them with undisguised awe.

When we had finished our meal we returned to the barrack block, where most of the others were changing into civvies in preparation for leaving the station to indulge in their various social activities which from their conversation seemed to be mainly confined to fraternising with what they referred to as the local talent. Soon the room was practically deserted apart from a few other airmen either lounging on their beds or talking shop among themselves, so I decided to take a walk around the station to get the lie of the land.

RAF Dishforth was a fairly new station, being part of the 1936 expansion scheme which included the formation of Bomber Command. 'T'-shaped, two-storey red brick barrack blocks lined three sides of a large square parade ground, on the fourth side was the airmen's NAAFI.

I walked along the road from the domestic area past SHQ to the hangar area and the aerodrome. It was not long before I reached the hangars, arranged in an arc around the airfield perimeter. They were all locked, but I could not resist having a look through the slight gap between the massive doors of one of them. In the dim interior I could barely see the aircraft parked within, but it gave me a great thrill to realise that from now on I would be working on and hopefully flying in them. The airfield area seemed to stretch for miles. At the side farthest away from the hangars was the Great North Road, which even in those days was a busy highway. I walked along the hangar apron past the watch tower (air traffic control) and made my way past the hangars through the technical area back to the barracks.

When I got back to my room I found Tam in conversation with some of the other airmen and joined them. I gathered that he was pumping them for 'gen' and listened to what they had to say. It seems we had arrived at a busy time, the squadron was converting from their old Mk.1 Whitleys to the new Merlin engined Mk.IVs. They also gave us the low-down on the squadron working routine. We learnt that every working day started with a parade, we airmen being marched from the barracks to the hangars area where the parade was held. This included a check for absentees and prayers before we were dismissed to our various sections for the day's work.

By now the train journey and the excitement of having finally made it to the real Air Force was having an effect. After writing home to let them know my new address I cleaned my buttons and boots in preparation for tomorrow and retired, or as the old sweats would put it in barrack room parlance, I collapsed on my charpoy.*

I was wide-awake in the morning and after the working parade we presented ourselves to the squadron W/T section. There we were greeted, or rather interviewed by the chiefy, Flight Sergeant 'Pincher' Martin, a very lean, blond man of average height, who asked us a few technical questions about the R1082/T1083 W/T equipment and our speed in sending and receiving Morse. We apparently gave him satisfactory answers because he told us that we would join 'A' Flight. To begin with we would work with senior operators until we got to know the routine. He dismissed us with the advice, "You'll be alright here as long as you keep your noses clean and keep out of trouble."

We left his office and joined the resident wireless-operators in the section who greeted us with a mixture of indifference, curiosity and

*From the Urdu for bed-stead.

bantering comment. "Where are you from?" one asked. "Oh no, not bog trotters and swede bashers!" "How's Cranwell these days?" asked another. "Old Billings still binding is he?" It was all quite friendly leg-pulling. It was obvious from the nick-names that the service tradition of calling all Whites 'Chalky', and all Clarkes 'Nobby' prevailed here. In the section we had two 'Loftys', one 'Ginger', one 'Scouser', two 'Paddys', two 'Geordies' and two 'Jocks'.

I discovered that my 'winger' (guide and mentor) was the 'Scouser' Johnny Fletcher, whom every one called 'Fletch'. He was about to carry out the daily inspections of his aircraft, so I tagged along with him. By this time the aircraft had been pulled from the hangars and parked on the apron. This was the first time I had been close to a Whitley and it seemed enormous. My first impression was that the coffin-shaped fuselage, thick wings, twin fins and rudders and lack of aerodynamic streamlining did little to enhance its appearance, but I couldn't wait to get airborne in one.

Fletch gave me all the gen as he carried out all the various checks included in the Daily Inspection: Examine the acid level in the two 12 Volt, 40 Amp accumulators; check the function and serviceability of the external lights; check the internal lights and so on. I did all the leg work, watching the lights as Fletch threw the switches in the cockpit. This was followed by a physical check of the W/T aerials and connections, then a functional check of the intercom and W/T equipment, which included a call on the station frequency. When Fletch was satisfied that everything was serviceable we returned to the flight office in the hangar where the Form 700 was kept. This was the serviceability record which was kept for each aircraft and had to be signed by all the relevant tradesmen before the aircraft could be flown and as all was well Fletch signed it.

I then rejoined Joe and Tam and spent the rest of the morning trudging around the station completing our official arrival procedure. The corporal in the station headquarters orderly room was especially pleased to see us. "Oh good," he said, "three more candidates for the guard and fire picket rosters." We eventually finished and returned to the W/T section where I pestered Fletch with interminable questions about the Whitley and flying. I must have driven him up the wall because I remember him saying to me, "You won't be so bloody keen after you've done a few sessions as 'Paraffin Pete' in the

No. 10 Squadron on exercise at Evanton in 1938. (Chaz Bowyer)

freezing cold while they're night flying." He was referring to the duty we WOPs were tasked with when acting as Aldis Lamp operators for the Duty Pilot, standing by the Chance Light adjacent to the first of the Goose-neck flares which marked the flare-path.

The first day on the station was made complete for me when Joe, Tam and myself were sent to the main stores where we were issued with our own personal flying kit. I was given a Sidcot outer suit with a Teddy bear inner, leather flying helmet, goggles, leather elbow-length gauntlets with inner silk gloves and the most impressive item of all, shiny black leather knee-length flying boots. From there we proceeded to the parachute section where we were fitted with parachutes and harness. Heavily laden we staggered back to the section where in the locker room we had our own mannequin parade in what the smart young aviator of 1939 was wearing.

I got my first flight two days later when Fletch came back to the section after he had signed the Form 700. "Grab your kit, our kite's required for flying. It's only local stuff so you'll only need your helmet, 'chute and harness." I collected my kit and followed him to the flight office where both our names were entered in the flight authorisation book, then went across the tarmac in front of the hangar to where our aircraft was parked.

The two officer pilots, Flying Officer Bagshaw and Pilot Officer Henry, were busy carrying out the external checks. Bagshaw told us to get on board and said that we were only doing a handling test so would not be long. It made no difference to me where we were going, the main thing was that we were going to get airborne in one of the RAF's latest heavy bombers. I followed Fletch through the fuselage door, then we clambered past the retracted mid-under gun turret and finally through the tunnel into the cockpit and seated ourselves by the W/T equipment.

It was not long before the pilots followed us and all the hatches were closed. After the preliminary checks were carried out, the engines were started and I experienced first hand the vibrant throaty roar of two Merlin engines as they burst into life. Soon we were taxiing across the grass to the take off point, the Whitley turned into wind and the throttles opened progressively to take off power, we were on our way. At first the aircraft trundled slowly across the grass, then as speed increased the tail came up and we sped down the take off lane until suddenly we were airborne. The undercarriage came up with a clunk as the Whitley climbed smoothly away from the airfield.

At this time Fletch was in the process of tuning in the W/T set to the local frequency. We had a dual socket and I was able to listen in as he established two-way communication. After a while he handed over the watch to me and I experienced a thrill of accomplishment as I called the various W/T stations, changing frequency and obtaining practice homing bearings. I was an operational key basher at last. Fletch eventually resumed control giving me the opportunity to wander around the aircraft.

I crawled through the tunnel to the rear fuselage and climbed into the mid-under turret which was nicknamed the dustbin because of its resemblance to that household object. This was the turret in the early Whitleys which would be manned by one of the WOP/AGs so I wanted to familiarise myself with it. I wound down the foot well, the small metal box to accommodate your feet, and sat down. Sitting there in that cramped and claustrophobic metal cylinder, I can't say that I relished the thought that it might be my fighting platform.

Before long I heard the pilot tell Fletch over the intercom to inform base that we were returning to land, so I vacated the turret and went back to the cockpit where I listened as he sent his X195 which was the code for, "I am reeling in my aerial preparatory to landing." Ten minutes later we landed and taxied back to the tarmac in front of the hangar, I had completed the first of what were to be many Whitley flights.

During the next few weeks I flew often as I was absorbed into the squadron's training programme, which included air gunnery training. At this time in 4 Group, air-gunners were trained at their Group Pool at RAF Leconfield or received on the job training with their squadrons. I came into this latter category. From time to time we spent sessions in the squadron's armoury where we received instruction, both theoretical and practical, on the Whitley Mk. IV armament. The hydraulically operated nose turret with its single .303 VGO machine gun, the hydraulically operated ventral (mid-under) turret fitted with two .303 Browning machine guns and the manually operated tail turret, also with a single VGO, were all studied in detail. We learned how to strip and re-assemble both types of machine guns until we could do it blind-fold, clear stoppages and fill the ammunition pans for the VGO and the belts for the Brownings. Our practical instruction also included flights to the local bombing and air firing range when we flew at low level firing at aluminium powder sea-markers in the sea. On one such sortie, during launch from the hatch in the nose of the aircraft, the sea marker burst prematurely and the powder was blown back into the aircraft, covering some of the unfortunate crew. When they got back to base and climbed out of the aircraft looking like so many 'Tin Men' they were butts of amused comment. The air training also included fighter affiliation exercises with our fighter squadron neighbours from Catterick. We were able to assess our air-gunnery competence by using camera guns as the fighters carried out mock attacks against us, exciting stuff for we sprogs.

By now we were settled in and getting to know the other members of the squadron. Each aircraft had its own fitter, rigger, armourer, instrument 'basher' and wireless-operator. We all had a personal pride in our own kites and accepted having to be on hand at any time of the day or night, without thought for extra remuneration or time off in lieu. We all had one thing in common, we were all peace-time regulars, volunteers and proud of it. Conscription at that time was a dirty word and in our estimation something only foreigners would tolerate.

The RAF trade structure in those days comprised five trade groups. Group one consisted of higher technical grades such as fitters, instrument makers, electricians (1st class), wireless-operator mechanics etc. The other groups contained trades in descending order of technical merit, wireless operators were in Group II. However, off duty in the barrack block trade groups counted for little, length of service held sway and any rash opinions expressed by sprogs elicited such remarks as, "What do you know about it? Your number's still wet." Or "Why don't you get some (service) in."

There were different personalities, we had different likes and dislikes, but we all got on fairly well together and I cannot recall any serious upsets. Mind you, when you are living cheek-by-jowl in a barrack room you soon learn to get on with each other. The squadron was the linchpin and we all mucked in together to keep it on top line. We, like all the airmen of the other squadrons in the RAF, knew that our squadron was the best.

Every barrack room had its characters and ours was no exception. There was Freddie, ACH/GD and part time air gunner. He was a small cheerful Yorkshireman who owned a 500cc motor bike nearly as big as himself on which he roared back and forth to his home town of Leeds whenever he could fiddle a sleeping out pass. Another was Ace, a dark, curly-haired flight mechanic and also part-time air gunner who was reputed to be God's gift to the local females. Fifi was a Geordie flight mechanic, built like a brick outhouse and formidable on the football field. I never did discover how he came by the nickname, I was too scared to ask. Tom was a flight rigger and excellent footballer. It was rumoured that the station commander, who was a soccer enthusiast, had engineered Tom's posting to strengthen the station team. Tubby was a Fitter II and air observer (a rare bird) and also a good pianist. He was popular with the NAAFI crooners and the vocalists of the Ripon pub circuit.

Although it was May, 1939, and only a few months before the outbreak of WWII, the pattern of life in the RAF continued at its peace-time tempo. Generally the working schedule was 8 am. to 5 pm. daily, except when night flying took place. On Wednesday afternoons there was organised sports and one a month week-end passes were issued on a rota basis, all in all a pleasant existence. The cricket season was well under way and as I was an enthusiast I took every opportunity to indulge.

Prior to joining the RAF my opportunities to travel outside my home area had been limited by how far I could go on my bike, but

28

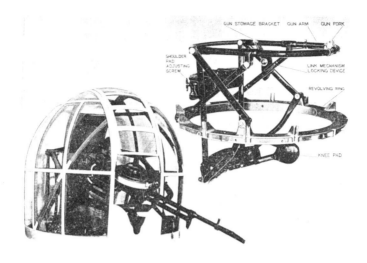

Detail of the tail turret fitted to the Whitley Mks I, II, III, and IV.

The author posing beside the tail turret of Whitley Mk.IV K9023 in July 1939.

since my enlistment I had explored the areas in which I was based and visited places of interest. Now being at Dishforth I explored Boroughbridge which was just over two miles away. There I discovered the three massive, 30 feet high, monoliths dating back to pre-historic times and known as the Devil's Arrows. I suppose the hotel nearby, The Three Arrows, was named after them. Ripon was easily reachable and I was able to visit the 12th century cathedral and the old market square. Here every night at 9 pm. the Wakeman, dressed in his long period coat and tricorn hat, sounded the forest horn. At Knaresborough I was able to walk along the banks of the River Nidd and, as well as ogling Yorkshire lasses, see the famous Dropping Well where all kinds of objects hung in the dripping water by members of the public are solidified by the lime. Nearby is Mother Shipton's Cave. According to legend she was a prophetess born in 1488. Among her prophesies was the development of aircraft.

However, there were sobering moments. I witnessed my first prang one day while working in the W/T section. I was engaged in my least favourite task, splicing lead weights onto trailing-aerials. I heard bells clanging and on looking out of the window saw the fire engine charging across the grass to a Whitley which had its undercarriage retracted and was doing its best to plough up the aerodrome. It slewed to a halt scattering clods of earth as the fire engine approached. The firemen were on the ball and had their hoses out in good time, however, there was no fire and both pilots escaped without injury. Our chiefy had also seen what happened and detailed Fletch and I to get out to the pranged aircraft and remove the W/T equipment. We made our way across the airfield to where the aircraft was lying forlornly on its fuselage. By the time we got to it other tradesmen were swarming all over it being directed by a harassed looking chiefy. After obtaining his permission Fletch and I climbed aboard and we set about removing the W/T transmitter and receiver. Then we set out to carry it back to the section, which was no easy task because of the weight and shape of the transmitter, and guess who got to carry it? By the time I got back to the section I was on my knees. The aircraft was recovered later that day after trenches had been dug under it, enabling jacks to be fitted and the undercart lowered. We never did learn why it landed with its wheels up, but rumour had it that it was due to 'cockpit trouble'.

On July 24th, the squadron moved en masse to RAF Evanton on the Moray Firth, Scotland, for our practice camp. Here we were to carry out an intensive period of training in our respective skills. We were fortunate with the weather and the aircraft were able to fly every day. The other air-gunners under training and myself were able to practice gunnery from all three turrets firing at targets in the sea as well as drogues towed behind aircraft. The Home Fleet of the Royal Navy was at that time based at nearby Invergordon and the Stringbags, as we called the Swordfish bi-planes of the Fleet Air Arm, from time to time shared the airfield at Evanton with us. The Swordfish pilots could not resist the opportunity of showing off in front of their RAF counterparts. However, our commanding officer was not amused when they carried out side-slip approaches between the lines of our parked Whitleys.

It was not all work and no play. Although we worked at full pressure during the weekdays we generally had the week-ends free. The more affluent members of the squadron took off to sample the high spots of Inverness, while the others including myself, spent our time visiting the local villages where we were able to sample that traditional Scottish dish of Haggis, Tatties and Neeps (Haggis, Potatoes and Turnips).

There were many places of interest for me to visit. Overlooking the village of Evanton is a hill some 1,500 feet high called the Fyrish, on top of which is a stone monument representing the gates of an Indian city. A local told us his version of the story of its building. He said that it represented the gates of Delhi, and was erected to commemorate the city's relief by a local regiment during the Indian Mutiny. The story continued that the local laird had given its builders a loaf of bread for each stone carried up the hill. I subsequently discovered that this was somewhat far from the truth for the monument was commissioned by Sir Hector Munro of Novar (1726-1805) a famous Scottish general who had a distinguished service record in India. It was a replica of the gates to the city of Negapatam which was the scene of one of his notable victories and it was built to help alleviate unemployment. Climbing the Fyrish was a must and after clambering to the top I had a fantastic panoramic view of the Home Fleet in the Moray Firth. There was no way of knowing, but this was one of the last occasions that the Fleet would be seen in its entirety and magnificence.

Our bombing and gunnery programme continued as planned and eventually reached its conclusion. For us would-be air-gunners this was a practical and oral examination and the award of the coveted Winged Bullet to the successful candidates. I was one of the successful ones and it was a great feeling to realize that I was now a fully qualified WOP/AG. I was now entitled to the financial increment of sixpence (2.5p) a day air-gunnery pay. The squadron returned to Dishforth on August 19th and we resumed what we thought would be normal routine. However, the increase in flights at night and the searchlight co-operation flights were a sign that things were hotting up. Ever since the crisis of September 1938, when Hitler had taken over Czechoslovakia, it had been accepted that if such aggressive acts continued it was only a matter of time before there would be a show down. This was despite the promise of 'Peace in our time' by Mr Chamberlain. Newspaper reports indicated that things were coming to a head and, during the last week of August 1939, it became obvious that a war in Europe was on the cards. On September 1st, Hitler's forces invaded Poland.

On the day of the invasion our squadron received orders to mobilise to war establishment. The station was sealed off by armed sentries and our aircraft were dispersed to nearby fields. Steel helmets and gas masks were issued to personnel and had to be carried at all times. Black-out screens were supplied to be fitted to the windows and masks to be fitted to the headlights of our vehicles. The installation of a Tannoy with speakers in barrack blocks, sections, offices and other strategic points began. In our crew-rooms and sections posters appeared showing Allied and German aircraft to aid recognition. All we WOP/AGs were tasked to ensure that our aircraft's W/T equipment was fully servicable and stocks of spares available. Throughout the station an air of suppressed excitement pervaded, rumour was rife and speculation reached the unbelievable.

At about 10.00 pm. on September 2nd, two SPs. invaded our barrack room and informed us that all available WOP/AGs were to report to their W/T section immediately. Altogether the SPs. mustered eight of us and we set off down the road to the hangar. As we trudged along in the darkness I am sure all our imaginations were working overtime, thinking, 'this is it!' and wondering where we would be come dawn. However, when we reached the section our fears were partially allayed by Chiefy Martin, who informed us that our immediate task was to re-calibrate all the W/T equipment to a new list of frequencies. After obtaining W39 wavemeters we set off and made our way by torchlight to where the aircraft were dispersed and set about our task. It was not until the early hours of September 3rd that we were able to finish the job. Despite this we were up early, had a hurried breakfast and all trooped off to our various sections. Then out to the aircraft where we carried out what I am sure were the most detailed and conscientious inspections of all time. After this it was back to the section to listen to the Prime Minister's broadcast. At 11 am. we heard Mr Chamberlain tell the nation that because of Hitler's refusal to withdraw his troops from Poland, we were now at war with Germany. In our section there was no great reaction, no visible excitement, but I am sure we all had a mental gulp, knowing full well that as regulars and aircrew it was highly likely that we would be called upon to put our peace-time training into practice before very long.

Shortly after the Prime Minister's proclamation one of the WOP/AGs came into the section and reported that a 'war' crew-list had been posted on the flight notice board. There was a concerted rush to see with whom we had been crewed. This institution of permanent crews was an innovation for previously crews had been selected in a haphazard manner. Tradesmen aircrew generally flew in the aircraft they serviced while pilots flew in whichever aircraft was available at the time. At that time aircrew other than pilots were looked upon as part-timers, so this meant that it was a matter of chance if the same crews flew together regularly. The new system was the first attempt to weld crews into efficient, cohesive groups who knew that they could depend upon each other. However, it would be some time before this was achieved because of the gulf which existed between officers and other ranks in the peace-time RAF. This uneasy mix often improved with time and perhaps a few hazardous operations when mutual respect could be won, but it is a sad fact that some crews flew and died together without really getting to know each other.

When we perused the new crew list I discovered that Fletch and I had been selected to fly with Flying Officer R. Bickford, one of the squadron's more experienced pilots, as first and second WOP/AGs. The other members of our crew were Pilot Officer M. T. Henry, second pilot/navigator and LAC. Freddie Gudgeon as tail gunner. We had all flown together previously, but not often.

The following morning, September 4th, we were informed via the BBC news that RAF aircraft had flown over Germany during the night and had dropped propaganda leaflets on towns in North-West Germany and the Ruhr. This announcement brought forth derisive comment from some, "I bet they won't bomb *us* with paper," or, "All we're doing is giving them free bog paper!" When we got to the section we found that the bush telegraph had been working overtime and we were told that the 'Bumph'* raid during the night had been the handiwork of our Whitley equipped compatriots of Nos. 51 and 58 Squadrons. This was a Whitley first as they were the first aircraft to fly over the German mainland in WWII.

Although we were not told it at the time the leaflet raids were part of a restricted bombing policy dictated by the Government that Bomber Command should restrict its activities during the initial phase of the war. Most of us, in our ignorance, were eager to get cracking with bombing Germany. This restriction would prove to be a blessing in disguise, because our first raids were to reveal many deficiencies in equipment and training. In peace-time, flying in adverse weather conditions and flying at high altitude was rarely attempted. This inexperience was to become patently evident during the leaflet raids of the atrocious winter of 1939/40 when aircraft began to fly at great altitudes. The lack of suitable heating, oxygen facilities and adequate flying clothing was to cause unimaginable hardships for the crews and especially the gunners in their unheated turrets. Airframe de-icing consisted of a compound smeared on the leading edges of the wings, an antidote which was less than satisfactory. The only aid to navigation was the M/F and H/F Direction Finding W/T stations. Their range and accuracy was limited to between 250 and 300 miles for the bearings and fixes and 100 miles for QDMs. (Homings) and bearings. Aircraft W/T equipment. The T1083/R1082 combination was difficult to operate. the main difficulty was the necessity of changing the coils every time a change in frequency was required. Outside the M/F and H/F direction finding range we had to rely on basic navigation, Dead Reckoning, which could prove to be fatal at night and in bad weather conditions. Despite the difficulties the crews made the best of what they had and their achievements are a testament to their courage and endurance. The lessons learnt by them during the leaflet raids were to prove of great value. Better techniques were developed to help overcome some of our deficiencies. When the bombing war really started in 1940, operations would be carried out during the full moon periods and, if possible, self illuminating targets such as blast-

*Leaflet.

furnaces and those adjacent to features such as rivers and lakes would be selected. But this was learning the hard way.

We had one thing to be thankful for. Unlike our comrades in 2 Group flying Blenheims, and 3 Group flying Wellingtons, we were not committed to daylight raids against the German Fleet which were to prove so disastrous and futile.

Chapter Two

The First Raids

The leaflet raid carried out by Nos. 51 and 58 Squadrons on the night of 3rd/4th September, was followed during the afternoon by daylight bombing attacks on the German warships in the Shillig Roads and Brunsbuttel, by Blenheims of Nos. 107 and 110 Squadrons from 2 Group and Wellingtons of Nos. 9 and 149 Squadrons from 3 Group. Both raids were ineffective and the RAF suffered its first casualties when five Blenheims and two Wellingtons failed to return. Seven Whitleys of No. 51 Squadron flew to the French airfield at Rheims, from where four of them carried out another leaflet raid over the Ruhr that night. They were supported by three aircraft of No. 102 Squadron from Driffield who made their debut in German skies. The other Driffield squadron, No. 77, got into the act the following night by sending three aircraft to drop leaflets over the Ruhr.

We at Dishforth were by now champing at the bit, eager to get cracking, even though we were only going to drop leaflets. We consoled ourselves by thinking, 'They're leaving the best squadron till last!' Listening to the radio reports, embellished by snippets of information which filtered through the grapevine did nothing to relieve our impatience. However, we didn't have to wait long. On the afternoon of the 7th, our skipper, Flying Officer Bickford, informed us that we would be going that night. Our reaction to the realization that we were now going to do our first raid was, I suppose, one of excitement tinged with a sneaking apprehension.

After the skipper's dramatic news Fletch, Freddie and myself trudged across the fields to where our aircraft K9023, 'E' for Easy was dispersed. Although we had carried out our DIs. on the W/T equipment and guns earlier in the day, we left nothing to chance and re-checked everything.

We assembled in the station operations room at 20.00 hours for briefing as instructed. It was an informal affair, the pilots and aircrew in separate groups swapping corny and macabre jokes in an attempt to disguise any apprehension. I recall that one of our SNCO (Sergeant) pilots, obviously influenced by superstition or trying to emulate the WWI air aces, was wearing one of his wife's silk stockings as a scarf.

Eventually order prevailed and the briefing commenced. We were given our take-off times and our targets which were located in North West Germany. The met. man gave us a general forecast of the weather we were likely to encounter and the height to fly over the target to obtain maximum scatter of the Bumph. The signals officer informed us that there would be wireless silence except in an emergency and the intelligence officer briefed us on what we could expect in the way of anti-aircraft opposition. Reports from previous leaflet raids carried out by other Whitley squadrons indicated that the opposition was light. Our particular target was the German naval base at Kiel, which was known to be well defended. There was the possibility of some opposition, but we would have the protection of darkness, unlike our Blenheim and Wellington counterparts who had attacked a similar target on the 4th with such disastrous consequences.

Our ebullient commanding officer, Wing Commander W. E. Staton MC, DFC and Bar, bolstered our morale. He had done it all before, being a fighter pilot in WWI and credited with twenty-five victories. Because of his massive build he was known as Kong, more affectionately than disrespectfully, by his officers and men. As usual he was leading from the front and had elected to take-off first.

After briefing we dispersed to our various messes for a pre-flight meal. In the airmen's mess, contrary to usual practice, the duty cook did not query our entitlement to a night flying supper. This was our first of what was to become the ritual pre-ops meal, labelled blasphemously by some of the less couth and un-godly crews as Last Suppers. The aircraft participating in the raid had been brought from the dispersal area and parked on the hangar apron. Fletch and I climbed into the fuselage of 'E' for Easy to inspect our load. The leaflets were contained in large brown paper packages which were stacked mainly forward of the dustbin ventral gun turret. It would be our job to off load the leaflets via the flare-chute and as we surveyed them Fletch observed laconically, 'We're going to earn our corn getting rid of this lot.'

Eight aircraft had been selected to take part in the raid, four from each flight. 'B' Flight were selected to take-off first and were now starting their engines. It was not long before they taxied out and we watched as they trundled into the darkness to the goose-neck flare-path before taking off at intervals. One by one they climbed away, were lost to sight and then the sound of their engines also faded. We climbed aboard 'E' Easy and our ground crew wished us luck as they closed the door behind us. We settled in at our positions and after the pre-flight checks were completed the skipper ordered the engine start. The two Rolls Royce Merlins crackled into life with their unmistakable throaty roar. Thank God we had them instead of the Tiger engines of the Whitley III. Soon the aircraft was bumping its way to the take-off point. We requested take-off clearance by flashing our aircraft letter 'E' on the identification lights and after receiving a green from the flare-path controller we lined up for take-off - the game was on. The skipper opened the throttles and the Whitley bumped along the grass rapidly passing the flares as its speed increased. Suddenly the bumping ceased and we were airborne, climbing away from the airfield. The time was 00.55 hours on September 8th, 1939, a time and date I have never forgotten.

We proceeded on course and after a while Pilot Officer Henry announced over the intercom that we were crossing the coast near Flamborough Head. Although it was quite dark we were able to see the white spume as the waves tumbled onto the shore. This would be our last pinpoint until we reached the enemy coast. When we were well out to sea I asked for permission to go aft and check the guns in the mid-under turret for, as second WOP/AG, this was my responsibility. The skipper gave the OK and I crawled through the interconnecting tunnel from the cockpit to the rear fuselage, groping my way with the aid of my shaded torch.

I scrambled into the turret with difficulty, my bulky flying kit making it a tight squeeze. Lowering the turret by touch alone I loaded the two .303 Brownings. Depressing the guns to point to the sea I cocked them, switched on the reflector gun sight and slipped off the safety catch. I looked through the sight and pressed the triggers. The two guns blazed away and I watched fascinated as the tracers and incendiaries curved away in a fiery stream, for this was the first time that I had fired the guns at night. Two bursts were enough to re-assure me that the guns were working correctly and I wondered if I might be using them in anger before the night was out. At that time we had no information on the German night-fighter capability, so we did not know what to expect. Meanwhile Freddie in the rear turret tested his single VGO machine-gun. I didn't envy him.

At least the mid-under turret and guns were hydraulically operated, but the tail turret and gun in Whitleys up to and including the Mk. IVs had to be manually operated. The turret seat, shaped like a motor cycle saddle, was attached to the frame incorporating a gun mounting. According to the operating manual:-

"The air-gunner is seated in a convenient position relative to the gun and by a system of links statistically balances it. He is thus able to train the gun in elevation with little exertion and is independent of the accelerations of the aeroplane. Rotation of the turret in the horizontal plane is affected by the reaction of the air-gunner's feet on the floor."

I wonder if the manual's author had ever attempted to turn the turret from aft to beam and felt the full effects of the slipstream? Obviously not. The turret was covered with a transparent perspex cupola which was fixed to the gun mounting and rotated with it. There was a gun aperture through which the elements, wind, rain, snow, you name it, entered when the turret was turned abeam. Getting from the turret to the fuselage when wearing full flying kit was almost an impossibility, so the Tail-End Charlie was incarcerated in his turret for the duration of the flight. As most of the flights over Germany were to last from seven to ten hours the unfortunate tail-gunners were left to suffer temporary paralysis of the their nether regions to add to the other physical discomforts.

We continued on our way, the aircraft droning its way through the skies over the North Sea. There was little cloud and so far the the flight had been smooth and uneventful. We were now flying at 18,000 feet and on oxygen. Eventually Pilot Officer Henry, who had been poring over his charts, announced that we should be crossing the enemy coast shortly. The excitement mounted when a few moments later the skipper reported that he had seen the coast. Henry moved forward to obtain a pin-point. Visibility was good and although it was dark and we were at altitude, we could clearly make out the outline of the German coast and even see the lights of neutral Denmark away to the north of our track.

After Henry had fixed our position we altered course for Kiel and Fletch and I prepared to go aft to drop the leaflets. Just as we were about to leave the cockpit the skipper announced that there were searchlights ahead, our first sight of the German defences. Craning forward we saw them, four ghostly white beams probing the night sky. The skipper commented that they were probably searching for the aircraft preceding us. It was re-assuring to see they had not illuminated any and there was no anti-aircraft fire.

Fletch and I left the cockpit and went aft where, by the light of our shaded torches, we opened the packages of leaflets and stacked them in readiness for dispatch down the flare chute. The aircraft was now flying at 20,000 feet and the physical effort was considerable. We were hindered by the fact that there was only one oxygen point available so we had to take turns using it, changing over whenever the non-user looked like flaking out.

We got the order to drop the Bumph so we got cracking. I had stationed myself by the flare chute and as Fletch passed the bundles I thrust them down the chute. Each bundle was secured by a rubber band which was removed by the slipstream after the bundle had left the aircraft.

Everything proceeded according to plan with Fletch and I heaving out the leaflets as fast as we could. Freddie in the tail turret reported that they were scattering behind us. We had the odd hiccup when one bundle lost its securing rubber band in the chute and we were engulfed in a snowstorm of paper thrown back at us, but we pressed on and completed our task. Afterwards I was busy tidying up when without warning, the rattle of machine-gun fire shook me rigid. I shot back to the mid-under turret and before you could say 'Red Baron' was whirling the turret in search of our attacker. I peered into the darkness, but as the field of visibility was severely limited called excitedly over the intercom, "Mid-under to tail. Where is he?"

"Where's who?" came Freddie's voice.

"Whoever you're shooting at!" I yelled.

"Oh, that. I was just warming up my gun to stop it freezing. Why, did I wake you up?"

I stayed in the turret until I had simmered down, by which time we were well on our way home.

We crossed the German coast and then the North Sea before making land-fall in Lincolnshire which was south of our briefed track that should have brought us in over the coast just to the north of Newcastle-upon-Tyne. Someone had to point out the error and a disembodied voice put him in his place, 'Why worry, at least we're back over England.' That about summed up our feelings, but we were running low on fuel which lead our skipper to head for RAF

Manby to re-fuel and report to base. Manby was still not operational at this time and we were the first aircraft to land there on return from operations over Germany. It was nearly 8 o'clock in the morning when we landed, but even at this time news travelled fast and it was not long before we became the focus of much admiring attention. While we basked in the limelight our aircraft was refuelled and our skipper had telephoned our commanding officer.

We were the last aircraft to return to Dishforth and our ground crew were eager to learn how we had fared. Somewhat rejuvenated and back on home ground it was easy to dismiss the whole affair as a piece of cake, but we had been airborne for eight hours and five minutes, the longest any of us had been up at any one time. The skipper and Pilot Officer Henry went off to operations to report while Fletch, Freddie and myself made our way to breakfast and then bed. It was mid-morning before I drifted off to sleep and in that time I had time to reflect on the events of the past few hours. Being an impressionable 18 year old and unduly influenced by the highly coloured accounts of WWI air warfare and dreams of glory I felt a little let down, for my first raid had turned out to be nothing like I had imagined. In the months to come I found out what war really meant and my dreams of glory were replaced by those of grim reality.

At lunch time the returning ground crew awoke me as they clattered into the room. The BBC 1 o'clock news came on and in that bulletin announced,

"RAF aircraft carried out raids over north west Germany and dropped propaganda leaflets on selected targets during the night. They all returned safely."

Although the announcement gave no details of the aircraft involved I am sure all the crews got the same thrill I did. Our raid also produced another first for 4 Group when it became the first group to have flown all its squadrons over Germany.

The leaflet raids continued with results that ranged from the tragic to the fortunate. On the night of September 8th/9th, the group suffered its first casualties when two of the six No. 102 Squadron crews failed to return from a leaflet sortie to the Ruhr. K8950 - Squadron Leader S. S. Murray, was shot down by Flak over Thurlingla, while K8985 - Flight Lieutenant W. G. C. Cogman strayed into Belgian territory where Fairey Foxes and Fireflies - two-seater biplanes - were scrambled from Nivelles to intercept. The Whitley was intercepted by Foxes of the 5e *Escadrille* flown by Lieutenant Jottard and Sous Lieutenant Offenberg. The Whitley was forced down at Nivelles, where the aircraft was captured and the crew interned. Another No. 102 Squadron Whitley, K8951 flown by Flight Lieutenant Connell, was engaged by Belgian fighters and although damaged returned with the tail-gunner claiming a fighter shot down. He had in fact damaged the Firefly flown by Daniel Leroy Du Vivier, and shot down that piloted by Adjutant Albert Genot. This aircraft crashed in flames after the crew baled out.

One of six crews sent out by No. 77 Squadron also became lost on the way home. Come dawn they were flying over Belgium and violating that country's neutrality. Further Fairy Foxes intercepted, but with a happier outcome. At first the skipper acknowledged their instructions, but then realized how close he was to the coast and gave a two-fingered salute as he whanged open the throttles and dived for the sea. The Fairy Foxes were left floundering in the Whitley's slip-stream, powerless to prevent the bomber's escape.

The miscreant crew, skippered by Sergeant T. G. 'Hamish' Mahaddie*, landed safely at RAF Manston and had some fast talking to do before being allowed to return to Driffield. Apparently the disgruntled fighter pilots had accused the gunners of firing on them, but fortunately their accusations were proved to be unfounded.

On the night of September 9th/10th a leaflet raid and reconnaissance was launched to the Ruhr, Frankfurt and Nuremberg by Nos. 10 and 58 Squadrons. For this raid the aircraft were to be previously moved to an advanced airfield at Rheims. The four aircraft sent by No. 10 Squadron carried out their task as briefed and reported the

---

* 'Hamish' Mahaddie was subsequently to become one of the stalwarts of Bomber Command Pathfinder Force. After being commissioned on April 1st, 1940, he completed his tour and was posted to No. 19 (Whitley) OTU at Kinloss as an instructor. He later returned to operations on Stirlings and went on to attain the rank of Group Captain and commanding officer of RAF Warboys, one of the Pathfinder bases. In 1943 he received the DSO, DFC and AFC from His Majesty King George VI and later the same day went to the Czechoslovakian Embassy where he was decorated with the Military Cross in recognition of his operations over that country in 1939 and 1940. Receiving so many awards at one time was a very rare distinction shared with the WWI fighter ace Billy Bishop, who had received the VC, DSO and MC from King George V who is reported to have said, "You have been a busy little bugger, haven't you."

opposition as light, but No. 58 Squadron was not so fortunate. Of their three crews only one successfully completed the sortie, one returned early because of a mechanical fault and the third crashed on take-off and burnt out, fortunately without injury to the crew. Leaflet raids were suspended on September 14th by the War Cabinet and the Air Staff because the value of the raids was being called into question by both political and service critics. However, they were resumed on September 24th. The war cabinet produced an explanation that the raids were only a secondary task, the primary function being reconnaissance and operational training, so the raids continued. No. 10 Squadron despatched two crews on September 24th/25th, one to Hamburg and the other to Bremen. Both encountered severe icing conditions and electrical storms, but they did their job and returned safely to boot.

Nos. 77 and 102 Squadrons sent out crews on the night of September 25th/26th, and No. 51 Squadron sent out six crews on the 27th/28th. On the last night of September No. 10 Squadron allocated four aircraft to reconnoitre Hamburg and Bremen. Joe Fahy, who was posted to the squadron at the same time as myself, was doing his first raid and had a lucky escape. They encountered severe weather conditions, but carried out their task although 'Ginger' Irving, the first WOP/AG, suffered frostbite to his hands in the process. On return they were misled by inaccurate W/T bearings and eventually pranged in the dark near Bolton. They had been airborne for nine hours and forty minutes. Luckily they all survived the crash unhurt the only casualty being 'Ginger' with his frostbite, from which he recovered.

On September 30th, No. 58 Squadron left 4 Group on temporary attachment to Coastal Command to carry out convoy escort duties and anti-submarine patrols. They would return to 4 Group in February, 1940, convert to Whitley Mk. Vs and resume bomber operations.

As the result of the general mobilisation which took place at the outbreak of hostilities RAF Reserve, Auxiliary Air Force and Volunteer Reserve personnel had reported to their allocated RAF stations. At Dishforth the first to arrive were for the most part administrative support staff and technical tradesmen. We would not receive our reinforcement aircrew until the middle of 1940, when they had finished their operational training. The first reinforcement to

Squadron Leader S. S. Murray (left) and Pilot Officer A. B. Thompson seen here in the hands of their German captors at Itzhoe, near Hamburg. Their Whitley, K9850 DY-M of No. 102 Squadron was shot down by Flak on the night of September 8th-9th, 1939. (Chaz Bowyer)

our wireless section was a grizzled old sergeant reservist wireless operator, whose last flying had been in airships! His entire service number comprised three digits and he claimed there were so few of the old timers they were on first name terms with each other.

The Volunteer Reservists and Auxiliaries were treated by we regulars with what I suppose can be described as condescending tolerance. Some of our old sweats were reluctant to show respect for their officers and I recall one of them who sported two good conduct stripes (denoting eight year's regular service) muttering darkly, 'Bloody weekend wonders, what do they know about our Air Force.'

However, some of our reinforcements were welcomed with open arms, the members of the WAAF. Even so there were some who looked askance at this intrusion of what was considered to be during peace-time, an exclusively male bastion. The story got around of one

Group Captain of that calling, who summoned the young WAAF officer in charge of the WAAF detachment posted to his station and telling her in no uncertain terms that he would tolerate no hanky panky. Tapping her forehead the young officer is supposed to have replied, "Don't worry Sir, all my girls have got it up here." To which the Groupy answered, "I don't give a damn where they've got it, my bloody airmen will find it, so keep your gals away from them."

So ended the first month of WWII, during which most of the Whitley crews of 4 Group had made their debut over the night skies of Germany, part of the nucleus of a night-bombing force which was to grow to awesome proportions during the next few years.

Summary of operations by 4 Group
September 1939

3rd-4th. Leaflet raid - Hamburg, Bremen and Ruhr.
51 Sqn. Three a/c all successful. Opposition negligible.
58 Sqn. Seven a/c all successful. Two a/c crash landed in France, but the crews were safe.

4th-5th. Leaflet raid - Ruhr.
51 Sqn. Seven a/c pre-positioned at Rheims. Due to unserviceability only four a/c took off, but they completed the sortie.
102 Sqn. Three a/c all successful. Opposition light.

5th-6th. Leaflet raid - Ruhr.
77 Sqn. Three a/c carried out the task as briefed.

7th-8th. Leaflet raid - north-west Germany.
10 Sqn. Eight a/c all successful, opposition negligible, mostly searchlights.

8th-9th. Leaflet raid - Ruhr.
102 Sqn. Six a/c, four successful, two failed to return.
(see loss table).
77 Sqn. Six a/c, one returned early unserviceable. Five a/c successful, but three landed in France where one collided with a French fighter.

9th-10th. Leaflet raid - Ruhr, Frankfurt and Nuremburg.
(All a/c pre-positioned at Rheims.)
10 Sqn. Four a/c completed task against light opposition.
58 Sqn. Three a/c, one crashed, one returned early, one successful.

24th-25th. Leaflet raid - Hamburg and Bremen.
10 Sqn. Two a/c, both successful despite severe weather.

25th-26th. Leaflet raid - Hamburg and Ruhr.
102 Sqn. Three a/c all successful, landed at Villeneuve.
77 Sqn. Two a/c, one returned early.

27th-28th. Leaflet raid - north-west Germany.
51 Sqn. Six a/c, one returned early, five successful and landed at Rheims. Searchlight and AA opposition encountered.

30th-1st. Leaflet raid - Hamburg and Bremen.
10 Sqn. Four a/c completed their tasks despite severe weather conditions. One crashed on return.

Chapter Three

The Phoney War

October started with another Whitley 'first'. On the night of the 1st/2nd, four of No. 10 Squadron's crews were detailed to carry out a reconnaissance and to drop leaflets on the German Capital. This was the first occasion on which RAF aircraft flew over Berlin during WWII. The raid was led, as usual, by our Commanding Officer, Wing Commander W. E. Staton.

Despite encountering severe weather conditions en route and over the target, three crews were successful and carried out their task as briefed. The Commanding Officer's aircraft was particularly affected by the adverse weather and equipment failure. While flying over Berlin at 22,500 feet, the oxygen supply failed momentarily and Leading Aircraftsman Stan Broadhurst and Aircraftsman 'Ivy' Ives, the two WOP/AGs who were dropping the leaflets collapsed. Pilot Officer 'Lofty' Willis, the second pilot went back to assist them. After making sure that Ives' oxygen tube was connected to the mid-under turret supply, he dragged Stan Broadhurst back to the cockpit and connected his tube to the main supply. He then went back to the fuselage and took on the task of dropping the leaflets, successfully distributing two-thirds of them before he too collapsed. The Wing Commander then brought the aircraft down to 9,000 feet at which height, Leading Aircraftsman 'Paddy' Turner, whose tail-turret had frozen up at altitude, managed the almost impossible task of scrambling out of his turret. He made his way forward and gave assistance to Lofty who recovered and returned to the cockpit after he had disposed of the rest of the bumph.

The fourth aircraft (K9018) flown by Flight Lieutenant J. W. Alsop failed to return. Its last reported position had been 180 miles from St. Abbs Head during the early hours of the 2nd. It was concluded that the aircraft had been forced to ditch in the North Sea after its fuel had run out. This was our squadron's first loss and it was deeply felt. Aircraftsman 'Dinger' Bell and Aircraftsman 'Jock' Hill, the two WOP/AGs. and Leading Aircraftsman 'Chippy' Ellison, the tail-gunner, were the first of our 'oppos' to be lost, a significant reminder to us that war was not all glory.

Whenever a crew went missing a Committee of Adjustment comprising generally the Padre and the Station Warrant Officer or another NCO (for other ranks), collected their kit for dispersal. Using their discretion, they examined and disposed of correspondence. Service equipment was returned to Stores but, as they weren't interested in clothing, it was an unwritten law that it would be disposed by holding a 'sale of kit' where their 'oppos' would pay inflated prices for items, this money going to the dependants. It was all done unemotionally, even though we were like a family, attached to each other. We had learned the necessity of concealing our feelings because we realised that we were all in the same boat and the same thing could, and probably would, happen to most of us when the Law of Averages caught up.

Some time later a service was held in the village church at Dishforth where a memorial plaque recording their names was installed. It has since been removed from the church and presented to the squadron where it is prized as part of its WWII memorabilia.

Bad weather over the Continent continued and precluded operations for the next two weeks, but Chiefy Martin made sure that we were fully occupied. Besides carrying out the daily inspections and day-to-day maintenance of the aircraft W/T. equipment, we were given other tasks. One of the more interesting was that of monitoring German W/T transmissions on selected frequencies. The Luftwaffe relied to a great extent on the use of wireless beacons as aids to aircraft navigation and they had established a system of beacons strategically positioned throughout Germany for direction finding purposes. Our signals intelligence service was aware of this and from listening out sessions information was obtained which resulted in the beacon coding system being cracked. Subsequently this information was given to our crews which enabled them to use the German beacons to obtain bearings when operating over Germany. However, because of the emphasis placed on Dead Reckoning navigation by the RAF and the lack of facilities for training in the use of radio beacons as a navigational aid, most observers were reluctant to use radio loop bearings unless they agreed with the DR. plot.

Despite the continuing bad weather, air operations were resumed on the night of October 15th/16th. We were one of the nine crews from No. 10 Squadron detailed to carry out a reconnaissance over the Elbe and to drop leaflets on Hamburg. After the usual preliminaries we took off at 17.20 hours. When we were safely airborne I got permission to go back and load the guns in the mid-under turret as I wanted to get it done in daylight instead of struggling to do it in the

Inside the aircraft things weren't always as organised when dropping leaflets as this posed photograph would suggest!

dark. I squeezed into the turret, lowered it and began loading the guns.

Meanwhile they had struck a problem up front. The front-turret had developed an oil-leak and was spewing oil over the pilot's windscreen which prevented them from seeing out. They decided to land as soon as possible. I can only assume that they were so pre-occupied with their problem that they forgot that I was in the mid-under turret and therefore neglected to warn me. I was so busy loading the guns that I didn't realise what was happening until there was a thump and the footwell was wrenched from the bottom of the turret. My feet hit the ground, my flying-boots were ripped off and my legs were jammed against the bottom edge of the turret. I

51

instinctively grabbed the turret pipelines above me and hung on for dear life.

When the aircraft came to a halt they extracted me from the turret and laid me on the grass - Freddie in the tail-turret must have warned them something was amiss when he saw my boots bouncing past the tail!

The Medical Officer arrived and after a preliminary examination I was strapped onto a stretcher and loaded into the back of a covered three-tonner to be transported to Catterick Military Hospital where the nearest X-Ray equipment was available. Before I left I recall our Squadron Commander warning me not to divulge any information concerning the raid. After a very uncomfortable journey I arrived at the hospital where I was stripped and my legs cleaned.

After being X-Rayed, I was tucked up in bed and given a sedative. When I awoke late in the morning they gave me the good news that there were no broken bones, only superficial injuries. The outcome was that after a further day I was discharged and sent on three days sick-leave.

I limped off for home where for the next three days I was able to take things easy and 'stoke up' on home cooking. This was my first time at home since the outbreak of war, so everyone was curious to learn what I'd been up to and I had to sing for my supper. I tried to convince them that my injuries had nothing to do with operational flying but I don't think they believed me. I was also at pains to convince them that the newspaper accounts of our operations were somewhat lurid and that in future they should take the reports with a pinch of salt. I don't think that they wanted to believe that either, for it was much more exciting to have a real live hero in their midst. My short break soon ended and I returned to Dishforth where I was pronounced medically fit to return to active duty. I was told that night of the 15th/16th had turned out to be a disastrous night for all concerned because of the filthy weather. Cloud had been forecast at all levels with outbreaks of rain, but it had turned out much worse than predicted and only one of the No. 10 Squadron crews were able to carry out the task. No. 77 Squadron had also encountered trouble that night when four of their crews were detailed to drop leaflets over Frankfurt. One of their aircraft (K8947) with Flying Officer R. Williams and crew on board failed to return.

The next raids were on the night of October 18th/19th to Hanover, Bremen and Hamburg. Once again the weather had the last word and four of the six aircraft despatched by No. 10 Squadron, turned back. Two crews were successful, but one of these was forced to make a crash-landing near Amiens on its return. There were no casualties among the crew, but the aircraft was damaged. The crew had to return to Dishforth by rail and boat. On arrival in the UK. they proceeded through customs carrying their parachute-bags in which they had secreted bottles of Champagne purchased cheaply in Amiens. Unfortunately when one of the crew put his bag on the ground, it 'clinked' suspiciously! The Customs Officer was inclined to be a little sceptical when told that the bag contained only parachute and harness. However when told the 'harrowing' tale of shot, shell and crash-landing, he turned a blind eye.

The weather continued to dictate the progress of air operations and in an attempt to overcome the bad weather over the UK aircraft were despatched to France to carry out raids from the French advanced bases. However it was to be of no avail, because the weather over France was no better. Despite this, operations were carried out, but the price proved to be high.

On the night of October 27th/28th, five crews from No. 51 Squadron were detailed to carry out a reconnaissance and leaflet drop over Stuttgart and Munich. They took off from their advanced base of Villeneuve in appalling conditions but with an assurance that conditions would improve.

After taking off and climbing away in cloud, they found that ice began to form at only 1,500 feet and continued to get worse and build up as they climbed to 12,000 feet. The cloud was thick from ground level upwards and shortly after take-off one crew turned back.

Flying Officer H. Budden and crew in K8989, one of the four remaining aircraft, pressed on over Germany in thick cloud. Over their target of Stuttgart the WOP/AG and front-gunner began to drop the leaflets, but with only one oxygen point available they suffered from anoxia but dropped the load despite their difficulties.

On the return flight they ran into conditions so severe that ice inches thick formed on the control surfaces, making control desperately difficult. The outside air-temperature was minus 38°C and ice forming on the pitot-tube made the airspeed indicator inaccurate. Huge lumps of ice flew from the propeller blades and crashed against the fuselage with alarming thuds. In the front turret the gunner only kept things going by continuously moving it around, even though he was frozen solid himself. Also in difficulty was the radio operator, but he was able to obtain fixes which brought the aircraft down safely at Villeneuve after a flight of over six hours of blind flying.

Sergeant E. Cotton flying K8980 fared no better. The front turret, mid-under turret and trim tabs had all frozen up by the time they dropped their leaflets, the dispatchers suffered the usual problem of anoxia which was made all the worse as the aircraft had taken off in haste and had not had a full supply of oxygen. On the way back the front gunner collapsed in a semi-frozen heap and the second pilot endeavoured to stay conscious by bashing his head repeatedly on the navigation table. Things were now so bad that Cotton decided to bring his aircraft down to a height where they would not need oxygen, but at this altitude anti-aircraft fire began to appear all around them. Miraculously the wireless operator managed to obtain sufficient bearings to get them back safely.

Flight Sergeant J. W. P. Wynton was the pilot of K9008 which in comparison with other aircraft was doing well until, that is, they were on their return flight. The mid-under turret had become stuck in the down position and both the dispatchers passed out in their efforts to raise it manually. In the cockpit Wynton was having trouble maintaining control after spending six hours flying on his instruments alone. He handed over the controls to his second pilot while he took a rest, but almost immediately the starboard engine caught fire and he was forced to re-take control. With the fire raging Wynton had no option but to stop the engine which caused an additional complication. The flight instruments worked on a vacuum system provided by two pumps, one on each engine, but already the pump on the port engine had failed and when the starboard engine was stopped all the instruments failed. To compound all their problems a large accumulation of ice, around six inches of it, had built up on the leading edges of the wings and the aircraft went into a steep dive. Both pilots pulled back on the control column in an attempt to bring the bomber out of its screaming dive, but to no avail. The starboard engine was still well alight and Wynton had no option but to order his crew to bale out. Calling the front and rear gunners to acknowledge the command he received no reply and concluded that they must have collapsed at the posts. With renewed vigour the two pilots heaved with all their might on the frozen and immovable controls and were bringing the nose of the Whitley up when they broke through the low cloud. Ahead of them was a belt of trees which skimmed by beneath the fuselage, but ahead lay even taller trees. The topmost branches of the trees scraped against the fuselage and dragged the bomber to earth in a small clearing where it slithered along on its belly before coming to grinding halt. Amazingly none of the crew were injured in the crash and they scrambled from the wreck to put the fire in the engine out. Gathering themselves together the five men walked up to a near-by farm house in the hope of finding aid and knocked on the door. An elderly French woman appeared and, after one look at their dishevelled appearance, slammed the door in their faces and shot home the bolts. With that it was back to the Whitley as there seemed to be no other houses in sight. A miserable and cold night was spent at the wreck with the men alternately keeping guard or sleeping. Come dawn a local appeared on the scene and asked, "When are you taking off?"

The crew of the last Whitley were in even deeper trouble on their return from Munich. The out bound flight and leaflet dropping had gone fairly well, even though they had the usual mid-under turret problems and oxygen failure. It was on the return leg of their journey that trouble really started for Scrgeant T. W. Bowles and his crew when a cylinder head of the starboard engine blew off somewhere near the Franco-German boarder. Unable to maintain height on one engine and encumbered by ice the Whitley went into a dive through thick snow clouds. The port engine then iced up and failed. Bowles had no option but to give the order to bale out and at 2,000 feet the crew began to extricate themselves.

The front gunner was out of his turret in a flash, but in his haste he forgot to disconnect his intercom and oxygen leads. He hung halfway out of his turret, slowly strangling himself, until the air observer came to the hatch and helped him on his way with his boot. He was free, but still not out of trouble for when he pulled his rip-cord his chest type parachute came up and hit him on the chin, knocking him out cold. He came to some time later surrounded by cows chewing their cud. Having kicked the gunner out the observer followed and was swinging safely beneath his parachute when he saw below a seemingly huge expanse of water. He splashed down in eighteen inches of water in a flooded field and sprained an ankle, but considered himself damn lucky in the circumstances.

The WOP/AG also had his troubles. He baled out successfully and landed safely in a field, but then had to do a hundred yard dash to escape a bull, no mean feat in full flying kit. The skipper, in spite of being the last to leave the cockpit, was the only one to land safely and without incident.

K8984 carried on in a shallow dive and burst into flames on impact. It was only then that the tail gunner realised that the aircraft was in trouble! He had been totally unaware of the drama in the cockpit because his intercom had failed. Miraculously he survived the crash and got out of his turret relatively unhurt and scrambled to the cockpit to free his crew. Somewhat bewildered the dazed, bruised and bleeding gunner left the wreck and limped to the nearest village where he discovered the rest of the crew drinking it up in a local estaminet. Eventually they were taken to the local hospital where the celebration continued.

No air operations were scheduled for 4 Group squadrons on 28th/29th October - they must have known that it was my nineteenth birthday. To celebrate, instead of the usual char and wads in the NAAFI, I went with two of my room-mates to Ripon where we indulged in a change from our usual cook-house fare in one of the restaurants. Afterwards we went to the Unicorn which was one of the local pubs.

At that time I was not enamoured of the taste of beer and I drank from bravado to prove that I was one of the boys. I think that evening two half pints were more than enough and lasted me the session. It is worth noting that then for sixpence (2.5p), you could obtain a half pint of beer, five cigarettes and a box of matches, and still receive an old half penny change.

The evening ended with a journey back to camp in a blacked-out local bus which weaved its way cautiously along the unlit roads. Then it was the usual booking in proceedure at the guardroom, being scrutinised by the beady-eyed service policeman who was looking for any excuse to put you on a Fizzer, and back to the billet to collapse on the charpoy.

The Group's last raid of the month was carried out on the night of October 31st by two of our squadron's crews. The objective was a reconnaissance of the Jade, Wesser and Hamburg areas and mine was one the crews selected. As luck would have it Pilot Officer Henry, Fletch and Freddie were on leave so they were replaced by Pilot Officer K. G. J. 'Dougie' Wakefield as second pilot, Leading Aircraftsman Arthur 'Lofty' Millington as 1st WOP/AG and Leading Aircraftsman Bob Hutton in the tail turret. I had flown with Lofty before, but not with the other two. Bob was a unique character, a peace-time regular who had served during WWI and one of the few remaining Fitter / Aero-engines. Wakefield was at that time filling the post of squadron adjutant.

We were airborne at 23.00 hours. During our passage over the North Sea, Bob and I tested our guns and after an uneventful two hours we approached the German coast. There was only a small amount of cloud so Dougie was able to get a good pinpoint and confirm our course. As we approached Jade Bay the cloud thickened, obscuring the area as it continued to do along the River Wesser so we set course for Hamburg. We were lucky for the cloud began to break up and when we reached the city it was clear. Our reconnaissance commenced and initially we were able to proceed undetected, but soon the searchlight activity increased. By de-synchronising the engines periodically, the skipper was hoping to fool the German ground defences into believing we were one of theirs. This worked for a while, but eventually our luck ran out and one of the probing searchlights picked us up in its beam. This was my first experience of being held in searchlights and I was amazed how exposed we were. Then the light flak opened up - my baptism under fire. At first I was naively fascinated by the different colours of the missiles as they hosed up towards us. It looked just like a firework display, until I was jolted back to the reality of just how lethal the fireworks were by Bob's voice over the intercom as he gave us his urgent commentary. His normal baritone changed to tenor as he reported, 'Tail gunner to pilot. The ack ack's getting closer, getting closer!'. We were flying at about 8,000 feet and by now other lights and flak batteries had joined in so the skipper heeded Bob's warning and took evasive action. The Whitley dived, climbed and weaved as our pilot attempted to extricate us from what was fast becoming a predicament. He finally succeeded and as we escaped into the darkness the relief was audible. The searchlights waved frantically about the sky attempting to pick us up again and the flak gunners continued their 'Brocks benefit' no doubt hoping to be lucky with a random shot. We left the immediate area without delay.

We steered clear of any further trouble and were soon crossing the German coast for our return across the North Sea. After an un-eventful two hours we reached the English coast where the cloud base was lowering, but with the aid of a few timely bearings from Linton-on-Ouse we were able to get back to Dishforth before the weather really clamped down on us. We had been airborne for eight hours and twenty minutes.

Both pilots were required for a full debrief during which Bick modestly under-played the opposition we had encountered over Hamburg. He reported it as 'light'. Bob's comment was, "It might have been light, but there was more than enough of it."

At around noon the next day we were rudely awakened by our room mates clattering in. They told us that we were required to report to the 'B' Flight hangar at 14.00 hours and we were to be in our best blue, No. 1 uniform.

"Come off it," I said, "We've only just got to bed. Don't you know that we were flying when you were snoring your heads off?"

Corporal Dick Still, who was in charge of the room, spoke up, "We've got some top brass coming, better get ready."

We got dressed and spruced up and wended our way to the hangar area with the rest of the squadron's erks. On arrival we were greeted by the squadron discipline officer who ordered us to line up in the hangar. The aircrews were lined up infront of the aircraft and our crew of the previous night were the second crew in line. As the VIP party entered the hangar the parade was brought to attention by the squadron adjutant. Out of the corner of my eye I saw the entourage approaching and as it got closer I discerned a slight figure in Air Force uniform accompanied by the towering figure of our commading officer, Wing Commander Staton and the other top brass. It was then I realised the identity of the VIP - it was His Majesty King George VI. He walked along the line of crews shaking hands with the officers and inspecting the airman aircrew. When it was our turn the CO informed His Majesty that we had just been over Hamburg and as I came under the Royal scrutiny I suppose my chest swelled visibly. It was one of those unforgettable moments which lives in the memory for the rest of your days. That evening in the barrack rooms pens worked overtime to pass the news of our honour to parents and girlfriends.

We continued to be plagued by bad weather over the UK and there was a series of nights when operations were first called for, but then cancelled. In an attempt to overcome this aircraft were again detached to Villeneuve in France. No. 77 Squadron was one of the units involved in these raids and sent five aircraft to France on the night of November 10th/11th to carry out a leaflet drop and reconnaissance over the Ruhr. One crew were forced to return shortly after take-off when their W/T equipment failed, but the remainder carried out the sortie. Tragedy struck on their return when Squadron Leader J. A. B. Begg and crew flying N1346 crashed in a forest near the town of Bouxurulles and burst into flames. All aboard were killed and the story goes that the rescue team discovered that the locals had placed flowers near the wreck in honour of the crew.

No. 10 Squadron was the next to send aircraft to Villeneuve. Ours was one of the crews detailed and we took off from Dishforth on November 20th. We were back to our original crew now, Pilot Officer Henry, Fletch and Freddie having returned from leave, and we had Wing Commander Staton along with us as force commander.

We arrived in France during the afternoon and fussed around our aircraft until Fletch, Freddie and I were taken to our billet in Avize, a few miles from the airfield. We discovered that our accommodation was, to say the least, primitive. It was a two-storey building which had been used by casual grape pickers at harvest time. The beds were just raised wooden boards placed each side of a central corridor and the bedding was only straw-filled palliases supplied by the French. These we found to be totally un-usable for they were already occupied - by bugs! We spent a very uncomfortable night on bare boards and wearing full flying kit. The things we did for England.

After our disturbed night we were glad to greet the new day, even if it meant washing and shaving in icy water. Our next priority was to get some breakfast inside us, but when we saw what the RAF temporary kitchen had to offer we decided to go hungry. Luckily we met a WOP/AG from No. 226 Squadron, which was equipped with Fairey Battles, who was also operating out of Villeneuve and who directed us to an establishment that served bacon and eggs. We lost no time in getting there and between the three of us we managed to resurrect from our school-boy French, "Des oeufs et bacon, S'il vous plait."

After finishing our meal we still had time left to explore before setting off for the airfield. The small town of Avise is nine kilometres from Epernay, the centre of the Champagne producing district. During our exploration we just happened to arrive at a warehouse where the locally produced Champagne was stored. We had been tipped off by the chap from 226 that this place was worth a visit. Fortunately the owner spoke better English than we did French and he took us on a guided tour. He lead us into the dark recesses of the massive cellars which stretched for some considerable distance and recounted the story of Avise in WWI. Apparently Marshal Foche, the French commander, had allowed the Germans to capture the town during the battle of the Marne, only to recapture it three days later without a shot being fired. There were 3,000 legless Germans still in the cellars! Much impressed with our tour we were given the opportunity to buy some bubbly at 14 Francs a bottle. With an exchange rate of 172 Francs to the Pound that made it cheap enough for even me to give it a try.

We stood by as a reserve crew that night, but were not required. The other two completed their sorties to Dusseldorf and Frankfurt successfully and we returned to the UK next day, keeping low all the way as Champagne is extremely pressure sensitive.

Shortly after our return a panic occured. A Coastal Command crew had reported sighting the German pocket battleship *Deutschland* proceeding on a westerly course from Germany, so a force of 24 Whitleys was despatched to Kinloss from where they could mount an attack. Seven crews from No. 10 Squadron, eight from No. 51 Squadron, five from No. 102 Squadron and four from No. 77 made the trip, but it was all to no avail for the sighting was not verified and the operation cancelled after several days waiting. During this detachment a very unfortunate accident occured to Pilot Officer 'Lofty' Willis who had flown with me before and was one of the squadron's very few 'Astro.' experts. He was attempting to hand start an aircraft using a crank when he fell off a ladder and struck his head on the turning propeller. Lofty was severely injured in the accident and spent many months in hospital, but happily he recovered and finished the war as a Group Captain with the DFC.

While the bulk of the group's aircraft were detached to Kinloss those left at home continued to carry out reconnaissance and leaflet raids over Germany. On one of these raids on the night of November 26th a crew from No. 102 Squadron had a very lucky escape. On return from a leaflet drop in the Wilhelmshaven area Pilot Officer Long and his crew in N1377 experienced icing problems during their slow descent from 15,000 feet. Levelling out at 2,000 feet they headed for the coast to carry out a reconnaissance and flew through snow storms all the way. They crossed the coast where they noted several boats and turned east to re-cross the coast again. Suddenly they were illuminated by searchlights and shortly afterwards there was a loud bang as though the bomber had been hit by flak. Long struggled for control and successfully turned the Whitley towards Heligoland, climbing to 19,500 feet as he did so. At this height the accumulation of ice became so bad that Long lost control and was not able to pull the aircraft up until they had dropped to 2,500 feet. The instruments were now covered with ice and the captain ordered the crew to ditching positions, but he was just able to keep the Whitley airborne at between 500 and 800 feet with an airspeed of 110 mph. The air observer was already at his ditching position and had opened the fuselage door in preparation to get out when he saw the source of their trouble. All the fabric had come off the upper surface of the wings and one flap was jammed in the down position. In spite of the crippled state of the aircraft they managed to cross 342 miles of North Sea and land safely at Bircham Newton where they concluded that the damage had in fact been caused by lightning. On December 12th both Long and his second pilot, Pilot Officer K. N. Gray, were awarded the Distiguished Flying Cross for their efforts, the first of many awards to be given to Whitley aircrew in 4 Group.

I was able to take some of my leave entitlement in November and it happily coincided with my return from France. I took home some of the Champagne, but I am sure that it was only the novelty of it that impressed, good ale being more to their liking. At that time my home was on the Northumbrian Fells which inevitably felt the force of the English winter and the 1939 winter was no exception. Despite the weather my leave was a welcome break from service routine and I was able to visit friends and relations and renew aquaintances with school friends who were now volunteering to join the services. They, like myself, thought that it was going to be a great adventure and were keen to hear from me what they could expect. I hope that I was able to put it in its correct perspective without laying it on too thick. They would find out for themselves soon enough what the reality of it was. Being the only one from the village on flying duties in the RAF also gave me a bit of glamour so during my leave I must admit to making the best of it with the belles. Suffice to say that I enjoyed every aspect of my leave and I was reluctant to return to Dishforth at the end of the month, but needs must.

When I got back I found that the weather was still affecting operations and that aircraft and crews were still going on detachment to France. Conditions marginally improved and on the night of December 6th/7th two crews from No. 10 Squadron, ours and another, were detailed to carry out a reconnaissance and leaflet drop in the Keil / Eckenforde area. Take-off was scheduled for 15.05 hours, so after lunch we began our preparations. We took off on time and climbed away from our snow covered airfield while it was still light. The flight over the North Sea as the light faded was uneventful, but as the aircraft climbed the temperature steadily got lower and lower. After two hours we passed to the north of Heligoland where the searchlights illuminated the sky about us in an attempt to pick us up. They were unsuccessful, but provided us with a good pin-point so we were on track when we crossed the enemy coast. Away to the north we could again see the lights of neutral Denmark. By now we were flying at 22,000 feet and the outside air temperature was minus 32°C - bloody chilly.

While the others up front got busy with their observations, Fletch and I made our way back to the fuselage and removed the outer wrappings from the parcels of leaflets stacked forward of the mid-under turret. Eventually we reached the Eckenforde area and were given the order to off-load the bumph. We decided to leave the turret raised as we did not want it to freeze in the down position as had happened so often before. This would make it more difficult to drop the leaflets, but we decided that it would be worth it in the circumstances. We adopted the usual dropping procedure. One passed the bundles to the other who dropped them down the chute, while coping with the oxygen problems caused by the single point and putting up with extremes of cold from which our flying clothing

Two photographs of Pilot Officer Long's Whitley N1377 after it had been struck by lightning.

gave scant protection. I was kneeling by the chute and losing all feeling in my feet even though I was wearing fleece-lined boots.

We finally got rid of the last bundle and Fletch returned to the comparative warmth of the cockpit. I attempted to follow him, but could not. I had lost all feeling in my legs as the circulation had been restricted as I knelt. Painfully I dragged myself passed the retracted turret and reached the Elsan, the chemical toilet which was whimsically referred to by aircrew as the thunderbox. Seated on the throne I began to pound my feet up and down on the fuselage floor in a effort to get the circulation going. I do not know how long it was before the blood got flowing again, but for the next half an hour I experienced the exquisite agony as it coursed in my frozen feet.

Back in the tail turret poor Freddie, more exposed to the cold than we were, finally admitted that he had lost all feeling in his hands and that his gun had frozen up. By now we were crossing the enemy

63

coast so the skipper could take us down to where the air was comparatively warmer, but still well below freezing. The return flight was without incident, but extremely uncomfortable and interminable. We were more than thankful when we landed at Dishforth at 21.15 hours, having been airborne for six hours and ten minutes. It seemed to have lasted twice as long. Freddie was carted off to the sick bay where they found both his hands were frost bitten, but I am glad to say that no permanent damage had been done and he eventually recovered completely. I was more fortunate. My pounding of feet on the floor had paid off, but I did not get away with it entirely as I had blisters on both feet. Dispensing propaganda leaflets was a painful business, and all for one and sixpence a day extra.

On December 9th, No. 78 Squadron, which had acted as group reserve and shared Dishforth with us, went to Linton-on-Ouse and swopped locations with No. 51 Squadron. We were able to renew acquaintance with old oppos with whom we had trained or met previously. Inter squadron rivalry was revived when we reminded them that we were the senior residents and pointed out that they should consider themselves lucky to join the Group's best squadron. It was all good natured stuff and they soon settled in without resort to violence.

In December the group's squadrons were given the additional task of carrying out offensive sweeps over the North Sea in an attempt to locate and attack enemy shipping. This was the first time that the Whitley squadrons were used on daylight operations and No. 77 Squadron led the way when three crews carried out a sweep on December 10th. On this occasion nothing was sighted or attacked. These sweeps would continue at intervals until February, 1940, without any degree of success, but it a made a change for the crews. At least we could see where we were going instead of groping in the dark, although we did run the risk of attack from German fighters.

Another new operation we were tasked with was security patrols over the seaplane bases of Borkum and Hornum in the Frisian Islands. Their purpose was to curb the activities of the enemy's mine laying sea-planes which were sowing magnetic mines in our coastal shipping lanes and causing havoc. A system of standing patrols was introduced whereby Whitleys operating in relays flew over the bases and bombed any sign of activity. Six aircraft of No. 77 Squadron and two more from No. 102 Squadron started the patrols on the night of

December 12th/13th. It was during these patrols that bombs were first dropped in anger by Whitley crews.

The patrols were carried out at a reasonable altitude where, although the temperature was low, it was still bearable and not the extremes experienced on high altitude leaflet drops. There were of course hazards in this cat and mouse game because the sea-plane bases were well protected. However, I think this was accepted by most of the crews as there was the chance of some offensive action. During patrols it was sometimes necessary to run the gauntlet of the defences when there were indications that sea-planes were about to get airborne. It gave us air-gunners the opportunity to retaliate by firing down the searchlight beams and at the flashes from the flak guns. On the whole we were a blood-thirsty lot. All the Whitley squadrons were involved at one time or another, but there were no casualties even though some came back with flak damage. It was subsequently reported that security patrols over the bases paid dividends, the Germans being forced to transfer the minelaying task to land-based Heinkel He111s flying from Germany.

On December 23rd ours and another crew carried out No. 10 Squadron's first offensive daylight sweep when we were detailed to search an area within 50 miles of the island of Sylt. This trip was to be my first of many as tail-end Charlie because of a change in crewing policy on the squadron which introduced air-observers to take over the navigation and bombing duties previously carried out by second pilots. These direct entry air observers, part of the peace-time expansion scheme, had been posted to the squadrons just prior to the outbreak of war. Since then they had only flown non-operationally and it was decided that they could become operational. It was rumoured that our commanding officer was not enamoured with the decision, but that Group had twisted his arm. So it was decreed that with the inclusion of an air observer the second WOP/AGs should man the tail turret instead of the tradesmen gunners who, to their disgust, were taken off flying duties and returned to their ground trades. I took Freddie's place as he was still recovering from frost bite and Sergeant Arthur Knapper joined us as air observer taking on the duties of Pilot Officer Henry.

We were told quite early on December 23rd that we would be required for ops. Our usual aircraft, K9023, was undergoing inspection and we had been allocated one of the squadron's spares,

K9035, so I went to the hangar area where it was parked to check the tail gun and turret. On the way I met Flying Officer 'Bick' Bickford who told me to make a good job of it because I might be using it in anger before the day was out. Our patrol would be in daylight and we would be in an area well within the range of enemy fighters. Bearing in mind the ill-fated armed reconnaissance carried out on December 18th when twelve out of twenty-four Wellingtons were shot down by fighters I needed no prompting.

At briefing when we met Arthur Knapper, Fletch and I decided that because he was the new boy and looked so young he would be known as the 'Nipper' and besides that rhymed with Knapper. We also thought that he had picked a hot one for his first trip.

A covering of snow lay on the ground as we prepared for take off. It was a Saturday and some of the tradesmen had been stood down so my room-mate Frank Ashworth gave me a hand getting into the turret. I remember that he gave me the thumbs up as the Whitley squelched through the slush covered grass. We were airborne at 11.30 hours and climbed away from the airfield. The saving grace of this sortie, and possibly the only one was that it would be at low level where the temperatures were not too bad, but cold enough in my draughty turret. We crossed the coast at Flamborough Head, our usual place of departure, at 2,000 feet and were able to see quite well despite the slight drizzle. How bloody cold and uninviting the North Sea looked. Bick gave Fletch and I permission to test our guns and soon tracers and incendiaries burned their way down as we let go. It was easy to imagine being over the trenches in a bi-plane, fighting the Red Barron in WWI. We passed to the north of Heligoland and began our 'creeping line ahead' search pattern. Bick exhorted us to keep our eyes skinned and I diligently scanned behind while the rest of the crew searched ahead. Freddie used to say, "In the tail you never see where you're going, only where you've been." How right he was. After about thirty minutes in the area north west of Sylt we were alerted by 'Enery', our pet name for Pilot Officer Henry, to a ship, "Ship off the starboard bow, heading north." The adrenalin began to surge again as Bick turned the aircraft towards it. Enery went forward to man the front turret while the Nipper went forward to the bomb aiming position. Fletch by this time was in the mid-under turret ready to lower it as and when required.

As we neared the ship it was recognised as a merchantman and up at the sharp end Enery and Nipper were endeavouring to identify the flag flying from its stern. Our feelings were mixed when Enery called, "It's Swedish, neutral." Leaving the ship unmolested we continued our search, but there were no further sightings. We reached our PLE (Prudent Limit of Endurance) and set course for home.

Back in the billet we had our de-briefing with our room mates. As always they were keen to hear our blow-by-blow account, which we were pleased to provide. We might have to do the flying, but without the expert help of the ground crews we would be lost and let's face it our safety depended on them. They worked all hours of the day and night in dispersals open to the elements, who could blame them if they moaned sometimes and wanted to hear of the real action.

The pre-war practice of granting block leave during public holidays had of course been discontinued at the outbreak of war so over Christmas most of us were on duty, but this did not prevent us entering into the festive spirit. Most barrack room lockers were festooned with Christmas cards and as we all had received our parcels from home, there was no shortage of home-baked cake. On Christmas Day most of us were stood down early and there was the traditional mid-day meal of roast turkey with all the trimmings. We did not have to queue for it because we were served by our officers and senior NCOs, the old service tradition. Another perk was free bottles of beer - if you did not want yours there were lots of takers. Later in the day the sounds coming from the ablutions pin-pointed the over indulgent.

It was back to work and business as usual the following day and we air-gunners were given the gen that we were going to get a new flying badge to replace the winged bullet. The new badge was to be a half-wing brevet to be worn over the left breast pocket, similar to the air-observer's brevet, but with the letters AG in the centre. This was the first of the brevets to be fashioned on the air-observers badge and marked the first step in a decision taken by the Air Council to finally improve the status of the air-gunner when it was foreseen that large numbers of us would be needed in the future.

Air Chief Marshal Sir Edgar Ludlow-Hewitt, Air Officer Commanding-in-Chief Bomber Command had written to the Air Council Member for Personnel early in November 1939, requesting that consideration should be given to introducing a new badge similar to that of pilots and observers which he could award to every operationally qualified air-gunner. He argued that the award of such a badge would not only raise the status and prestige of the gunners, but also give greater recognition to the increasing responsibility which rested on them as vital members of aircrews. His views were endorsed by the Air Council and within three weeks a badge had been designed and specimens circulated among members before formal submission to the King for his approval. When the badge reached the Chief of Air Staff, Marshal of the RAF, Sir Cyril Newall, he noticed that the wing comprised of thirteen feathers. His reaction was that in the interests of those who might be superstitious, there should be twelve or fourteen feathers, but not thirteen. The remedy was dispensed by Wing Commander E. H. Hooper in the Directorate of Personnel Services, who had designed the badge. He cut away the smaller root wing, reducing the number to twelve and the badge was sent to the King in Buckingham Palace, who approved it.

At the end of December, 1939, Air Ministry Order A547/39 was promulgated authorising the issue and award of the new badge to all operational air-gunners. On No. 10 Squadron the news had a mixed reception, some approved, but most of the old sweats did not like it and continued to wear the winged bullet until well into 1940. Unfortunately the new brevet was not accompanied by any change in status or rank. We would have to wait until June, 1940, before that deficiency would be rectified and it was decided that the minimum rank for operational aircrew would be that of sergeant. Until then we would continue to fly on operations in our trade status and there would be many who would not survive to get their well deserved promotion.

We saw the old year out in style when ours was one of four crews from No. 10 Squadron detailed to patrol the sea-plane bases in the Frisian Islands. This would be our first 'go' as airborne sentries and though we did not look forward to stooging back and forth over the islands for hours, there was always the possibility that we might drop some bombs and do some strafing. The flight over the North Sea was uneventful and when we got over the islands we started the patrol. For the next few hours we flew back and forth over the bases, daring them to start something. No take-offs were attempted, but whenever we got within range of the defences they had a go at us. At midnight Bick, now newly promoted to the rank of Flight Lieutenant, wished us a happy New Year. Usually he was a stickler for crew discipline over the intercom, no chit chat. Some of the answering remarks to his New Year greetings bordered on the insubordinate, but he let them pass. Since the beginning of the war when our crew had come together as comparative strangers, the officer / airman gulf was diminishing as we did more raids and got to know each other better. Mind you we other ranks dare not take liberties. Fletch and I might refer to the skipper as Bick or Charles (after Charles Bickford, the American film actor) and to our second pilot as Enery, but we did so only between ourselves and when they were well out of earshot. Our peace-time discipine did not allow us to get that chummy. Having been indoctrinated to believe that the RAF was exclusively for pilots, we part-time fliers knew our place. We left the patrol area at 00.20 hours on January 1st, 1940, and landed at Dishforth a couple of hours later.

During the months of January and February the weather reached its worst and temperatures dropped to their lowest for 45 years. The River Thames froze hard for eight miles of its length. The main-line trains were sometimes a day late. Huge falls of snow added new perils in the blacked-out cities and cut off villages and towns from the outside world. Although these conditions curtailed operations the reconnaissance, leaflet raids and security patrols continued until the heaviest of the weather brought everything to a grinding halt.

On the night of January 4th/5th two crews from No. 10 Squadron were sent out on a reconnaissance and leaflet drop over Hamburg and Bremen. They both carried out their tasks, but Flying Officer V. R. Patterson crashed K9020 on landing at Dishforth. The crew escaped serious injury, but the aircraft was badly damaged. Much later there was to be a droll sequel. The WOP/AG Aircraftsman W. R. 'Charlie' Armstrong was recommended for a commission in 1944 and during his medical the examining officer discovered an entry in Charlie's records stating that he received fatal injuries in the crash. "Welcome back," he said. "I know you lot are supposed to be living on borrowed time, but this is ridiculous." Duly resurrected Charlie received his commission, survived the war and in 1946 was seconded to BOAC.

The next night our crew was back on sentry over the sea-plane bases when we were one of four sent by No. 10 Squadron. Apart from having to endure the intense cold, the temperature was minus six, the flight over the North Sea was uneventful. When we got to the islands we found them covered with snow. There was no sea-plane activity, but as we flew over the bases the searchlights and flak opened up. Now that I was flying as tail end Charlie I discovered that the best way of relieving any moments of temporary concern (fright in other words) as the flak got close was to get permission from Bick to belt a few rounds down the searchlight beams. It also had the effect of taking my mind off the discomfort caused by having to sit on the uncomfortable turret sadle in sub-zero conditions. That night I gave the defences at both Hornum and Borkum a ration of .303. Sometimes during these retaliatory bursts we had the satisfaction of causing the lights to go out. Whenever a Whitley Mk III or IV landed after a trip over Germany and the crew disembarked it was easy to spot the tail-gunner, he was the bow-legged one frantically massaging his numb bum.

On January 12th/13th another Whitley first was chalked up when two crews from No. 77 Squadron, Flying Officer T. J. Geach in N1357 and Flying Officer G. E. Saddington in N1347, were tasked to carry out a reconnaissance and leaflet drop over the Austrian capital, Vienna. A third crew, Flying Officer J. B. J. Boardman in N1348, was detailed to make a similar sortie to the Czechoslovakian capital, Prague. These were the first RAF aircraft to fly over these countries in WWII. All three aircraft took off from Villeneuve just before 17.00 hours. They crossed the frontier at 14,000 feet over Karlsruhe. It was minus 20°, but a clear and starry night with good visibility. The Vienna bound crews set course for their next pin-point at Munich, while the Prague crew proceeded via Nuremburg to their target. Both tasks were carried out as planned after which all aircraft landed safely, thus completing the deepest penetration of German occupied territory to date. The crews reported that the black-out precautions at both Vienna and Prague were very poor and that the opposition en route and over both targets was negligible.

By January 25th winter was well and truly with us and the Group's operations were halted when bases were blanketed by heavy falls of snow which ploughs, supplemented by the muscle power of every one available, failed to remove. We were well and truly earth

The pre-war 'winged bullet'   *The new air-gunner's badge*

bound. The weather was so bad that we were confined to camp so our social activities were somewhat curtailed. Our off duty time was being spent in the barrack room or the crowded NAAFI where, to the accompaniment of a battered beer-washed piano, budding crooners attempted to emulate Bing Crosby. Hoagy Carmichael's 'Stardust' took a terrible beating and the washing was hung on the Siegfried Line nightly. These decorous renditions took place before the NAAFI ale took effect. When that happened the musical repertoire changed to 'Salome', 'One eyed Riley', 'There's a Troopship leaving Bombay', 'T'was on the good ship Venus' and other obscene service 'classics'.

In the barrack room we had our radio set and the BBC had thankfully relaxed some of the restrictions on broadcasting. The Home Service resumed something like a normal balance of radio programmes and a new Forces Programme based on light entertainment was introduced. Daily newspapers leading the barrack room circulation were those with strip cartoons, the Daily Mirror topping the popularity poll with Jane, who was always guaranteed to be in some stage of undress. Heading the Sunday league was the News of the World, known to us other ranks as the Picadilly PORs (Personnel Occurence Reports) because of its tendency to report the juiciest and most lurid sex cases. And talking of sex cases even our Group had its moments.

On one station an incident occured involving two flight commanders and two sergeant WAAFs. By the time the tale got to our level it resembled the script from a Whitehall Farce, but on this occasion it was not Brian Rix who was doing the trouser dropping. Apparently two SPs. on night patrol noticed a light shining from a first floor room window in the officer's mess, thus infringing black-out regulations. The two policemen entered the mess where they were met by the station Padre who offered to assist. He suggested that they should accompany him and pin-point the room from where the light was shining. They did so and when the room was indicated the Padre knocked on the door and entered. There was a squadron leader in flagrante delicto. The Padre, attempting to recover his composure, immediately shut the door, telling the two SPs. (whose eyes were standing out like organ stops) that they had got the wrong room and suggested it was the one next door. He again knocked on the door and entered, not thinking that lightning would strike twice, but it did. There was the second squadron leader caught in the act, with again the two SPs. as boggle-eyed witnesses. The unfortunate outcome was courts martial all round, resulting in both Squadron Leaders being reprimanded and one of them being posted from his squadron. Both Sergeant WAAFs were dismissed the service. However they did not leave the area, but set up an establishment in one of the local towns from where it was alleged they continued to dispense their favours.

In civvy street the population were inflicted with rationing which began on January 8th, 1940, for foodstuffs such as bacon, ham, butter and sugar. The weekly ration for each person was four ounces of ham or bacon, four ounces of butter and twelve ounces of sugar. Petrol had been rationed since September 16th, 1939, and there was only one grade available at one shilling and sixpence a gallon (7.5p).

The dreadful weather continued to dominate the scene. Dishforth was the worst affected of the group's airfields, first by snow and then by flooding. It was not until February 17th, that operations were resumed and No. 77 Squadron sent two crews on a daylight reconnaissance of Heligoland. One aircraft suffered low oil pressure and came back on one engine, but the other reported eight large warships escorted by twelve destroyers five nautical miles west of Heligoland. On the 19th, No. 102 Squadron repeated the mission, but found only pack ice for a distance of five miles around the islands.

We were still earth-bound at Dishforth, but were delighted by the news which reached us on February 21st. Wing Commander Staton, our Commanding Officer, had been awarded the Distinguished

*Loading Bumph into a Whitley for a raid on January 12th, 1940.
(Chaz Bowyer)*

Service Order and Sergeant A. S. 'Johnnie' Johnson the Distinguished Flying Medal. These were the first awards to the squadron in WWII.

Detachments to France continued to make the best of the slightly better weather over there. On the night of February 22nd/23rd, No. 102 Squadron sent Squadron Leader J. C. MacDonald in N1378 and Pilot Officer J. J. McKay in N1381 to Vienna. They took off from Villeneuve and climbed to 10,000 feet where, because of the beautifully clear moonlit night they flew in loose formation. Over Vienna they descended to drop leaflets and flares before climbing back to 10,000 feet without any opposition. On their return they dropped to 3,000 feet over Munich and plotted an airfield with aircraft on it to the west of the city. The Flak then opened up so they made their seperate ways back.

Back in the UK the weather was improving and operations began to get underway again. At the end of February, No. 58 Squadron returned to the 4 Group fold when it returned from detachment to Coastal Command and commenced its conversion to Mk. Vs. We at Dishforth got back to the war on March 1st/2nd when No. 10 Squadron was ordered to send two crews to drop leaflets on the German capital, Berlin. Ours was one of the crews selected and it gave us a big kick to be going to 'The Big City' as it was called even in those early days. We took off from Dishforth at 20.00 hours in Old Faithful, K9023, and made our way through the clear night with excellent visibility. As we climbed so the temperature began to drop and I began to stamp my feet up and down on the floor of my draughty turret in an attempt to keep the circulation going. It crossed my mind that I might have to stamp all the way to Berlin, quite a walk I mused. We crossed the enemy coast and saw the bright lights of neutral Holland. Because of Hamburg's poor black-out we were able to skirt around its defences and made use of the excellent visibility to avoid other well defended areas. We arrived over Berlin without incident and I had a grandstand view as Fletch and the Nipper dropped the leaflets which scattered behind me in a white flurry. The searchlights and flak defences now opened up at us, but sitting in my little turret, very exposed and detached from the rest of crew, I got the distinct impression that it was all directed at me. I kept my eyes skinned for German fighters, but luckily there were none. The German night-fighter force was, like the British, in its embrionic stage but they did send the odd Me109 or Me110 up on clear nights.

My main problem was the cold. It was well below freezing and I was very glad when Fletch announced that the last of the bumph had gone. We set course for home, but before we left the Big City I had to give it my personal baptism of fire and belted off a few rounds. I told Bick that I did not want my gun to freeze up! We landed at 06.00 hours after a flight of ten hours and to say that I was relieved when they prised me out of my turret is an understatement. The other crew on the operation was Sergeant Johnson's in K9026. They had a similarly uneventful trip, but ran into trouble just a quarter of a mile short of Dishforth's runway when their engines cut as they ran out of fuel. The Whitley was wrecked, but I am glad to say that the crew got away with it. That lunch-time, on the 1 o'clock news, the BBC reported, "Last night the RAF carried out a reconnaissance and dropped leaflets over Berlin. All our aircraft returned safely." This was a great boost to our egos and something to write home about.

The leaflet raids and reconnaissances continued and included another Whitley 'first' when on the night of March 7th/8th No. 77 Squadron sent two aircraft, N1366 flown by Flight Lieutenant B. S. Tomlin and N1365 flown by Flying Officer G. L. Raphael* from

*Raphael was later to transfer to Fighter Command, where he would distinguish himself flying nightfighter Havocs during the 'Blitz'

Flight Sergeant Tomlin and how the press pictured his adventure.

They had to ask Nazis the way home . . . .

The R.A.F. boys who landed in Germany after a reconnaissance flight. They thought they had passed over the French boundary until they asked villagers. Then they dashed for their machine after the Germans had pointed the way. They had been fifteen minutes on German soil. Picture taken when they landed in France.

"I told you edelweiss didn't grow in France."

Villeneuve to drop leaflets over Poznan. They were the first RAF aircraft to fly over Poland during World War II. This raid was followed by others on March 9th, 10th and 15th, over Vienna and Warsaw. The raid over the Polish capital on the 15th resulted in a unique aftermath. One of the two No. 77 Squadron aircraft involved, N1387 flown by Flight Lieutenant B. S. Tomlin, after successfully dropping the leaflets, set off on the return flight to Villeneuve. As dawn approached their fuel stocks were getting low and they were lost - or in navigation parlance uncertain of their position. Thinking they were over France, Tomlin landed the aircraft in a large field. After stopping the engines and getting out of the Whitley the crew discovered to their horror when attempting to converse with some civilians who had appeared on the scene, that they were in Germany. This fact was confirmed by the approach of a number of German troops on bicycles.

Dashing back to the aircraft they piled aboard, fortunately managed to get both engines started, and hauled the Whitley back into the air as the enemy troops fired their rifles. Once airborne they established their position and crossed the German/French border. When they arrived back at Villeneuve to tell their story, the newspapers had a field day.

In Nazi Germany the repercussions were, however, more serious. The day after the incident a Hauptmann and three German soldiers from the local Wehrmacht unit arrived at Niedersalbach, the village near to which the Whitley had landed. They apprehended Albert Kartes, a seventeen year old who had, unfortunately for him, conversed with Sergeant Ron Charlton, the Whitley's air-observer. He was carted off to the headquarters of a military unit where he was interrogated and then incarcerated in the remand prison at Volklingen, some six miles away. A week later he and another eye-witness of the incident were brought to trial, accused of 'giving support to the enemy'. They were found guilty and sentenced to two years imprisonment, the judges commenting that the 'leniency' was due to Kartes youth. However, thanks to the village pastor and some influential members of the local community there was a re-trial, during the course of which the defending counsel was able to convince the judges that those responsible for the escape of the Whitley and its crew were actually the fully armed German soldiers who had appeared on the scene and had done nothing. The outcome was that the sentence was quashed and Albert Kartes and his co-defendant were released six weeks later. During a renewed hunt for scapegoats, they even tried to nail the village policeman for not being on the scene quick enough.*

Our next trip took place on the night of March 16th/17th, when we were one of No. 10 Squadron's crews detailed to reconnoitre Germany's industrial Ruhr complex. We took off from Dishforth in

*Herr Albert Kartes survived to recount the above description of his adventure to Herr Werner Eckel.

K9023 at 20.15 hours. The weather was cloudy and we ran into the odd rain shower as we crossed the North Sea, where as usual we checked the guns and turrets. Reaching the enemy coast without incident and taking care to avoid the now well-known defended areas, we set course for what was to become known in bizarre aircrew jargon as 'Happy Valley'. The area allocated for our attention was Düsseldorf and we approached from the north, flying at approximately 10,000 feet. As the Ruhr was the heart of Germany's industrial area, it was well defended and we constantly weaved to avoid the searchlights and Flak.

Over Düsseldorf itself the Flak opposition was quite severe and the aircraft bucketted as it absorbed the effects of the heavy stuff. In the area were about thirty to fifty searchlights endeavouring to illuminate us, but luckily we escaped undetected. This was the first time we had seen so many searchlights operating in 'cones' in co-ordination with the Flak batteries; very frightening and I was glad when we left the area.

We landed at Villeneuve in the early hours of March 17th. The other five aircraft also landed there, the crews similarly reporting heavy opposition over Düsseldorf. It was an indication of Germany's increasing defensive potential and of how seriously they were regarding our nightly intrusions over the Fatherland.

Two days later, March 19th, our room-mates took great delight in pulling our legs about an article which had appeared in the newspapers. It read:-

Gunners - RAF Call

More men of high courage, determination and powers of endurance, aged between 28 and 35 years are needed for the RAF's most dangerous job - the rôle of Air Gunner, who is both the eyes and teeth of the RAF. Development of warplanes equipped with multiple gun turrets has increased the importance of the air- gunner in modern warfare. That is why commissions for the duration of the war are being granted to air-gunners for the first time in the history of the RAF.

Suicide Squad

Although this branch is sometimes called the 'suicide' squad, there has been no shortage of recruits. The extra men are needed owing to the expansion of the RAF.

Applicants for commissions as officer air-gunners must be of first-rate physique, good education and able to handle men. The initial rank is Acting Pilot Officer with pay of eleven shillings per day with regulation allowances. On posting to duty after satisfactory completion of training they are regarded as Pilot Officers with pay of fourteen shillings and sixpence per day.

After twelve months service as Pilot Officers they are promoted to Flying Officers with pay of eighteen shillings and twopence per day. After a further year they are promoted to Flight Lieutenant (pay twenty-one shillings and ninepence per day).

You can imagine the ribbing we had to take; "First-rate physique, high courage, determination, good education, powers of endurance and able to lead men. You lot haven't a chance!"

Later notices were to appear on POR's inviting experienced WOP/AG's to be trained as Gunnery Leaders. We discussed it but didn't apply. Joking apart, as peacetime regular airmen we didn't consider we had the high standards we attributed to officers. Of course, we could have been wrong. One ambitious WOP/AG in the group did apply, was accepted and became so successful that he commanded his own squadron later in the war. We thought that we were getting a raw deal considering that 'Sprog' officers were going to be paid up to twenty- one shillings and ninepence a day for doing the job that we had been doing since the first day of the war for a bonus one shilling and sixpence per day.

Later that day, March 19th, we discovered that we were going to take part in the first bombing raid against a German land target, namely the seaplane base of Hornum on the Friesian Islands. The change in bombing policy was in retaliation for the air raid by the Luftwaffe on Scapa Flow in the Orkney Islands on March 16th, during which a civilian was killed. This retaliatory raid was to be a 'one off'; we would attack no further land targets until the Germans invaded Scandinavia and the Low Countries.

We were called to briefing early in the evening, during which we were given the gen on the impending raid. The 4 Group force of Whitleys comprised eight aircraft from No. 10 Squadron, with twenty-two more from Nos. 51, 77 and 102 Squadrons. 5 Group were sending twenty Hampdens and this combined force of fifty aircraft would be the greatest number of RAF bombers to concentrate on a single German target to date. The atmosphere during briefing was charged with anticipation and excitement at the prospect that we were going to drop bombs instead of those 'bloody leaflets'.

The flight over the North Sea went smoothly, but the excitement mounted when 'Nipper' announced over the intercom that we would soon be near the island and the target. This was confirmed when 'Enery' reported that he could see searchlight and Flak activity ahead, indicating that the leading aircraft were already carrying out their attacks and no doubt stirring up trouble.

'Nipper' went to the bomb-aiming position in the nose of the aircraft to prepare for the bomb-run from 4,000 feet. The adrenalin flow increased when he reported that he had identified the target and called "Bomb doors open!" We started the bomb-run and the litany commenced: "Left, left, steady...ri-ight, steady," as we ran the gauntlet of the Flak and searchlight defences. The Whitley lurched as the bombs dropped away. We were now receiving the attentions of the defences, but the skipper kept the aircraft straight and level to enable 'Nipper' to plot the bursts. Some of the Flak got uncomfortably close to the tail and I was being blinded by the searchlights, so I opened fire down the beams.

We got away unscathed from our first bombing sortie. Although the bomb-run had lasted only a few minutes it had seemed much longer. As we set course for home I had a grandstand view as more aircraft attacked the target. It was an exciting spectacle, with multi-coloured Flak curling its way upwards, dark eruptions of the heavier stuff and the searchlights probing the night sky. Fletch came on the intercom, reporting that one of our bombers had just transmitted an 'X' signal to base which, when decoded, read 'The natives are hostile'. The WOP/AG responsible must have been an old sweat who had previously spent some of his overseas service bombing recalcitrant natives in the Middle East or tribesmen on the North West Frontier of India.

All the aircraft of our sister squadrons participating in the raid claimed to have attacked the target as briefed, with the exception of a crew from No. 102 Squadron which returned early. One crew from No. 51 Squadron, Flying Officer Birch in K9043, successfully evaded an attack by an Arado float-plane without sustaining damage. During their bomb-run, however, they encountered severe Flak opposition and the tail gunner, Corporal J. C. MacIntyre, was slightly wounded. No. 51 Squadron also suffered the only loss when N1405 flown by Flight Lieutenant J. E. Baskerville failed to return and was claimed by Luftwaffe Flak batteries in the target area.

The afternoon following the raid we were exposed to the national press and newsreel cameras as they gave us the full publicity treatment. Unfortunately, exaggerated claims had been made, but it is worth recalling an article published on March 25th 1940, which goes some of the way to putting things into perspective:-

The Attack On Sylt

A great deal of bother has been caused by the reports that the RAF did not do as much damage as at first we were led to believe. Well if this is true, there is nothing surprising in that. Sylt is a heavily fortified air base and it is said we attacked with forty-nine aircraft and forty-eight got back safely - that in itself is a considerable achievement. The brave men who flew the machines deserve the praise for it. The politicians claimed too full a measure of success before all the facts were known.

There was good-natured rivalry between Nos. 77 and 102 Squadrons at Driffield and Nos. 10 and 51 Squadrons at Dishforth, which was further stirred by the publicity. One newspaper report stated that our CO, Wing Commander 'Crack 'em' Staton had led the raid. This was strongly disputed by the Driffield boys, who claimed that Squadron Leader J. C. MacDonald of No. 102 Squadron had been first over the target. Subsequently, three officers of the squadron drove from Driffield to Dishforth and surreptitiously distributed some home-made leaflets poking fun at the newspaper description of the Dishforth squadrons' participation. On the following day two aircraft of Nos. 10 and 51 Squadrons dropped leaflets over Driffield containing an appropriate retaliatory reply.

Whitley N1357 which was shot down by Dutch fighters on the night of March 27th/28th 1940.

My participation in the raid also had an amusing sequel. I went home on leave shortly afterwards and one night took my girl-friend to the cinema in a small town some miles away. The programme as usual included a British Movietone newsreel showing some of the more important events of the week. The maiden voyage of the liner *Queen Elizabeth* was featured, the meeting between Hitler and Mussolini in the Brenner Pass, the aftermath of the Russo-Finnish war and 'RAF Heroes Return From Sylt'. This latter included an interview with four of the tail-gunners, one of whom was asked, "Did you fire your guns?" The gunner nonchalantly replied, "Only once Sir, to warm it up." The effect on my girl- friend was electric, she called out excitedly, "That's you!" We were at the back of the cinema (where else?) and with her outburst a sea of white faces turned towards us in the gloom. On the way back to our village in the bus that night, we were the subject of much whispering and head nodding. For the rest of my leave I was the recipient of a lot of well-intentioned curiosity and interest. Of course, I modestly played it down - like Hell I did, I played my new-found fame for all it was worth!

After the bombing raid on Sylt it was back to the 'paper round'. On the night of March 27th/28th one of No. 77 Squadron's aircraft, N1357 flown by Flying Officer T. J. Geach, strayed over neutral Holland and Fokker G-1 twin-engined fighters were scrambled to intercept. It was sighted by an aircraft of the 3e JaVa and was shot down south of Rotterdam by Lieutenant P. Noonan. Unfortunately the air- observer, Sergeant J. E. Miller, was killed, but the rest of the crew survived as internees. Because of bad weather there were no further operations during the remainder of March.

Summary of 4 Group Operations
October 1939 - March 1940

October 1939

1st-2nd. Leaflets and Reconnaissance - Berlin.
10 Sqn. Four a/c. Three successful, one FTR. Slight opposition, but weather severe.

15th-16th. Leaflets - North-West Germany.
10 Sqn. Nine a/c. One returned early U/S. Only one successful due to severe weather.
77 Sqn. Four a/c operating from Villeneuve. Slight opposition, weather severe. One FTR.

18th-19th. Leaflets and Reconnaissance - Hanover - Bremen - Hamburg.
10 sqn. Six a/c. Four aborted due to icing and/or equipment failure. Two successful. One force landed near Amiens.

24th-25th. Leaflets and Reconnaissance - Wilhelmshaven - Magdeburg - Berlin.
10 Sqn. Four a/c. One returned early U/S, three successful. Slight opposition.
77 Sqn. Four a/c. Three successful, one FTR. Opposition moderate.

27th-28th. Leaflets and Reconnaissance - Stuttgart and Munich.
51 Sqn. Five a/c from Villeneuve. One returned early with severe icing, four successful despite very bad weather. One crashed on return and another was abandoned over France.

31st-1st. Reconnaissance - Jade - Weser - Hamburg.
10 Sqn. Two a/c both successful. Opposition light to moderate in the Hamburg area.

November 1939

10th-11th. Leaflets and Reconnaissance - Ruhr.
77 Sqn. Five a/c. One returned early with W/T failure, one crashed on return.

21st-22nd. Leaflets and Reconnaissance - Frankfurt - Dusseldorf.

10 Sqn. Two a/c from Villeneuve successful. Opposition light.

24th-25th. Leaflets and Reconnaissance - Wilhelmshaven.
10 Sqn. Two a/c successful despite severe weather conditions.
77 Sqn. One a/c successful despite severe weather conditions.

26th-27th. Leaflets and Reconnaissance - Wilhelmshaven.
102 Sqn. Three a/c. Weather appalling. One a/c struck by lightning and badly damaged.

December 1939

6th-7th. Leaflets and Reconnaissance - Kiel - Eckernforde.
10 Sqn. Two a/c. Weather extremely bad, one rear gunner frost-bitten. Opposition light.

10th. Daylight Anti-Shipping Sweep over North Sea.
77 Sqn. Three a/c. Nothing sighted.

12th-13th. 'Security Patrols' - Hornum - Borkum.
77 Sqn. Six a/c. One bombed a flarepath, one damaged by Flak. Two enemy aircraft seen, but these did not attack.
102 Sqn. Two a/c. One bombed a flarepath.

13th-14th. 'Security Patrols' - Hornum - Borkum.
51 Sqn. Three a/c. One bombed a British submarine but missed. One strayed over Heligoland and heavily engaged by defences.
10 Sqn. Four a/c. Opposition moderate.

14th-15th. 'Security Patrols' - Hornum - Borkum
77 Sqn. Two a/c. Opposition light.
102 Sqn. Two a/c. Opposition light.

15th. Daylight Anti-Shipping Sweep over North Sea.
77 Sqn. Two a/c. Nothing sighted.

16th. Daylight Anti-Shipping Sweep over North Sea.
102 Sqn. Three a/c. Nothing sighted.

16th-17th. 'Security Patrols' - Hornum - Borkum.
77 Sqn. Three a/c. Four Flak-ships bombed without result. Much searchlight activity over Norderney.

17th-18th. 'Security Patrols' - Hornum - Borkum.
10 Sqn. Six a/c. Flares dropped over Borkum. Searchlights very active, but Flak light. Two enemy aircraft seen but these did not attack.

18th-19th. 'Security Patrols' - Hornum - Borkum.
51 Sqn. Two a/c. Medium to severe opposition.
77 Sqn. Four a/c. Three enemy aircraft seen but these did not attack.
102 Sqn. Four a/c. One machine-gunned lights at Hornum.

19th-20th. 'Security Patrols' - Hornum - Borkum
10 Sqn. Four a/c. Opposition light. Two enemy aircraft seen but these did not attack.

20th-21st. 'Security Patrols' - Hornum - Borkum.
77 Sqn. Two a/c. Bombs dropped on flarepath.
102 Sqn. One a/c. Bombs dropped on flarepath.

23rd. Daylight Anti-Shipping Sweep over North Sea.
10 Sqn. Two a/c. No enemy shipping sighted.

23rd-24th. Leaflets and Reconnaissance - North-West Germany.
51 Sqn. Four a/c. Opposition light.

26th. Daylight Anti-Shipping Sweep over North Sea.
77 Sqn. Two a/c. No enemy shipping sighted.
102 Sqn. Two a/c. No enemy shipping sighted.

29th. Daylight Anti-Shipping Sweep over North Sea.
77 Sqn. Two a/c. No enemy shipping sighted.
102 Sqn. Two a/c. No enemy shipping sighted.

31st-1st. 'Security Patrols' - Hornum - Borkum - Norderney - Heligoland.
10 Sqn. Four a/c. Moderate opposition.

January 1940

4th-5th. Leaflets and Reconnaissance - Hamburg - Bremen.
10 Sqn. Two a/c. Severe opposition over Bremen. One a/c crashed on return.

'Security Patrols' - Hornum - Borkum.
51 Sqn. Two a/c. Opposition moderate.

5th-6th. Leaflets and Reconnaissance - Hamburg - Bremen.
51 Sqn. Two a/c. Opposition moderate.

'Security Patrols' - Hornum - Borkum.
10 Sqn. Four a/c. Opposition moderate, cold intense.

9th-10th. Reconnaissance - Rheine - Emmerich - Hamm -
Osnabruck. 77 Sqn. Two a/c. Opposition slight.

'Security Patrols' - Hornum - Borkum.
102 Sqn. Four a/c. Flarepath bombed. Opposition light.

10th. Daylight Anti-Shipping Sweep over North Sea.
77 Sqn. Two a/c. No enemy shipping sighted.
102 Sqn. Two a/c. No enemy shipping sighted.

11th-12th. 'Security Patrols' - Hornum - Borkum.
77 Sqn. Three a/c. Lights and Flak positions machine-gunned.
Opposition light.

Leaflets and Reconnaissance - Hamm - Frankfurt.
102 Sqn. Two a/c. Opposition light.

12th-13th. Leaflets and Reconnaissance - Vienna - Prague.
77 Sqn. Three a/c from Villeneuve. No opposition

'Security Patrols' - Hornum - Borkum.
102 Sqn. Two a/c. Opposition light.

14th-15th. 'Security Patrols' - Hornum - Borkum.
51 Sqn. Two a/c. Opposition light. Two enemy aircraft seen, but
these did not attack.

20th-21st. 'Security Patrols' - Hornum - Borkum.
51 Sqn. One a/c. Opposition light.

February 1940
17th. Daylight Reconnaissance - Heligoland area.
77 Sqn. Two aircraft. One returned early U/S, the other sighted eight
warships escorted by twelve destroyers. Heavy opposition.

19th. Daylight Reconnaissance - Heligoland area.

102 Sqn. Two a/c. No ships sighted. Heavy opposition from shore batteries.

22nd-23rd. Leaflets and Reconnaissance - Vienna.
102 Sqn. Two a/c from Villeneuve. No opposition over Austria, some en route.

23rd-24th. Leaflets and Reconnaissance - Prague - Pilsen.
77 Sqn. Two a/c. No opposition.

24th-25th. 'Security Patrols' - Hornum - Borkum.
77 Sqn. Two a/c. Moderate opposition.
102 Sqn. Two a/c. Moderate opposition.

26th-27th. Leaflets and Reconnaissance - Berlin.
10 Sqn. Two a/c. Moderate opposition.

27th-28th. Leaflets and Reconnaissance - Berlin.
51 Sqn. One a/c. Moderate opposition.

28th-29th. Leaflets and Reconnaissance - Berlin.
51 Sqn. Two a/c. One returned early U/S. Moderate opposition.

March 1940

1st-2nd. Leaflets and Reconnaissance - Berlin.
10 Sqn. Two a/c. Moderate opposition. One crashed on landing.

3th-4th. Leaflets and Reconnaissance - Berlin.
51 Sqn. Two a/c. Light opposition. One enemy aircraft sighted, but this did not attack.

7th-8th. Leaflets and Reconnaissance - Poznan.
77 Sqn. Two a/c. No opposition.

Leaflets and Reconnaissance.
77 Sqn. Three a/c. Moderate to severe opposition. One enemy aircraft sighted.

9th-10th. Leaflets and Reconnaissance - Vienna.
102 Sqn. Three a/c from Villeneuve. No opposition.

10th-11th. Leaflets and Reconnaissance - Warsaw.
77 Sqn. Two a/c. Opposition en route, but none over target area.

15th-16th. Leaflets and Reconnaissance - Vienna.
77 Sqn. Two a/c from Villeneuve. One landed in Germany, but

escaped.

Leaflets and Reconnaissance - Ruhr and Rhine.
51 Sqn. Six a/c from Villeneuve. Some opposition, weather bad.

16th-17th. Leaflets and Reconnaissance - Prague.
10 Sqn. Two a/c from Villeneuve. No opposition.

Reconnaissance - Ruhr.
10 Sqn. Six a/c. Heavy opposition over Dusseldorf.

19th-20th. Bombing - Hornum.
10 Sqn. Eight a/c. Moderate opposition.
51 Sqn. Seven a/c. Moderate opposition. One gunner wounded, one a/c FTR.
77 Sqn. Seven a/c. Moderate opposition.
102 Sqn. Eight a/c. One returned early U/S. Moderate opposition.

22nd-23rd. Leaflets and Reconnaissance - Ruhr.
10 Sqn. Six a/c. Two returned early due to icing. Opposition heavy. One a/c shadowed by enemy aircraft but was not attacked.

25th-26th. Reconnaissance - Borkum - Wanne-Eickel - Thionville - Ruhr.
102 Sqn. Two a/c. Heavy opposition over the Ruhr. One a/c damaged by Flak.

27th-28th. Leaflets and Reconnaissance - Ruhr.
77 Sqn. Nine a/c detailed, five took off. One returned early U/S, another shot down by Dutch fighter.

Chapter Four

Norway - Right Up The Fjord (Creek)

The first indication that the military stalemate might be coming to an end was when a Blenheim, carrying out a daylight reconnaissance over the Elbe estuary on April 4th, reported a large number of merchant vessels and warships, estimated at about seventy, moving northwards in the Schillig Roads. A small force of Blenheims was sent out immediately to attack this fleet, but they failed to achieve any results. Another sortie was mounted on the morning of April 5th, but was abortive due to adverse weather conditions. The leader of this force, flying just below cloud at 500 feet, reported that the ships had gone. Next day further reconnaissance discovered elements of the German fleet at Wilhelmshaven.

That night (April 6th/7th) Nos. 10 and 51 Squadrons sent aircraft out to reconnoitre over north-west Germany and the Ruhr. On their return, the crews reported that there were long columns of motor transport on the Hamburg to Lubeck roads and at Eckernforde, near Kiel, all with their headlights blazing. A major loading operation seemed to be in progress. One of our No. 10 Squadron aircraft, K9032 skippered by Flying Officer G. W. 'Pinpoint' Prior, ran out of fuel on return and force-landed near Grimsby; the aircraft was damaged but luckily there were no casualties.

The following day, April 7th, a Blenheim squadron on armed reconnaissance over the North Sea spotted a German cruiser and four destroyers. After shadowing them for a few minutes the main body of the enemy fleet was sighted. A cruiser, believed to be either *Scharnhorst* or *Gneisenau* was attacked by the Blenheims without effect. The leader of the Blenheim force sent back a signal giving the position and course of the German fleet, but this was not received. Thus the information that the Germans were at sea in strength was not given until the Blenheims returned to base. Immediately a squadron of Wellingtons was sent to attack the warships, but failed to find them. A second attempt next day also failed.

It became evident that all this activity by the German fleet and the loading operations reported by our reconnaissance aircraft were preliminaries to the invasions of Denmark and Norway. On the morning of April 9th, Denmark was completely over-run in a very short time and, by the end of the day, most of the southern Norwegian ports and airfields had been captured. The Germans were now able to carry out continuous air attacks against our Home Fleet, already at sea, with relays of Heinkel He111s and Junkers Ju88s from the captured airfields. During the afternoon of the 9th, the destroyer *Ghurka* was sunk and the cruisers *Southampton, Devonshire* and *Glasgow* were damaged. These air attacks prevented our Home Fleet from taking any offensive action against the German warships at Bergen, so at dusk a squadron of Wellingtons and another of Hampdens carried out an attack. They claimed two hits on a cruiser, which turned out to be the *Konigsberg*, which was finally sunk on April 10th by Fleet Air Arm Skuas operating from the Orkneys.

From the newly captured Norwegian airfields of Sola (Stavanger), Fornebu and Kjeller (Oslo) and Vaernes (Trondheim), the Luftwaffe were able to control the approaches to the vital ports of Bergen, Trondheim and Narvik. Stavanger was the base from which the Luftwaffe mounted most of its attacks against our Home Fleet, so it became a prime target for attacks by Bomber Command. It was attacked at dusk on April 11th by Six Wellingtons escorted by Coastal Command Blenheims, the latter preceding the bombers with strafing attacks. Three bomber crews claimed to have started a large fire, but another was shot down.

While this was going on we were listening to reports and wondering when we were going to get into the act. We had been brought to readiness on April 9th when the invasion began and all our aircraft had been bombed-up and armed, but it wasn't until the night of April 11th that we were sent as part of a force of twenty-three Whitleys detailed to search for and bomb enemy shipping in the Skaggerak. Despite bad weather, there was some slight success; a No. 102 Squadron crew, Squadron Leader J. C. MacDonald in N1420, attacked and destroyed a ship estimated to be of 8,000 tons, carrying ammunition. Two more aircraft attacked shipping, one from No. 51 Squadron and us.

We had taken off from Dishforth at 18.45 hours, with Squadron Leader D. P. 'Pat' Hanafin, the new commander of 'A' Flight, flying with us as second pilot. Fletch and Nipper had been given the night off and were replaced by Enery doing the navigation and Lofty Millington as 1st WOP/AG. The bad weather worsened as we crossed the North Sea and when we reached the Skaggerak we started a 'creeping line ahead' search, heading north to Oslofjord.

We flew in and out of snowstorms which got more numerous as we continued the search. However, after about an hour we struck it lucky and spotted an enemy vessel heading for Oslo. We attacked, but Enery was having problems with the weather as we made our run-in. He was prevented from seeing any results due to cloud as the ship disappeared from view. We hoped that we had been lucky.

Continuing on our northerly course, we found the weather deteriorating as the frequency of the storms increased. Ice formed on the wings and chunks flew off the propellers, banging with resounding thuds on the fuselage. Snow swirled into the tail turret and I had to keep moving the breech-block of my VGO back and forth to prevent it from freezing up. By this time we were well up the fjord (creek) and in the vicinity of Oslo, where we were subjected to opposition from Flak-ships. Some of it was fairly accurate and the aircraft lurched as the shells burst nearby with ominous thuds. On our return we discovered that we had been hit, but only slightly. I was more than relieved when the skipper decided that we had had enough and set course for home. Fortunately the weather improved and we landed at 03.30 hours, having been in the air for nearly nine hours.

One aircraft from No. 77 Squadron, N1347 flown by Pilot Officer G. E. Saddington, was forced to ditch in the North Sea on its return sixty miles from the English coast. They were presumed lost after a long and fruitless search by RAF and Royal Navy Rescue Services. The Runnymede Memorial is a poignant reminder of the hazards that crews flying over the North Sea had to face.

During daylight on April 12th, Wellingtons of 3 Group and Hampdens of 5 Group undertook sorties to find and attack the *Scharnhorst, Gneisenau* and the *Leipzig,* units of the German fleet which were reported to be heading south across the entrance to the Skaggerak. The adverse weather conditions made their search fruitless and they encountered severe opposition from enemy fighters. One formation of twelve Hampdens was attacked by Bf109s and Bf110s which shot eight of the bombers down. After this operation the Hampdens were restricted to night sorties, the first being a mining excursion to the Danish coast on the night of April 13th/14th.

An attempt by twelve Blenheims to attack Stavanger during daylight was again frustrated by weather, only six finding the target.

However, the following night six Whitleys of No. 102 Squadron, operating from Kinloss, attacked the same target and claimed to have hit airfield installations. It was our turn to have a go at the occupied airfields on April 16th/17th, when six aircraft were sent to Stavanger, one to Kjeller and one to Fornebu. They were badly hampered by the weather. On that same night No. 77 Squadron sent four aircraft to Vaernes airfield at Trondheim, which was claimed to have been successfully bombed. One aircraft, N1387 skippered by Squadron Leader M. Hastings, ran out of fuel and was crash-landed by the pilot after the rest of the crew had baled out. The aircraft was wrecked, but Hastings escaped unhurt.

On April 17th/18th, both Nos. 77 and 102 Squadrons flew abortive sorties to Vaernes whilst No. 58 Squadron had similar fortune at Fornebu and Kjeller. One of the latter crews, whose air-observer was making his operational debut, had to fly blind for most of the flight and after groping their way for hours gave it up as a bad job. They returned safely to Linton-on-Ouse after a flight lasting nine and a half hours, not exactly an auspicious beginning to an operational tour.

On the following night (April 18th/19th) it was our turn to endure the bad weather and the frustration when six of our No. 10 Squadron aircraft plus three from No. 58 Squadron were detailed to raid Fornebu and Kjeller airfields. Leaving Dishforth at 20.15 hours we headed for Norway, hoping that the weather would be kind to us for a change, but it wasn't to be. As we proceeded over the North Sea, cloud cover increased and the occasions when we could see the clear sky above and the sea below became less frequent.

This was my eleventh raid and by now I was realising what flying on bomber operations really meant. At that time I thought I was invulnerable and the suspicion that I might not survive was not entertained. It would always be the 'other bloke' who would 'bite it', not me. I can only conclude that this optimism was a method of concealing the fear that I might be the 'other bloke'.

During these outward sea crossings there were long periods of silence on the intercom and, with the Merlins droning mesmerically, there were times when the imagination conjured up frightening possibilities, but on the other hand there were less unpleasant distractions. I recall sitting in my tail turret, catching glimpses through the perspex cupola of a crescent moon riding the cumulus

Squadron Leader Raymond Chance survived a harrowing experience when he was forced to ditch his Whitley in the North Sea on April 19th, 1940. (Raymond Chance)

The aircraft Raymond Chance ditched was N1352, seen here in earlier markings. (Chaz Bowyer)

clouds, and remembering a line from a poem I had learnt not so very long ago at school. Like most misguided lads I had considered most poetry to be 'cissy' and it was only the heroic ones that appealed; 'The Charge of the Light Brigade' or 'The Burial of Sir John Moore at Corunna'. The poem I recalled was 'The Highwayman' by Alfred Noyes and the line "The moon was a ghostly galleon tossed upon cloudy seas." I'll bet Mr Noyes never thought when he composed his verse that sometime in the future it would stir the imagination of a nineteen-year-old watching the moon from a bomber on its way to a target in Norway. I would also like to wager that my old English teacher would be most surprised to know that I had even remembered it.

I was jerked back to reality when Enery announced "Crossing the coast in ten minutes." By the time we were on our way up Oslofjord, the weather conditions were very bad and worsened as we attempted to find Kjeller airfield. The whole area was obscured by snowstorms and although we descended, sometimes as low as 500 feet, we were unable to locate the target. After searching the area for as long as our fuel stocks allowed we gave it up and, frozen and fed-up, set course for base. It was some thirty minutes after landing that any feeling returned to my numb nether regions. Only two of the other aircraft involved in our part of the operation were able to bomb.

While we were searching for airfields, No. 77 Squadron had sent three aircraft to attack shipping in Trondheimfjord. None were sighted and two of the Whitleys returned safely. The third, N1352, crashed whilst attempting to ditch in the North Sea. The following harrowing account by Squadron Leader Ray Chance, who was one of the survivors, graphically describes what happened:

"We were approaching the Norwegian coast flying at about 10,000 feet when the port engine failed - flames flickered from it - decided it was hopeless to go on and turned onto the reciprocal, but the aircraft failed to maintain height on the one engine. Came to the conclusion ditching was inevitable and asked the crew who could swim. Two couldn't so I told them to stick near me when we touched down - I fancied myself as a good swimmer. In an effort to maintain height everything moveable was thrown out, but to no avail. Told everyone for ditching to get near the back door and brace themselves against the bulkhead. I went down the fuselage and chopped off the rear door with the fire-axe, then went back to the pilot's seat again. At about 2,000 to 1,500 feet I was told that the wireless operator was still transmitting the distress message. I handed over the aircraft to Pilot Officer Hall and got the WOP/AG to clamp down his Morse key, then took him to join the others at the 'step' near the rear door. They asked me how high we were and I went to look through the open door - I told them about 1,000 to 800 feet. Then suddenly the aircraft, which had been in a shallow gliding attitude, dived steeply towards the sea.

I knew we had only seconds to live and, trying to be as calm as possible, told the others we were levelling off. Then bang! She blew up and I was flung somewhere into the wreckage in the nose and knocked unconscious. I hallucinated, imagining I was in a long dim corridor which led to a ballroom lit by dazzling lights, which I decided to make for.

"This experience faded and later I thought, without any qualms, that I was in the aircraft on the bed of the ocean and, if I could get to the back door, I would hold my nose and reach the surface. I started to crawl along the fuselage but this experience faded and I was back in the heavenly corridor. I reached the door and suddenly the reality of the situation hit me. I was in an aeroplane which was on fire!

"I was stung into action. The engine and wing were on fire and the water seemed on fire with the fuel spreading from the ruptured tanks. I could see no-one in the aircraft and was about to jump into the sea, when I saw the dinghy still folded lying down towards the tail inside the fuselage. My reactions were instantaneous. I knew the men were outside somewhere but hadn't got the dinghy. I dived for it like a rugger tackle, dragged it to the door and - with one idea uppermost, that the fire would destroy the rubber and no-one would then get away - flung it with all my strength into the dark towards the tail and immediately plunged in after it.

"My Mae West shot me to the surface; I found the dinghy, pulled the cord, and it started to inflate. As it did the two whom I understood couldn't swim (Aircraftsman O'Brien, WOP/AG and Aircraftsman Douglas, tail-gunner) started to climb in - think they had been hanging on the tail. We were joined by Sergeant Tindall, the bomb-aimer, who I was told was now hanging on the other side of the dinghy. I didn't know then that I had a crushed ankle, a broken leg and a hair-line skull fracture.

"There then followed the tense, desperate moments of super-human effort to gain release from the cords of the dinghy, push it away from the flames of the sinking aircraft and give succour to Pilot Officer Hall, who was some fifty yards away crying for help.

"I told the survivors I would have to wait to get my breath back before I would be able to get back into the dinghy. It may have been fifteen minutes before I could clamber in.

"Eventually I was hauled in and collapsed inside the rim of the dinghy. I hadn't the strength to lift my head out of the water in the bottom and was saved from drowning by one of the survivors putting his boot under my chin. I heard Pilot Officer Hall shouting, but more faintly, and conceived the idea of going over the side and trying to drag the dinghy towards him. I got up on one elbow but fell back exhausted. I had the agony of listening to him drown.

"In the small hours of the morning Leading Aircraftsman O'Brien and Aircraftsman Douglas appeared to be on the verge of passing out so, sitting on the rim, I supported both with an arm around each neck. I thought they would fall backwards into the sea which was getting choppier now.

"It was unbelieveably cold. I had lost my flying boots, which must have come off when I pulled the dinghy from the fire. Teeth chattering and knees knocking. I saw one of the two I was supporting was going to be sick. As he was being sick I put my hands in front of his mouth and found that it warmed them. About half an hour later I noticed the other was also about to be sick. This time I pushed my face in front of his mouth. (Looking back over my life that, I think, was when I reached rock bottom. I believe it's called survival).

"To try to keep up our spirits - and our warmth - I led the crew in singing 'Roll Out the Barrel'. It must have sounded strange in the dark in the choppy North Atlantic.

"In the hour before dawn I heard a noise which I thought was an aircraft. Suddenly Sergeant Tindall pointed to a dark shape in the water. A searchlight came on and started picking its way over the water and finally settled on us. It was a British destroyer *HMS Basilisk.* A whaler was lowered and started to row towards us. On reaching the destroyer a rope-ladder was lowered. My crew scrambled up, but on putting my foot on it I promptly fell back into the whaler. In the intense cold I had become unaware of my broken ankle and crushed foot. I was carried to the wardroom where I found the rest of the crew on mattresses. There being no doctor, my foot was put in a box of cotton wool. It was jet black and barely recogniseable. A bottle of whisky and two hundred cigarettes were put at my elbow.

"The First Officer told me they were in action against a submarine and were some 100 miles off course chasing it. He added that, with a break in the cloud, a moonbeam had shone on the water and an AB had shouted to the bridge on seeing us, thinking we were a floating mine. That's when they put the searchlight on the water. It was thought that there wasn't another British ship within 400 square miles of us.

"It was on the second day that we reached Scapa Flow. I was in hospital for a long time. One may ask how it is possible to survive so long in the water in those latitudes with severe head injuries, a crushed foot and a broken ankle. The answer is quite simple. You decide quite calmly whether 'to go now', in which case that's it. Or you look at the vast black ocean and say to yourself, "You'll get me sometime, but I'll give you a run for it. You will have to get me, I'll never surrender."

"There's a spiritual quality in it. You know there can be only one answer - death. You are looking straight into eternity. You are quite peaceful. You are not brave or courageous because there is no fear, that is over. You are looking into eternity and just wait. You feel growing closeness to the forms of the universe.

"In this experience, suddenly there was the blinding flash of the searchlight from nowhere. The trumpets had sounded on the other side. But it was not to be. If it be the hand of God, I know not - but I like to think, and believe, it was.*

Because of the bad weather persisting over Norway, reconnaissances were flown over Hamburg next night, but on April 20th/21st it was back to Norway. Raids in the Trondheim area were foiled by the weather, but further south it was slightly better, Nos. 10, 51 and

*"The Chance Papers", by Sqn Ldr Raymond Chance, Norwich, 1984. Published in "Out of the Blue," edited by Laddie Lucas. Hutchinson 1985. Grafton Books 1987. Ray Chance eventually recovered and returned to flying operations, flying Blenheims with No. 21 Sqn during the Battle of France. He served on the staff of the Air Ministry before a posting to Bengal and Burma. After the war he entered the legal profession and was called to the Bar in 1958.

58 Squadrons mustering a total of eleven aircraft to attack Kjeller, Fornebu and heavily defended Stavanger with varying degrees of success. The situation was similar two nights later (22nd/23rd). No. 77 Squadron, operating to the north, failed to find a frozen lake south of Trondheim that was being used as a landing ground, but Nos. 51 and 10 Squadrons operating against the southern bases were luckier and claimed hits on all the airfields attacked. The single No. 10 Squadron crew flying that night, was that of Sergeant 'Johnnie' Johnson in K9029. They were particularly successful at Kjeller where in addition to hitting the airfield installations with bombs they strafed and extinguished searchlights. Aircraftsman George Chalmers did most of the damage from the rear turret.* A damper on the night's work was the non-return of one of the No. 51 Squadron crews, Flying Officer J. R. Birch in K9043. They were engaged and shot down over Aalborg by the Flak gunners of Reserve Flakabteilung 603.

And so it continued the following night, with Nos. 77 and 102 Squadrons operating in the north while Nos. 10, 51 and 58 kept the pot boiling in the south. Ours was one of the No. 10 Sqn crews detailed and our target was the airfield at Fornebu. Because K9023 was U/S we were given K9029. Just as you get used to old clothing and you are reluctant to change it, so it is with aircraft. I suppose that subconsciously we looked upon K9023 as our lucky rabbit's foot.

We took off at 19.30 hours and had what was becoming a routine sea crossing - that is if you can call sitting in a draughty tail turret hoping that the 'fans' will keep on turning and you don't end up in the 'Oggin', routine.

As we headed up Oslofjord we ran into the usual Scandinavian 'clag'; snowstorms which got more and more frequent until we reached the Fornebu area, where everything was obscured. Bick decided that we would try our alternative target, the airfield at Kristiansund. The weather improved slightly and during a rare clear period we were able to drop our bombs, but it did not last long enough for us to assess the results. A consolation was that we did not have to contend with any great amount of opposition.

Shortly after we left the target area and were homeward bound, Fletch came on the intercom. The weather at Dishforth had

---

* George Chalmers joined No. 617 Squadron in 1943 and flew on the Dams Raid, being awarded the Distinguished Flying Medal.

deteriorated and we were to divert to Kinloss. Our new course took us across the Norwegian mainland and the glimpses I got of the rugged terrain were not at all inviting. My main concern for the next few hours as we crossed the North Sea was to keep my circulation going. To add to our difficulties Fletch had problems obtaining homing bearings from Kinloss, but we managed to scramble in before the weather clamped down. It had not been our night. This time we had been in the air for ten hours and had failed to achieve much.

One of our crews was more fortunate than we had been. Squadron leader Pat Hanafin, making his debut as an operational captain and flying the squadron's only Mk V, spotted two enemy ships in Oslofjord. He attacked the first ship and scored a direct hit near the funnel. Having no bombs left they descended to low level and flew around the second ship while Aircraftsman S. Oldridge, the tail gunner, fired some three thousand rounds from his four Brownings into it at close range. The ship was forced to run aground.

No. 51 Squadron suffered the only loss that night when the single aircraft sent to bomb shipping in Oslofjord, Flying Officer T. K. Milne and crew, failed to return. Their Whitley, K9048, fell to the accurate gunfire from Reserve Flakabteilung 603 at Aalborg. Other operations included three No. 58 Squadron crews to Aalborg, only two of which bombed, and six crews from No. 102 Squadron all of which failed to locate their target of Trondheim due to the bad weather.

Because of the fruitless attempts to attack the landing grounds at Trondheim, Nos. 77 and 102 Squadrons were switched to southern targets on April 25th/26th, attacking Kjeller, Fornebu and Aalborg airfields and shipping in Oslofjord. An aircraft from No. 102 Squadron, N1383 skippered by Flying Officer O. G. Horrigan, failed to return from Aalborg. Again it fell to the guns of Reserve Flakabteilung 603, the third Whitley to be brought down by this unit in four nights.

The next sorties were on April 29th/30th, when No. 102 Squadron set out to raid Fornebu. They faced severe opposition which claimed Flying Officer K. H. P. Murphy and his crew in N1421. This was the second loss to the squadron in less than a week. This aircraft was engaged and shot down at Sylling by the gunners of I/Flakregiment 611.

Pilots and observers being briefed for the coming nights operation.

The last night of April proved to be a busy one for the Whitley squadrons. Nos. 10 and 51 Squadrons were detailed to attack Fornebu. Two of our No. 10 Squadron crews were recalled, abandoning their sorties when it was discovered that the bomb safety pins had not been removed. As you can imagine, the 'buck' was passed around like a hot potato. The remaining four aircraft successfully attacked through heavy resistance, and started some fires. No. 51 Squadron were also successful, but one aircraft, K9039 flown by Pilot Officer E. Cotton,   crashed on Burnside Fell on return.

Meanwhile Nos. 77 and 58 Squadrons raided Stavanger again, flying through the intense Flak put up by II/Flakregiment 33 which is believed to have shot down the No. 58 Squadron aircraft, N1465, of Sergeant R. Heayes and crew over Sola at 23.55 hours.

The not-so-merry month of May started with continuing attacks on the Norwegian airfields. Nos. 77 and 102 Squadrons raided Fornebu while we in No. 10 Squadron were briefed to attack Stavanger. Six crews were selected. We were one of those assigned and we were off at 22.10 hours, again in K9029 because K9023 was still U/S. As we were climbing away from Dishforth Bick, our skipper, informed us that although we had taken off second with a bit of luck and extra boost we could get there first and surprise them. "We can be in and out before they realise what's hit them!" The weather forecast was good for a change and he was determined to take full advantage of it. As we flew over the North Sea it looked like our luck was in; the skies were clear and the visibility good. Because of the Northern Lights, the bods up front were able to see the Norwegian coast while we were still well out to sea. As we approached the coast, Nipper was able to get a good pin-point and it was not long before he reported, "Stavanger ahead!" There was no searchlight or Flak activity so it looked as if Bick had achieved his aim of being first to target.

Bick throttled back the engines and we commenced our glide attack from about 4,000 feet. During the descent the bomb doors were opened and the bomb-aimer commenced chanting his directions, "Left. Left. Steady," to get the target in his bombsight. He finally called, "Bombs gone!" and the Whitley lurched as the bombs fell away. Bick whanged open the throttles and we roared across the airfield at low level going like the clappers. I had an uninterrupted view from the tail and saw the bombs bursting in the hangar and installations area. At the same time the defences opened up. Three searchlights came on attempting to pick us up and Flak hosed after us, but I was ready for them and retaliated with my VGO, belting away until I had used up all the rounds in the pan. As we escaped out to sea unscathed and I was able to report that, as a result of our bombing, fires had started in the target area. The crews following us now had something to aim at, but we had also stirred up a hornets nest for them.

Highly elated, we made our way home. Even Bick was indulging in chit-chat. For a change we felt that we really had achieved something.

Our other five squadron aircraft all got back safely despite having to contend with the worsening weather back at base. Four of them also claimed success and confirmed that there were fires in the hangar area and adjacent buildings. They also reported the opposition as severe - we certainly had stirred it up!

The last raids to be carried out by the Whitley force during the ill-fated Norwegian Campaign took place on May 2nd/3rd. Nos. 51 and 58 Squadrons went to Fornebu and Stavanger, which were successfully attacked despite some opposition. One Whitley of No

51 Squadron, N1406 captained by Squadron leader G. P. Marvin, ran out of fuel and the crew baled out near Easingwold, Yorkshire. Marvin suffered a broken leg and unfortunately Aircraftsman Hepburn was killed. The final fling in the campaign came on May 9th/10th, when five of No. 77 Squadron's crews were recalled en route to Stavanger. Apparently there were indications that the Germans were about to switch their attentions much further south - the Blitzkrieg against France and the Low Countries was about to begin.

While we in the RAF had carried out air attacks against shipping and the airfields occupied by the Luftwaffe throughout the Norwegian Campaign the Army, assisted by the Royal Navy, had attempted to launch a counter attack by land and sea.* A week after the German invasion, on April 9th, a British brigade and three battalions of French troops were landed at Namsos. A second British brigade was landed at Aandalsnes with the objective of taking possession of the well equipped port of Trondheim and its nearby airfield (Vaernes). The idea was to land sufficient troops to prevent the progress of German troops northwards. Unfortunately the Germans, with their overwhelming air superiority, beat them to it. Having captured all the airfields in southern Norway, the Luftwaffe had built up a force of bombers and fighters that the RAF could not match. We tried - eighteen RAF Gladiator fighters of No. 263 Squadron were flown to operate from a frozen lake at Lesjaskog, forty miles from Aandalsnes, but they were heavily outnumbered and were wiped out both in the air and on the ground within four days. Hurriedly re-equipped, No. 263 Squadron returned to Norway, this time accompanied by Hurricanes of No. 46 Squadron. Although they fought courageously, the result was inevitable and most of the surviving aircrew were lost in the final evacuation when the aircraft carrier *Glorious* was sunk by German battlecruisers.

The Bomber Command squadrons did the best they could, but were hampered by the continuing atrocious weather conditions and the disadvantage of having to fly a round trip of approximately 1200 miles over open sea. Any hope of giving direct support to the ground forces was out of the question.

*It had became clear early in April that an invasion of Scandinavia was looming some time earlier and an Expeditionary Force had been in the process of assembling - but the Germans struck first.

The British brigade at Aandalsnes pushed sixty miles inland to the railway station at Dombaas, where it joined with Norwegian Army units. The combined force then headed south-east to harrass the German troops advancing from Oslo. They met them on April 21st, but after a day of very stiff fighting during which they were completely out-gunned by the German artillery, tanks and aircraft they were forced to withdraw back to Aandalsnes. There they fought a valiant rear-guard action until they were evacuated by the Royal Navy on the night of April 30th. The Namsos force was evacuated the next night, both operations being carried out while under heavy and continual air attack.

With the evacuation the Germans were left in complete control of southern and central Norway. There were still Allied troops fighting further north in the Narvik area, but these were to be evacuated on the night of June 7th when events in France were reaching a critical state. So ended the disastrous Norwegian Campaign.

It was towards the end of the campaign that the first of the VR (Volunteer Reserve) aircrew appeared on the operational scene with the 4 Group Whitley squadrons. Up to this time, the peacetime regulars had borne the brunt of the raids. Commissioned air gunners, whose training courses were of a shorter duration than those of the pilots and navigators, were the first to join us, but only in small numbers - one or two to each squadron. The initial reaction of the surviving regular airmen rear gunners, was one of derisive reluctance, tempered by the necessity to keep within the bounds of discipline, 'Bloody jumped up sprogs!'. Happily, common sense prevailed and they were grudgingly accepted with the comment, "At least they're willing to have a go," said one of our chaps.

One of these commissioned rear gunners was Pilot Officer Harry Welte, an Australian who, like other air-minded young men from the Commonwealth, came to the UK before the war with the intention of becoming a pilot in the RAF. He failed in his attempts to become a pilot, but was determined to fly and after refusing the offer of a commission in the Equipment Branch, accepted one as an air-gunner, commencing his training in September 1939. After successfully completing the air-gunnery course at Manby, he progressed through the Whitley Operational Training Unit and joined No. 58 Squadron in April 1940. He commenced operations on April 30th with a raid on Stavanger airfield. This was the first of twenty-eight raids he carried out on Whitleys during which he qualified as a member of the 'Goldfish Club' by surviving a ditching while returning from a bombing raid on the Skoda Works at Pilsen, Czechoslovakia, on the night of October 20/21st 1940. Because of the heavy cloud cover too much time was spent in the target area resulting in them having to take the short way home, which meant that they had to cross the heavily defended Ruhr (Happy) Valley. While doing so they were coned by searchlights and subjected to concentrated fire from both light and heavy Flak batteries. After twenty minutes of violent evasive action they managed to escape. Although no-one was hurt, the poor old Whitley had taken a battering. One engine was out of action and the radio and hydraulics had been damaged. They managed to limp back across the North Sea on one engine until they were forced to ditch two miles from Sheringham, Norfolk. The aircraft, P5089, broke in the middle when it hit the sea, but miraculously all the crew escaped and got aboard the dinghy before the aircraft sank. It went down in two minutes. Their amazing luck held and after about six hours they were picked up by the Sheringham life-boat, just two hours before a fog bank rolled in and remained in the area for several days.

After his twenty-eight 'trips', Pilot Officer Welte was posted to become Gunnery Leader at No. 10 (Whitley) OTU, and while there he participated in the two 'Thousand Bomber Raids'* on Cologne - May 30th/31st 1942 and Essen - June 1st/2nd 1942.

In December 1942, he was posted back on operations with No. 78 Squadron, then equipped with Halifaxes, but after two raids he was grounded due to medical reasons. For the remainder of the war he served in various ground appointments, leaving the RAF in 1945 to return to Australia, where he happily survives.

*Operations 'Millenium I and Millenium II'.

Summary of operations by 4 Group
6th April - 9th May 1940

April

6th-7th Reconnaissance -north-west Germany and the Ruhr.
10 Sqn. Two a/c to the Ruhr. Slight opposition. One a/c force landed near Grimsby on return.
51 Sqn. Six a/c to NW Germany. Convoys of motor transport sighted on Hamburg- Lübeck road, also loading operation taking place at Eckenforde.

11th-12th. Bombing - Shipping in the Kattegat.
10 Sqn. Six a/c. One returned U/S, one bombed ship without result.
51 Sqn. Five a/c. One bombed ship without result.
77 Sqn. Six a/c. One returned U/S. No ships sighted. One FTR.
102 Sqn. Six a/c. One bombed and destroyed an 8,000 ton ammunition ship.

15th-16th. Bombing - Stavanger Airfield.
102 Sqn. Six a/c attacked successfully.

16th-17th. Bombing - Stavanger, Fornebu, Kjeller and Trondheim Airfields.
10 Sqn. Six a/c to Stavanger. Only one bombed due to weather. Hits claimed causing fires. One a/c to Fornebu and one a/c to Kjeller. Both unable to locate targets due to weather.
77 Sqn. Four a/c from Kinloss to Trondheim. All attacked. One crash landed on return after four crew abandoned a/c.

17th-18th Bombing - Trondheim, Kjeller and Fornebu Airfields.
58 Sqn. Two a/c to Kjeller and Fornebu. No bombing due to weather
77 Sqn. Three a/c to Trondheim. No bombing due to weather.
102 Sqn. Three a/c to Trondheim. No bombing due to weather.

18th-19th. Bombing - Kjeller and Fornebu Airfields; Shipping in Trondheimfjord.
10 Sqn. Three a/c to Kjeller and three to Fornebu. No bombing due to weather.
58 Sqn. Three a/c to Kjeller and Fornebu. No bombing due to weather.
77 Sqn. Three a/c to attack shipping in Trondheimfjord. None sighted. One aircraft ditched.

19th-20th. Reconnaissance - Hamburg.
51 Sqn. Task carried out as briefed. Considerable searchlight activity, but Flak negligible.

20th-21st. Bombing - Kjeller, Fornebu, Stavanger and Trondheim Airfields.
10 Sqn. Five a/c. One returned U/S, two bombed Stavanger.
51 Sqn. Three a/c. One returned U/S. Two bombed Stavanger, claiming hits on installations. Heavy opposition.
58 Sqn. Three a/c bombed Stavanger.
102 Sqn. Three aircraft to Trondheim. No bombing due to weather.

22nd-23rd. Bombing - Fornebu, Kristiansund, Aalborg and Trondheims Airfields.
10 Sqn. One a/c to Kjeller. Airfield bombed and machine-gunned.
51 Sqn. Seven a/c. Six bombed Kjeller, Fornebu and Aalborg. 1 FTR.
77 Sqn. Two a/c to Trondheim. No bombing due to weather.

23rd-24th. Bombing - Fornebu, Kristiansund, Aalborg and Trondheims Airfields. Shipping In Oslofjord.
10 Sqn. Four a/c bombed Kristiansund, one bombed Fornebu, one bombed and hit a motor vessel and machine-gunned another in Oslofjord.
51 Sqn. One a/c to bomb shipping but FTR.
58 Sqn. Three a/c to Aalborg. Two bombed.
102 Sqn. Six a/c to Trondheim. No bombing due to weather.

25th-26th. Bombing Kjeller, Fornebu and Aalborg Airfields.
77 Sqn. Six a/c. One returned U/S, two attacked shipping without result, three attacked airfields.
102 Sqn. Two a/c to Aalborg. Intense opposition and one FTR.

29th-30th. Bombing - Fornebu Airfield.
102 Sqn. Six a/c detailed, five took off and bombed. One FTR.

30th-1st. Bombing - Stavanger and Fornebu Airfields.
10 Sqn. Six a/c. Two recalled, four bombed Fornebu starting fires. Opposition fierce.
51 Sqn. Six a/c bombed Fornebu. One crashed on return.
58 Sqn. Six a/c. Three bombed Stavanger. 1 FTR.
77 Sqn. Six a/c to Stavanger. Five bombed.

May

1st-2nd. Bombing - Stavanger and Fornebu Airfields.
10 Sqn. Six a/c bombed Stavanger, fires started.
77 Sqn. Three a/c bombed Fornebu. Severe opposition.
102 Sqn. Three a/c bombed Fornebu. Severe opposition.

2nd-3rd. Bombing - Stavanger and Fornebu Airfields.
51 Sqn. Six a/c. All bombed Fornebu. Severe opposition. One crew abandoned a/c on return.
58 Sqn. Six a/c to Stavanger. One returned U/S, four bombed. Light opposition.

9th-10th.
77 Sqn. Five a/c all recalled.

Chapter Five

Blitzkrieg and Bedlam

After the Norwegian debacle, No. 10 Squadron flew a fruitless Security Patrol over the German seaplane bases at Hornum and Borkum on May 4th/5th, then came a short lull - the calm before the storm.

During this respite, the squadrons continued the progressive conversion onto the Merlin engined Mk Vs. By this time those originally equipped with the Mk IIIs (Nos. 58, 77 and 102 Squadrons) had received and were operating Mk Vs. Our squadron and No. 51, equipped with Mk IVs, were the last to convert, but by now the re-equipping was nearing completion. In between operational flights, crews had carried out training flights in order to familiarise themselves with the differences in equipment and operation. The Mk V was a direct descendant of the Mk IVA, the main difference being the defensive armament. The mid-under turret had finally been discarded and the manually operated one-gun tail turret replaced by a four-gun hydraulically operated Frazer-Nash unit. Other improvements included the fitting of rubber de-icing boots on the wing leading edges and a fairing over the DF loop.

As far as I was concerned, the most important change was the new tail turret. It was fully enclosed, no more icy draughts whistling through it as they had on the Mk IVs, and with much easier access. The seat, while not as comfortable as your favourite armchair, was a great improvement on the cycle-type seat fitted to the Mks III and IV turrets. Access and departure was through two split doors which could be opened and closed from both inside and outside the turret, making it easier to evacuate in an emergency. In the event of the tail-gunner having to bale out, after obtaining and clipping on his chest-type parachute, he could rotate the turret onto the beam, open the doors and fall out of the turret backwards. This enabled him to fall clear of the aircraft without risk of hitting it. Also, the four Browning .303 inch belt-fed machine-guns, each with a cyclic rate of 1,150 rounds per minute, were a vast improvement on the single VGO 'popgun' defence of the earlier marks, even though still inferior in range and hitting power of the cannon-equipped German fighters. After carrying out air-firing and bombing exercises over Filey Bay, I now felt I had a much better chance of giving a good account of myself, should the occasion arise during future operations.

The fully enclosed tail turret of the MkV Whitley - a great improvement on the draughty MkIV's.

Meanwhile the political and military situation had changed dramatically. On May 10th, Hitler's forces broke through the Allied defences of the west to invade Holland, Belgium and Luxemburg, soon to be followed by the break-through into France. The 'Phoney War' was finally at an end. The initial break-through commenced during the early hours of the 10th, with an airborne attack on The Hague and Rotterdam, while the Luftwaffe attacked seventy-two Allied airfields in Holland, Belgium and France. Formations of Heinkel 111's, Dornier 17's and Ju88's flew sorties throughout the day against our airfields and communications. RAF and French Air Force fighters managed to get airborne in time to break up some of the enemy formations and their losses were fairly light, but the Dutch and Belgian Air Forces suffered serious losses.

Advanced Air Striking Force (AASF) Fairey Battle crews had been brought to immediate readiness at their French bases at 06.00 hours, but it was noon before they were able to carry out their first operation. The French Air Force Commander proved indecisive and Air Marshal Sir Arthur Barratt (Air Officer Commanding the RAF Forces in France), on his own initiative, committed the Battles of the AASF without French assistance in order to give some support to the hard-pressed Allied ground troops

Up until now neither the two Blenheim squadrons of the AASF nor the UK-based light and heavy bombers had been used in the battle. This was because of the indecision and lack of agreement between the British War Cabinet and the French War Council on how such forces should be used. It was only when Air Marshal Barratt requested assistance that the UK-based heavy bombers were finally committed to battle. On May 10th/11th, thirty-six Wellingtons attacked Waalhaven airfield and nine Whitleys bombed German communication lines to southern Holland.

It was at this time that the ban on the bombing of German targets was lifted and next night (May 11th/12th), again at the request of Air Marshal Barratt, Bomber Command mounted its first large raid. Thirty-six bombers from 4 and 5 Groups attacked road and rail communications around Mönchen-Gladbach, losing two Hampdens and one Whitley - N1366 with Flying Officer T. H. Parrott and crew on board.

While the Battle and Blenheim crews of the AASF were fighting desperately during the day, the 4 Group Whitleys carried out attacks on the night of May 12th/13th against communications targets in the Kleve and Mönchen-Gladbach areas. Six aircraft from No. 10 Squadron participated and all crews claimed to have bombed the primary targets. There was considerable opposition, especially around Mönchen- Gladbach, where numerous cones of searchlights and their associated Flak batteries were very active. Even the light Flak was reaching up to 9,000 feet. However, we all thanked our lucky stars we weren't flying in Battles and Blenheims like our less fortunate colleagues who were suffering terrible losses in France .

Our crew took off at 21.15 hours on May 12th in our new Mk V, P4953, 'F for Freddie'. Although I welcomed the additional armament and increased comfort of the Mk V, I hoped that it would be as lucky for us as our old Mk IV, K9023, which had served us well since the outbreak of war and in which we had survived eleven raids. It boosted my morale to test my four Brownings and watch the concentrated stream of tracers and incendiaries as they burned their way to the waves beneath us. At that time our ammunition belts were made up from four types of bullets. They fired in the order of two ball, one armour-piercing, one tracer, one incendiary and so on - an impressive sight when fired at night as long as you weren't on the receiving end!

We crossed the Dutch coast in the region of Amsterdam and to the south we could see gun flashes as the ground battle continued. There was little opposition until we reached the Mönchen-Gladbach area where searchlight and Flak activity was well under way, indicating that some of the preceding aircraft were already bombing. This helped to give Nipper a good pin-point and although the weather was hazy he was able to map-read to the target. After a while the bomb-aimer came on the intercom confirming that he could see the target and we began our run-in. Up to then we had been flying at about 9,000 feet to keep out of range of the light Flak, but as we commenced the bombing run we had to descend through it. The final few minutes, as always, were a mixture of trepidation and relief until those welcome words 'Bombs gone!' when we were able to dive away from the target. As we did so I boosted my flagging bravado by cutting loose at the defences with my new guns, even though I realised that from our altitude I would be very lucky if I hit anything.

Shortly after leaving the target my nerves were given another jangle when I sighted a Bf110. The adrenalin flow went into hyperdrive. I gave a running commentary over the intercom as I lined it up in my reflector sight. The skipper told me to hold my fire and the fighter continued on its way without seeing us. The relief was audible. I needed no urging to be on the alert for the rest of the flight, but it continued without further incident.

During May 13th, as a result of the crippling losses of the previous days, the AASF Fairey Battles were able to carry out only one operation in an attempt to support French troops under heavy pressure from a German Panzer division in the Breda area. That night two out of six Whitleys despatched bombed targets in the Maastricht and Eindhoven areas. Three crews who were unable to locate their targets brought their bombs back in accordance with existing regulations. Later the regulations were amended to allow us to bomb any other identifiable military targets, which were termed 'Self Evident Military Objective' (SEMO) or 'Military Objective Previously Attacked' (MOPA).

During the night of May 14th/15th, Nos. 77 and 102 Squadrons bombed road and rail communications near Mönchen-Gladbach. All got back, reporting successful attacks under moderate to severe Flak opposition. It was becoming evident that no matter what the target, the German anti aircraft defences were becoming increasingly

The bomb-aimer's position in a Whitley Mk V.

formidable. Returning crews also reported that flames from burning Rotterdam could be seen for some considerable distance. That afternoon fifty-seven He111s from KG54 had dropped one hundred tons of high explosive on the city, devastating a large area and killing nine hundred civilians.

As a direct result of that raid the British War Cabinet concluded that the unwritten 'Gentleman's Agreement' of the early months of the war, restricting bombing to strictly military targets where there was little chance of civilian casualties, was at an end. From now on, Bomber Command was authorised to mount attacks against targets such as oil plants, steelworks and railway marshalling yards in the Ruhr and the area east of the Rhine, Germany's natural border.

So on May 15th/16th, thirty Whitleys attacked Wanne-Eickel, Gelsenkirchen and Dusseldorf as well as communications targets near Dinant. Two returned early and the rest claimed to have bombed successfully, only one had been hit by Flak.

We were one of six No. 10 Squadron crews detailed for the road/rail targets at Dinant. During the briefing the announcement that from now on we were free to bomb targets in the German homeland was greeted with the reaction, "About bloody time." The Germans had proved by their bombing of Rotterdam that they had no scruples about killing civilians to achieve their ends. Even so, we were not to bomb indiscriminately and on occasions bombs would still be brought back. However, even the highest moral standards are subject to circumstances and I can't imagine any crew which was getting seven colours knocked out of them being reluctant to jettison their load to escape. When the need for survival takes over, morals go overboard.

We took off at 20.30 hours, again in P4953 - 'F for Freddie'. As we proceeded to the target area the flashes of gunfire on the ground indicated the bitter struggle taking place as the Germans continued to advance. We reached Dinant and, although the weather had been generally good, the visiblity was limited by haze. We spent some time flying around while Nipper attempted to identify the target which was a road and rail crossing. Eventually he pin-pointed it and we carried out a glide attack from 5,000 feet. There was some resistance from light Flak, most probably from the mobile 20 and 37mm guns, but we made our run without much interference. I am sorry to say that our bombs overshot the target. After we had left the area it was discovered that one of the 250 lb bombs was still on the rack and stayed there despite all attempts to release it. When we got back to base Bick made an extra smooth landing and taxied carefully back to our dispersal. The armourers replaced the safety-pin and removed the 'rogue' from the aircraft - sighs of relief all round.

The following day we were informed that the 4 Group squadrons were to operate on a 'one night on, one night off' roster to enable round the clock bombing support for our ground forces fighting for their lives in France and the Low Countries. That night, May 16th/17th, most of the crews from Nos. 10 and 51 Squadrons at Dishforth took off for Ripon and Harrogate to sample big eats, big licks and anything else available. Although we would have been reluctant to admit it the gravity of the military situation in France and the news of the appalling losses suffered by our counterparts, some of whom had trained with us pre-war, was probably having an effect. The thought of defeat never entered our minds, but I suppose we realised more than ever before that, as aircrew, the odds against us were decidedly shortening. It was a case of eat, drink and be merry, for tomorrow ......?

While we were whooping it up, nine Whitleys from Driffield operated against targets in the Maastricht-Aachen area without loss.

On the morning of May 17th, we learned that three of our squadron pilots had been awarded the Distinguished Flying Cross; Squadron Leader J. N. H. Whitworth, 'B' Flight's commander,*

*Later Group Captain Whitworth DSO DFC, commanding RAF Scampton at the time No. 617 Squadron operated from there to carry out their epic 'Dam-busting' raid.

112

Flight Lieutenant A. S. Phillips, one of the squadron's senior pilots and our skipper Flight Lieutenant Richard Bickford. We basked in his reflected glory. That night it was our turn to be 'on' with Nos. 51 and 58 Squadrons. Our ground crew pulled out all the stops and we were able to muster fourteen of the twenty-five aircraft operating. The target was an oil storage depot at Bremen. Both the other squadrons claimed successful attacks. One crew from No. 58 Squadron reporting that they saw tanks exploding followed by sheets of flame.*

Our squadron had what could be described as a very eventful night. During the briefing our CO, Wing Commander Staton, emphasised the importance of the target to the Germans and how its destruction would severely affect oil supplies to the invading panzers and mechanised forces in the Low Countries.

Things didn't start off very promisingly. One aircraft, P4957 flown by Squadron Leader Pat Hanafin, crashed on take-off, fortunately without casualties. We were sitting in our aircraft waiting to taxi out and saw it happen. Just as the Whitley got airborne the undercarriage retracted, but then the aircraft sank and slithered along the grass on its belly. When it eventually came to a halt with the engines stopped and props bent, the hatches flew open and the crew were out quicker than rats up a drainpipe. With full bomb and petrol load, who wouldn't? Luckily P4957 didn't blow up or catch fire, so the rest of us were able to get off.

That night we were flying P4967 'J for Johnny' and were airborne at 20.55 hours, on our way to Germany. Approximately two and a half hours later we were sneaking in over the German coastline taking care to avoid the defences at Wilhelmshaven and Bremerhaven which were quite active. Following the River Weser we headed for Bremen and as we approached it the bods up at the 'sharp end' of the aircraft were reporting that the defences seemed to be very busy and that fires were burning in the target area.

Our CO, who had been first off, had apparently teamed up with Sergeant 'Johnny' Johnson and they had carried out a combined attack. In total they spent thirty minutes over the target, making no less than six bomb-runs. They dropped their bombs during glide attacks from 5,500 feet down to 1,500 feet, each aircraft acting as a decoy for the other as the attacks were carried out. They were

*The sighting was accurate; six fires were started, the largest being in the dock area where a warehouse was set ablaze.

eminently successful, starting fires, but both aircraft were hit repeated by Flak. Fortunately there were no casualties and they got back safely in spite of the damage.

Heeding the Wingco's exhortations given us during briefing all the other crews bombed from low level, carrying out attacks from heights ranging from two to six thousand feet. They all claimed success and although six sustained Flak damage, there were no casualties. The crew in P4963 captained by Flight Lieutenant Phillips, also shot up the hangars and defences at Oldenburg airfield from 2,000 feet. Was he getting 'Flak happy' or just celebrating the award of his gong?

When we arrived on the scene, the fires enabled Nipper to pick out the aiming point and we commenced our run-in, gliding in from about 4,000 feet. The Flak and searchlights were intense and we had to run the gauntlet of what is usually described as a 'wall of Flak'. During the final agonising minutes we were flying straight and level in order to give the bomb-aimer a steady bombing platform, the searchlights picked us up and the Flak batteries gave us their undivided attention. The tracers and incendiaries hosed upwards and seemed to be all around us - I know it sounds incongruous, but at times I ducked. From time to time the aircraft bucked as shells burst in our immediate vicinity - I'm sure that this was the night I discovered the colour of adrenalin. The cry of, 'Bombs gone' signalled the relief that we had been longing for and gave Bick the opportunity to take evasive action to get us out of the lethal web of searchlight and Flak. As he dived, turned and climbed the aircraft I was thankful to be able to use my four Brownings against the defences. In situations such as this there was something to be said for being 'Tail-end Charlie'. At least I could retaliate while the bods up front had to sit there and take it.

After what I am sure had been, up till then, one of the most anxious periods of my young life Bick managed to extricate us from our predicament and we found refuge in the comforting cloak of friendly darkness. We thankfully set course for home. However, during the subsequent checks we found that we hadn't got away scot free. None of us had been hit, but it was evident from the way that the aircraft was flying that it had suffered. It was flying sluggishly and during an inspection it was discovered that all the fabric had been shot and torn away from the port wing. Up front both pilots were having their work cut out to keep it on an even keel. As we limped away from the enemy coast I ventured out of my turret into the fuselage from where I was able to see the damage through the narrow slits of the side windows. What I saw wasn't reassuring, but the old Whitley did us proud and kept flying across the North Sea without losing height. It was a great relief when the English coast hove into sight and an even greater relief when we touched down at Dishforth at 03.45 hours.

In dispersal we vacated the aircraft and spent some time prowling around inspecting the damage. In addition to losing the fabric from the port wing, there were holes in the fuselage caused by shrapnel and my bravado quickly diminished as I saw how close some of them were to my turret. In my estimation Bick had really earned his DFC for getting us back.

The raid, especially from the squadron's point of view, had been very successful in that all our crews estimated that they had hit the target. Although most of our aircraft had been damaged by Flak, some of them severely, there had been no casualties and we considered that we had done all that the CO had asked for at briefing. Nearly all our Whitleys required repairs, thus we were unable to operate on the following night, May 18th/19th. Some of the comments we got from our sister squadron at Dishforth (No. 51), were less than complimentary: 'You lot will do anything to get a night off'.

After sleeping off the excitement of the the previous night, most of us were off to indulge in the diversions in Ripon and Harrogate whilst the other Whitley squadrons set out to attack an oil refinery near Hanover. Twenty-three bombers were despatched, most reporting successful attacks through heavy Flak, but one crew from No. 51 Squadron, captained by Squadron Leader W. H. N. Turner in N1408, failed to return. One crew from No. 102 Squadron fired on an enemy aircraft without apparent success. N1388 of No. 77 Squadron, flown by Flight Lieutenant G. L. Raphael and crewed by Pilot Officer R. P. Brayne (2nd pilot), Sergeant Prescott (air-observer), Leading Aircraftsman Storey (WOP/AG) and Aircraftsman Parkes (tail-gunner) was intercepted on its outward flight by a Bf110 about sixty miles from the Dutch coast. A heavy burst of cannon and machine-gun fire wounded Flight Lieutenant Raphael and set fire to one engine, but as the enemy fighter crossed the Whitley's tail, Aircraftsman Parkes got in a long burst from his four Brownings which resulted in the Messerschmitt bursting into flames and plunging into the sea.

While Leading Aircraftsman Storey transmitted an SOS and position report, the two pilots brought the aircraft down to the sea and achieved a successful ditching. The dinghy was launched and the crew got safely aboard. Five hours later they were picked up by a Royal Navy destroyer which took them to Yarmouth where Raphael was detained in hospital. The rescue was due in no small measure to the crew of another No. 77 Squadron Whitley, N1410 captained by Flight Lieutenant J. A. Crockett. Fortunately they saw Raphael go down and circled the area while directing rescuers to the ditched crew.

On May 18th, our skipper Flight Lieutenant Bickford DFC was promoted to acting Squadron Leader, and moved to 'B' Flight where he was to assume command. Having been our skipper since the beginning of the war and done sixteen raids together we were sorry to see him go, but pleased about his promotion. His place as our new captain was taken by 'Enery' (Flying Officer Henry) our original second pilot. We didn't have the problem of breaking him in; we already knew what made him tick.

On the night of May 19th/20th the 4 Group attacks were switched from communications to industrial targets at Gelsenkirchen and Dorsten in the Ruhr. Both Nos. 58 and 77 Squadrons were successful and all got back without casualties although Pilot Officer 'Hamish' Mahaddie's aircraft, N1348 of No. 77 Squadron, was badly shot-up by Flak after bombing an oil installation. No. 102 Squadron, on the same target, were not so fortunate and lost two of their four aircraft, N1376 flown by Flight Sergeant E. L. G. Hall and N1417 flown by Flight Lieutenant W. C. G. Cogman. Cogman had been released from his internment in Belgium only a short while earlier. All the returning crews reported the opposition as being extremely severe.

The following night, May 20th/21st, it was back to communications targets; road/rail bridges at Catillon/Hannapes and Julich as well as bridges over the River Oise. One of seven aircraft from No. 77 Squadron sent to Catillon/Hannapes was N1384, captained by Flight Lieutenant D. D. Pryde. This was badly damaged and the crew baled out near Amiens, from where four of them managed to reach Allied lines and eventually return to the squadron. The fifth man, Sergeant A. C. Thompson, didn't make it and was captured. Of the five crews from No. 102 Squadron sent to attack the Oise bridges, N1380, captained Flight Lieutenant D. H. W. Owen, failed to return.

On the night of May 21st/22nd, Group called for a Maximum Effort* from the squadrons to attack road/rail communications at Euskirchen, Julich and Rheydt. This was to support our land forces who were in deep trouble. The squadrons mustered fifty aircraft between them. The Driffield squadrons Nos. 77 and 102, sent sixteen crews to Euskirchen. One of the No. 102 Squadron aircraft, N1528 flown by Pilot Officer G. H. Womersley, crashed in France on the return flight. There were no injuries and all the crew returned safely to the unit. Nos. 51 and 58 Squadrons sent twenty-four crews to Rheydt and Julich, losing one Whitley, P4980 from No. 51 Squadron flown by Sergeant T. W. Bowles.

No. 10 Squadron's contribution was ten aircraft to Rheydt and Julich. All our crews returned and claimed successful attacks from altitudes between two and six thousand feet. One aircraft, attacked by four fighters, escaped with only slight damage and no casualties. Another avoided the unwelcome attentions of what was identified as a Henschel Hs126 observation aircraft, while others sustained Flak damage. One aircraft, P4960 flown by Flying Officer H. V. Smith, encountered severe opposition over the target and the tail-gunner, Aircraftsman J. P. Atkinson, was slightly wounded.

This was Enery's debut as our new skipper and we were detailed to attack Julich. Nipper Knapper was temporarily indisposed so his place as air-observer was taken by Sergeant N. R. Johnston, while Flying Officer K. G. J. 'Dougie' Wakefield had joined us as our new second pilot/bomb-aimer. We got off in P4953 'F for Freddie' at 20.55 hours and set course. The weather conditions were fairly good and as we flew across Holland towards the German border we could again see gunflashes on the ground. As we neared the Julich area, the bods at the sharp end reported considerable searchlight and Flak activity. After a short while we located the target and we ran in from 6,000 feet. Although the defences were heavy, I am glad to say they were nothing compared to those defending Bremen which had given us such a fright on our last trip. We knew that some of the Flak had come quite close and when we got back we discovered some Flak damage to the fuselage. The bomb-aimer estimated that our bombs had fallen in the target area and before we left I had given the defences a ration of .303. As I had four thousand rounds in the new

*Maximum Effort. Every aircraft that could be mustered.

tail turret I figured that I had enough for the defences and any fighters which may have appeared. In the early afternoon of the next day (22nd) we were told that the game was on again that night. Communications at Givet and Hirson on the Franco-Belgian border were the targets assigned to Nos. 10, 51 and 58 Squadrons. We were again in P4953 and Nipper had rejoined us after his brief absence. We got off at 20.50 hours and after a smooth outward flight we crossed the Belgian coast and headed for Givet. On the way we encountered little opposition, but in the target area it was a different story. Givet was an important junction through which the Germans were supporting their breakthrough, and they were defending it with batteries of mobile 20 and 37mm Flak guns. When we arrived the battle was in full swing with fires burning in the town and Flak coming up thick and fast. However, we pressed on making our bomb-run and getting through unscathed. It was estimated that our bombs were on target. Leaving the area without delay we headed for home. From the tail turret I watched the Flak, mentally thanking our lucky stars that we had got through successfully yet again. As we crossed the coast on our homeward flight, Fletch came on the intercom saying that he had received a W/T message diverting us to Kidlington because the weather at Dishforth was closing in. Kidlington was a Flying Training Command station and numerous Tiger Moths were carrying out night circuits and bumps, but we managed to avoid them and land safely at 03.00 hours. While the higher ranking members of the crew made their way to their respective Messes, Fletch and I went to the airmen's transit billet where we were to be accommodated. Understandably, Kidlington was not geared up to cope with operational diversions and there were problems, especially in the early hours of the morning.

At the beginning of the war all of our aircraft were fitted with IFF (Identification Friend or Foe) transponder sets for air defence purposes. These sets were security classified and were not a permanent fixture, being installed in the aircraft prior to operations and removed again after landing to be placed in safe custody. Unfortunately for Fletch and myself, at that early hour, Kidlington had no such place of safety. Nobody wanted to know. So we were lumbered with having to remove the set and take it with us to our transit accommodation. There was no transport and by the time we

118

Wireless operators and air-gunners 'tradesmen aircrew' receive their briefing before another operation.

got there we were on our knees. However, that night we were the only airmen in the billet so we were able to get an uninterrupted sleep. After doing two raids on the trot we needed no rocking. During the following afternoon the weather cleared up and we were able to return to Dishforth.

That night, May 23rd/24th, Nos. 10 and 51 Squadrons were 'stood down'. For some of us it was a chance to relax, for others another 'whoop up' in Ripon and Harrogate, where the depressing news of the German break-through into France and the Low Countries was having its effect on civilian morale. It was said that even in 'toffee-nosed' Harrogate some were affected by the 'eat, drink and be merry' attitude and some of them were letting more than their hair down!

Meanwhile it was the turn of the Driffield squadrons to join No. 58 keeping up attacks on the road/rail communications in an effort to stem the German advance. Twenty-four Whitleys went out, but one of the five crews from No. 58 Squadron briefed to bomb La Capelle, Flight Lieutenant I. L. MacLaren and crew in N1361, was reported missing.

No. 58 Squadron were more fortunate the following night (24th/25th) when they attacked the same target. This time only one of the seven aircraft was damaged by Flak and there were no casualties. Our squadron, after the short respite, sent twelve crews to bomb the communications centres at Asvesnes, Mons and Binche. Eleven crews claimed successful attacks and we all got back, but one sustained Flak damage and had a 250lb bomb 'hang up'; it was ours!

We had got airborne at 22.00 hours and our specific target was Binche, some twenty kilometres from the Franco/Belgian border. Sitting in my lonely tail turret I now found the periods of silence on the intercom, which had sometimes stimulated poetic reverie, were now breeding times for more realistic conjecture: "Let's hope this is an easy one and our luck holds out." No more thoughts of Mr Noyes' 'Galleons tossed upon cloudy seas'! Nipper's laconic comment "Crossing the coast in five minutes," was the signal for increased alertness and added adrenalin flow as I slowly traversed the turret, visually sweeping each sector of the sky and at times doing a 'double- take' as my imagination conjured up a Bf110 out of 'spots before my eyes'.

The weather was fairly good, part cloud cover but with haze limiting the visibility, so after crossing the enemy coast, Nipper took us to the town of Charleroi, which was larger than Binche and as such easier to locate. His ploy paid off and we were able to follow the road from Charleroi to Binche. As we got near it was obvious from the chat on the intercom from up front that the target had been identified, apparently aided by the defence activity in its vicinity which had probably been stirred up by another of our squadron's crews who had beaten us to it - thanks a bunch chums!

At this time it was seldom that the three groups of heavy bombers of Bomber Command could muster even one hundred aircraft between them for operations on any one night. Instead of concentrating this small force on a single target it was split up to attack numerous objectives. Each squadron would be given its target or targets and left to work out their own tactics. Unlike future raids, those from 1942 onwards when the force often involved as many as one thousand aircraft bombing a single target in less than twenty minutes, we were given an attack time of an hour or more. This policy turned out to be somewhat unfortunate for us because it meant that each aircraft attacked the target singly in most cases and had to run the gauntlet of the defences on its own. Human nature being what it is, it was soon considered legitimate to attempt an attack when the defences were knocking hell out of some other poor so-and-so. As survival has no scruples, some crews succumbed to the temptation of hanging about, waiting for some unfortunate crew to act as their decoy while they made their attack. That night there were no 'legitimate' decoys for us. They had all left the target area before we commenced our bomb-run, so we received the undivided attention of the defences. The Flak hosed up as we glided in from 7,000 feet and we felt the effects of the shells as they burst near us (we were to discover that we had been slightly hit - again!). Despite this deterrent we pressed on, dropping our load which the bomb-aimer estimated had fallen in the target area. With the call of 'Bombs gone!', it was then 'Let's get out of here', which we did with alacrity, even quicker than that! By taking evasive action Enery got us clear of the defences and when we had settled down he did a 'body count and damage check'. During the seemingly interminable two minutes of the bomb-run, the intercom was restricted for the use of the bomb-aimer (except in extreme emergency) to enable him to pass instruction to the pilot without interruption. So after dropping the bombs it was standard practice for the skipper to call each crew member in turn to check for casualties and damage.

On this occasion after we had all called 'alive and kicking', the bomb-aimer reported that there was a 250lb bomb left on the rack, just to cheer us up. This was the second time this had happened to us. Was someone trying to tell us something? There were many such instances of bomber aircraft having 'hang ups' which failed to budge in spite of violent attempts by the crew to dislodge the offending bomb or bombs. How often had the bomb fallen off and exploded the instant the aircraft touched down, no matter how gentle the landing? During our return flight such a possibility was shut in the back of our minds and our apprehension was only relieved when the 'rogue' was removed by the armourers when we had landed safely back at base.

When we tumbled out of the aircraft the ground crew swarmed over it to carry out the post-flight checks and inspect it for damage. When they found the Flak holes in the fuselage they were more accusing and concerned with the repairs they would have to carry out than with our well-being. However, at four o'clock in the morning who could blame them?

On the night of May 25th/26th communications targets in France and oil installations in the Ruhr were the objectives for the 4 Group Whitleys. Two aircraft from No. 102 Squadron were damaged by Flak over their target at Bapaume and one, N1420, flown by Sergeant J. J. Gall, crashed at base on return, fortunately without casualties. Our squadron and No. 51 were briefed to raid the Ruhr and our crew was one of eleven sent to attack the oil plants at Mannheim, Reisholz and Emmerich. Reisholz was our particular objective and we took off in P4953 at 20.50 hours. The flight was uneventful and on this occasion we climbed to 12,000 feet before crossing the enemy coast. Having been hit on our last trip we had discovered that the light Flak was now getting up to 10,000 feet and, at important targets, the Germans had established concentrations of Flak batteries and searchlights making it increasingly hazardous to attack from low level. The 'Valley' was getting less happy with every raid!*

We stayed at 12,000 feet and attacked from there instead of gliding down as usual. Although there was opposition at that altitude we managed to stay out of trouble and dropped our bombs in the target area. Shortly after we had left the target area I sighted a Bf110 flying on a parallel course to ours. I got him in my sights, estimating the range to be about two hundred and fifty yards, but Enery told me to hold my fire unless he turned in to attack. He stayed there for about two or three minutes then turned away - he obviously hadn't seen us. I suppose I was relieved despite my fantasies, but of course after we had left the area and were safely on our way across the North Sea I was convinced that I could have shot it down. As ever, hindsight can be the basis for self-deception. We got back without further incident and landed at 03.35 hours. This was the second time that week that we had carried out raids on consecutive nights so by the time we had finished de-briefing, had our post-flight meal, trudged back to barracks and got into bed, I reckon I was asleep before my head hit the pillow!

When we surfaced during the late morning of the May 26th the news bulletins broadcast by the BBC concerning the land battle in France were anything but reassuring. As a result of the seemingly unstoppable German advance, the British Cabinet decided to allow

*One Whitley was observed by the Germans to emerge from cloud over Cologne and accurately bomb one of the railway bridges, the Sudbrucke, closing it to traffic and igniting a gas main underneath.

Lord Gort, the C-in-C of the BEF, to evacuate the remnants of his force which was now cut off and with its back to the sea. Thus 'Operation Dynamo', the evacuation of the surviving British troops from Dunkirk, was initiated.

Following the concentrated efforts by the 4 Group squadrons during the previous week the Whitley crews were given the night off. Most of us headed for our favourite haunts, the Linton boys to 'Betty's' in York, the Driffield squadrons to the 'Stag' in the village while we and No. 51 Squadron headed for the 'Bluebell' at Dishforth and the 'Unicorn' in Ripon. By now most of us, who at the beginning of the war seldom did so, were frequenting the local pubs on our stand-downs. The black-out and petrol rationing restricted travel so we were generally limited by how far we were prepared to walk. It was now the practice to assemble in the local for a few drinks with our 'Oppos' to relax away from the station for a few hours. Sometimes a party would develop if we had an excuse and could afford it - our airmen's rates of pay limited any tendency to be prodigal. That night we and the boys from No. 51 Squadron had an excuse; during the day it had been learned that our CO, Wing Commander W. E. Staton had been awarded a Bar to his DSO and was now, with DSO and Bar, MC, DFC and Bar, one of the most highly decorated officers in the RAF. Also among the awards to our 'sister' squadron, No. 51, was the Distinguished Flying Medal to Temporary Corporal R. 'Jacko' Jackson, the first WOP/AG of a 4 Group Whitley squadron to be so honoured during World War II.* 'Hero' Jackson took a lot of leg-pulling from his oppos for the next few days.

We were back 'on the job' on the following night, May 27th/28th, attacking marshalling yards in the Ruhr with thirty-five Whitleys being despatched. Some returned with technical problems, but the majority got through. Two crews attacked airfields as secondary targets and one of No. 51 Squadron had to evade a night-fighter attack. During the raids two aircraft were damaged, but there were no casualties.

---

*It is a sad but true fact that the award of the DFM, for which NCOs were eligible, was made far more rarely than that of the DFC to officers. It can be only a matter for conjecture why this should have been yet the fact remains that for the first few years of the war the majority of aircrew, including pilots, were NCOs. However, between 1939 and 1945, the number of DFCs awarded far exceeded those of DFMs.

No. 10 Squadron's targets were the marshalling yards at Neuss, Dortmund and Duisburg. Ten of the eleven aircraft bombed as briefed. One crew, that of Squadron Leader Pat Hanafin in N1483, was attacked by a fighter after leaving the target. The tail gunner, Aircraftsman Stan Oldridge, managed to get in accurate bursts and claimed to have shot it down. All ten crews reported severe opposition in the target area and it was estimated that fifty searchlights with associated Flak batteries were concentrated against us during this raid.

The eleventh crew from our contingent failed to find their primary target and bombed what was thought to be an airfield in Holland. This was not the case. After carrying out their bomb-run they set course for home, but after flying for some time, and when the Dutch coast failed to show up, it was thought that something was amiss. This was confirmed when W/T bearings indicated that the aircraft was over England and flying on a westerly course. With the aid of further W/T assistance they were able to scramble back to base. A re-plot of the sortie was instigated and the unfortunate conclusion was reached that the airfield they had bombed must have been British! This was confirmed when communication with Air Ministry revealed that the RAF airfield at Bassingbourn, near Cambridge had been attacked at the same time the No. 10 Squadron crew presumed they were bombing an enemy airfield. Luckily there had been no casualties and only slight damage at Bassingbourn. Subsequently the story got around that one of the bombs had hit the W/T rest hut at the side of the airfield, passing through one wall, over the top of a sleeping airman and out the other side before exploding. The said airman then woke up!

Repercussions followed. The unfortunate skipper was demoted to second pilot and he and his crew subjected to much leg-pulling by the other Dishforth and 4 Group crews. This included the dropping of a home-made 'Iron Cross' constructed from a tea-chest lid and some brown coloured cloth, by one of the other squadrons in 4 Group. It was addressed to 'Herr von (name withheld) from a grateful Fuhrer'!*

During the night of May 28th/29th, Nos. 77 and 102 Squadrons carried out the last Whitley operation of what had been a sad month

---

*During the subsequent investigation it was discovered that the magnetic compass had been rendered U/S when the aircraft had flown through an electrical storm after crossing the English coast on its outbound flight.

of May. Fourteen bombers raided communications targets and one of
the No. 77 Squadron crews, that of Flying Officer T. J. (Trevor)
Geach in N1342, failed to return.

Meanwhile in France and the Low Countries the bitter land battle
was coming to its tragic conclusion. 'Operation Dynamo' continued
in the face of constant air attacks by the Luftwaffe. Our friends in
the depleted Fairey Battle squadrons of the AASF went on fighting
as the French and the remaining British troops moved south and
west, but for the AASF the German advance made things
increasingly difficult for the crews. It proved impossible for them to
be given precise targets and all they could do was to take off, fly in
the general direction of the enemy and bomb targets of opportunity.

Coupled with this depressing news from the Continent, there came
rumours that all surviving and future WOP/AGs and AGs were to be
promoted to the rank of Sergeant to bring their status in line with the
other aircrew categories. This was tragically ironic, especially
bearing in mind the beating that our friends in the AASF Fairey
Battles and Bristol Blenheims had taken during the last few weeks.

Summary of operations by 4 Group
10th - 31st May 1940

10th GERMANY INVADED HOLLAND AND BELGIUM

10th-11th Bombing - Road/Rail Communications in Cleve Area.
77 Sqn. Four a/c bombed as briefed. Slight opposition.
102 Sqn. Five a/c bombed as briefed. Slight opposition.

11th-12th. Bombing - Road/Rail Communications Mönchen-Gladbach.
51 Sqn. Six a/c all bombed, one damaged by Flak.
58 Sqn. Three a/c all bombed, opposition severe.
77 Sqn. Three a/c all bombed, one FTR.
102 Sqn. Six a/c all bombed, one damaged by Flak.

12th-13th. Bombing - Road/Rail Communications Cleve and Mönchen-Gladbach.
10 Sqn. Six a/c all bombed. Severe opposition, one enemy aircraft
sighted, but no combat.

13th-14th. Bombing - Road/Rail Communications - Maastricht and Eindhoven.

58 Sqn. Six a/c. One returned early U/S, two bombed, three brought bombs back.

14th-15th. Bombing - Road/Rail Communications Mönchen-Gladbach.

77 Sqn. Seven a/c, all bombed, moderate opposition.

102 Sqn. Five a/c, all bombed, moderate opposition.

15th-16th. Bombing - Industrial Targets in Germany - Wanne-Eickel, Gelsenkirchen, Reisholz, Dusseldorf. Rail Targets - Dinant.

10 Sqn. Twelve a/c. Six bombed German industrial targets, six bombed road and rail targets at Dinant.

51 Sqn. Nine a/c. One returned early, seven bombed.

58 Sqn. Nine a/c. One returned early, eight bombed, one hit by Flak.

16th-17th. Bombing - Road/Rail Communications and Troops - Maastricht, Aachen.

77 Sqn. Six a/c. One returned early, six bombed.

102 Sqn. Three a/c. All bombed.

17th-18th Bombing - Oil Storage Depot at Bremen.

10 Sqn. Fourteen a/c. One crashed on take-off, Twelve bombed primary target from low level, one bombed secondary target. Severe opposition, six aircraft damaged by Flak.

51 Sqn. Six a/c. Five bombed primary, one bombed Delmenhorst airfield and was damaged by Flak.

58 Sqn. Six a/c. Five bombed successfully.

18th-19th. Bombing - Oil Refinery at Hanover.

51 Sqn. Four a/c. Three bombed, one FTR.

58 Sqn. Four a/c. Three bombed.

77 Sqn. Seven a/c. Six bombed, one shot down by Bf110, crew rescued. Bf110 claimed destroyed.

102 Sqn. Eight a/c. Seven bombed.

19th-20th. Bombing - Oil Targets at Gelsenkirchen and Dorsten.

58 Sqn. Six a/c. All bombed from low level (2 - 8,000 feet). Severe opposition.

77 Sqn. Two a/c. Both bombed, one badly damaged by Flak. 102 Sqn. Four a/c. Extremely severe opposition, two FTR.

20th-21st. Bombing - Road/Rail Communications at Catillon-Hannapes, Julich and Bridges over River Oise.

10 Sqn. Six a/c. Five bombed from low level (2 - 6,000 feet).

51 Sqn. Six a/c, four bombed.

77 Sqn. Seven a/c. Six bombed, one FTR.

102 Sqn. Five a/c. Four bombed, one FTR.

21st-22nd. Bombing - Road/Rail Communications at Euskirchen, Julich and Rheydt.

10 Sqn. Ten a/c all bombed (2 - 6000 feet).

51 Sqn. Twelve a/c, all bombed. One FTR.

58 Sqn. Twelve a/c, all bombed. Moderate to severe opposition.

77 Sqn. Seven a/c. One returned early U/S, six bombed.

102 Sqn. Nine a/c. Two returned early U/S, one FTR.

22nd-23rd. Bombing - Road/Rail Communications at Givet and Hirson.

10 Sqn. Eleven a/c, all bombed.

51 Sqn. Eight a/c, all bombed. 58 Sqn. Six a/c, all bombed.

23rd-24th. Bombing - Road/Rail Communications at Avesnes, Maubeuge, Aulnoye and La Capelle.

58 Sqn. Five a/c. Four bombed, one FTR.

77 Sqn. Ten a/c, all bombed.

102 Sqn. Nine a/c. One returned early U/S, eight bombed. One damaged by Flak.

24th-25th. Bombing - Road/Rail Communications at Avesnes, La Capelle, Mons, Binche and the Ruhr.

10 Sqn. Twelve a/c. Eleven bombed, one damaged by Flak and returned with hung-up bomb.

51 Sqn. Eleven a/c. Two aborted, eight bombed.

58 Sqn. Seven a/c. All bombed, one damaged by Flak.

25th-26th. Bombing - Road/Rail Communications at Bapaume and Oil Targets Ruhr.

10 Sqn. Eleven a/c. All bombed. Moderate to severe opposition.

51 Sqn. Ten a/c. Nine bombed. Moderate to severe opposition.

77 Sqn. Eight a/c. Seven bombed. Moderate to severe opposition.

102 Sqn. Seven a/c, all bombed. One damaged by Flak and one crashed on return.

27th-28th. Bombing - Dortmund, Duisburg, Dusseldorf and Cologne.

10 sqn. Eleven a/c. Ten bombed. One enemy aircraft claimed destroyed by

tail-gunner. One bombed Bassingbourn in error.

51 Sqn. Nine a/c. Eight bombed, one attacked by enemy aircraft but evaded undamaged.

58 Sqn. Five a/c, all bombed. One damaged by Flak.

77 Sqn. Nine a/c. One returned early U/S, eight bombed.

102 Sqn. Two a/c. One returned early U/S, one bombed.

28th-29th. Bombing - Road/Rail Communications at Givet, Avesnes, Guise and Hirson.

77 Sqn. Eight a/c. One returned early U/S, one FTR.

102 Sqn. Six a/c. One returned early U/S, four bombed.

Chapter Six

Promotion The 'Hard Way'

The speculation concerning our promotion to the rank of Sergeant ended with the promulgation of an extract from Air Ministry Orders in Station Personnel Occurrence Reports on June 1st. This made it official by stating that all we operational WOP/AGs and AGs were to be promoted immediately and that in future the rank would be awarded on successful completion of training. The promotion was accompanied by a new rate of pay of eight shillings and three-pence per day (41p).

As soon as our names appeared on PORs we lost no time in obtaining our 'stripes' from stores and sewing needles worked overtime. The camp tailor may have made a neater a job of it, but we couldn't afford to wait. We worked on the premise that, if we were going to get shot down, it would be as Sergeants. This was understandable for, under the terms of the Geneva Convention, prisoners of lower ranks could be made to work for their captors, while senior NCOs were given the option.

For we surviving 'bob a day' fliers this was an improvement in status, pay and living conditions. There was no room for us in the Dishforth Sergeant's Mess, so we were moved from the Squadron barrack-room dormitory to occupy separate rooms in the peacetime airmen's married quarters, which had been vacated by the families at the outbreak of war. The family furniture had gone and we were given the usual airmen's single bed, locker, chair and if you were lucky, or well in with the stores bashers, a table and chest of drawers. The main advantage was that now we would have the opportunity of some uninterrupted sleep - an impossibility in a crowded barrack-room.

Before moving to the Sergeant's Mess and our new accommodation, we were given 'the treatment' by our barrack-room mates. "Don't go pulling rank on me, Sprog," and, "Put in a good word for me with the Chiefy." It was all good-natured, even when they referred to us as 'jumped-up' and suggested we had better go on a 'knife and fork course' before attempting to eat in the Sergeant's Mess.

It was with a certain amount of trepidation that we made our debut, but we needn't have worried. I suppose the gloomy news of our forces fighting for their lives in France, and the fact of us having to carry out an increasing number of raids, tempered the resentment of some of the 'Old Sweat' SNCOs to our quick promotion. While I could sympathise that they had possibly waited years for their promotions it was us, not them, that had 'made it the hard way'. We were all on our best behaviour and our squadron SNCO pilots and air-observers rallied round to give us their support and guidance. The Chairman of the Mess Committee, a senior Warrant Officer who had obviously been briefed by the Station Commander - as we had by our Squadron Commander - welcomed us with other senior Mess members. The food was a great improvement on that in the Airmen's Mess and there was the added luxury of waitress service - no more having to queue with 'mugs and irons'.

Another advantage of our new rank was that we were no longer required to book in and out of the guardroom with the SPs breathing down our necks as we entered and left the base and we were not restricted by the midnight curfew. Despite these advantages, for which we were grateful, the gap between the pay, career prospects and rewards of we SNCO WOP/AGs and those of our fellow SNCO crew members (pilots and air-observers) continued to be very wide.

Unfortunately for some, promotion had come too late. Between September 3rd 1939 and June 1st 1940, two hundred and one Bomber Command 'tradesmen aircrew' (WOP/AGs and AGs) had been killed in action and a further seventy-one taken prisoner, the latter of course were promoted, which improved their lot as captives.

There was further good news for the Dishforth squadrons in another official publication released on June 1st, which stated that Squadron Leader P. A. Gilchrist of No. 51 Squadron and Flying Officer W. H. Nelson together with Pilot Officer H. G. Cattell of our squadron had been awarded the DFC. Leading Aircraftsman A. J. 'Tich' Heller of No. 51, was awarded the DFM. Official sources also revealed that Squadron Leader W. H. N. Turner of No. 51 Squadron, missing since May 19th, had been reported safe as a prisoner.

The weather at the outset of June was anything but 'flaming' over the continent, especially France and the Low Countries, so the Whitley squadrons were restricted to attacking targets in Germany. As it turned out, the weather over there wasn't much better.

Our squadron sent eight aircraft of the twenty-eight despatched on June 1st/2nd, but few successes were claimed. On the following night however our squadron had another go at the oil plant at

Hamburg. Squadron Leader Bickford, our ex-skipper, joined forces with two crews of No. 51 Squadron and made the first attempt at 'pathfinding'. Each aircraft carried thirty flares and, after positively identifying the target, they flew back and forth dropping a series of parachute flares to illuminate it. While carrying out this manoeuvre they came under intense gunfire. Bick's aircraft, P4962, was badly damaged and his tail-gunner, Sergeant Jimmy Cornforth, was seriously wounded.*

That same night Osnabrück and Hamm were attacked by Nos. 58 and 77 Squadrons, one aircraft of No. 77 Squadron, N1356 flown by Squadron Leader Tomlin, was hit by Flak and two men were wounded.

Next night oil targets were the priority when forty-six Whitleys were sent to Hamburg, Gelsenkirchen and Kamen. The defences were severe and several aircraft were hit by Flak, one No. 10 Squadron aircraft, P4963 flown by Flight Lieutenant A. S. Phillips crashed at Battisford, Suffolk, on return with one fatality.

On June 4th the evacuation of the remnants of the British Expeditionary Force from Dunkirk was successfully completed. Meanwhile the French fought on as the German advance continued. What was left of the gallant Advanced Air Striking Force continued to operate from bases near Le Mans. The Fairey Battle crews gave what support they could by hitting at railways, ammunition dumps, troop concentrations and the airfields at St. Hubert and Guise which were being used by Stukas pounding the Dunkirk beaches. Back in England a German bomber caused the first damage to the British railway system by bombing the Northallerton railway station, not far from Dishforth - getting close!

That night our attacks against the oil targets continued when seventeen Whitleys from Nos. 58, 77 and 102 Squadrons raided Buer-Kamen and Gelsenkirchen. One of the four crews from No. 77 Squadron , that of Pilot Officer A. C. Meigh in N1522, sent a radio signal that they were on fire and baling out over Ghent.

Tactical targets were given priority on June 5th/6th. No. 10 squadron sent five aircraft, joining six from No. 51 Squadron to bomb troop and transport concentrations near Doullens. No. 102 Squadron was detailed for similar duties in the Somme-Aisne area and No. 77 Squadron was to bomb troops and transport around Bapaume. One of the No. 77 Squadron crews, Pilot Officer A. W.

---

*Happily Sergeant Cornforth recovered, and returned to operations four months later.

Dunn in N1476 didn't make it. Shortly after taking off from Driffield and setting course, a parachute flare ignited in the aircraft and Pilot Officer Dunn ordered his crew to bale out. Sergeant Malcolm Lucas, the air-observer recalled:

"We were only thirty-five minutes out from Driffield when the incident occurred, in fact after I'd baled out I came down in the grounds of Bawtry Hall, a country mansion not far from Finningley. It was dusk, but on the way down I could see people below me with shotguns. I landed fairly heavily, having had to dodge some high tension cables as I got near the ground. While lying flat on my back I had a shotgun pointed at me from close quarters, but fortunately a lady appeared on the scene and said "Can't you see he's one of ours?" and gave me a swig from a bottle of Scotch she was carrying. Eventually I was transported to RAF Finningley where I spent the night in the guardroom! I returned to Driffield the following day."

Pilot Officer Dunn flew the damaged aircraft to Finningley, where he made a safe landing.

As a matter of interest, the 'postings-in' to No. 102 Squadron on June 5th had included a certain Pilot Officer Leonard Cheshire!*

On June 6th/7th, Nos. 58, 77 and 102 Squadrons had a welcome night off while Nos. 10 and 51 Squadrons kept the Whitley flag flying with attacks against marshalling yards, transport and enemy troops. While crews from No. 51 squadron attacked troops around Doullens, we were one of the nine crews assigned to bomb the yards at Rheydt. As this was the first trip for Fletch and I as Sergeants, we had to put up with a certain amount of leg-pulling from our skipper and second pilot concerning our 'meteoric rise' through the ranks.

We took off, again in P4953, at 21.15 hours, passing over York and crossing out near Hull. It was a fine night for a change and we passed to the north of Amsterdam heading inland for the industrial heart of Germany; the Ruhr.

After we had crossed the German border we encountered sporadic Flak, but avoided it without difficulty. However as we approached the target area the increase in defensive activity was a good indication that we were on the right track. The Germans were determined to protect the industrial heartland at all costs and now the searchlights and Flak batteries were more numerous and concentrated. More nightfighters were also being deployed, but it was fortunate for us that the Germans had not, at that time, developed

*Later Group Captain Leonard Cheshire VC, OM, DSO, DFC.

airborne radar. Combats were rare and the result of visual sightings as direction came from ground control only.

There was a slight haze in the target area, but after groping around for a short while Nipper announced that he had pin-pointed the target. With the light Flak now reaching 10,000 feet the skipper decided, prudently in our opinion, that we would make a single bomb-run from 11,000 feet: "Did you hear that, bomb-aimer? One run. No going around a second time." He must have read my thoughts.

During the bomb-run we had to contend with the blinding effect of searchlights and the thuds as the heavy stuff exploded near us, but we were lucky and carried out our attack without difficulty. All the same, that straight and level bit was always a nail-biting time. From that height the bomb bursts were just brief flashes of light. I could see them and the bomb-aimer assured us that they had fallen in the target area. We lost no time in getting out of the area and setting course for home. This time I resisted the temptation to spray the Ruhr valley with .303 - we were a little too high.

No. 58 Squadron was the only Whitley unit to operate on June 7th/8th by raiding rail targets at Hirson. Thus with the night off most of us headed for the local towns or villages, some going to the cinemas, others to the local pubs and dance halls. Now that we WOP/AGs were Sergeants as well as 'flying men', our glamour and what is now referred to as 'bird-pulling' influence had increased accordingly. This of course was sometimes resented by the local male civilian population. Also, at this time we had another element of discontent thrust upon us, namely some of the troops evacuated from Dunkirk who were now stationed in the area. They wanted to know where we 'Brylcreem Boys' had been when they were being bombed on the beaches. It was sometimes difficult trying to convince some fourteen stone 'brown job', awash to his back teeth with brown ale, that you had been doing your best to help him by bombing some place in Germany that he had never even heard of!

All the Whitley squadrons were back on the job on June 8th/9th, attacking road and rail communications, troops and marshalling yards to support the land battle. Our squadron mustered ten aircraft which were detailed to attack marshalling yards at Rheydt, Wedan and Essen. At this time we were using Topcliffe airfield near Thirsk as our satellite base where some of our aircraft were dispersed. After briefing at Dishforth and getting kitted-up we were transported in three- tonners to Topcliffe. That night our old skipper, now Squadron Leader Bickford, pranged P4962 on take-off from Topcliffe - fortunately only two of the crew were slightly injured. We were one of the ten crews detailed for the operation and got airborne at 21.35 hours. We were soon heading for our target at Essen, which even then was one of the most heavily defended targets in the Ruhr valley. With every raid all the routine tasks were now becoming second nature, evidence that our 'on the job' training was paying dividends. Crews were being welded into efficient teams with every member confident that he could rely the others no matter what happened. Our crew discipline was relaxed without impairing efficiency. From time to time someone would make a comment or reply that helped to relieve the tension, but it was never allowed to get out of hand.

Around midnight we entered the Ruhr area and as we approached Essen the numerous searchlights sweeping the skies and the multi-coloured Flak was a sure indication that an attack was in progress. The bomb-aimer was now at his position, guiding us in with his target map to a point from where he could set up the run-in. Luckily for us the defences seemed to be concentrating on one of the preceding aircraft so while they were thus engaged, he took us in and we were able to drop our load relatively unmolested. Mind you, the time to "Bombs gone!" seemed to get longer with every trip - no doubt a figment of the imagination stimulated by the ever-present apprehension - I'm not as brave as I used to be! However, that night we again got away without a scratch, landing at 04.15 hours. Then it was back to Dishforth, debrief, bacon and eggs and bed.

The bombing attacks against road and rail communications continued on the night of June 9th/10th. For the second night in succession all the 4 Group squadrons were engaged, thus for us it was a case of bed, carry out checks and air tests, then stand by for the night's raid.

No. 51 Squadron despatched eleven crews all of which claimed successful attacks, but in doing so one crew, that of Squadron Leader W. B. Tait* in N1414, ran into severe opposition and their aircraft was hit several times. Sergeant McNeil, the tail gunner, was wounded in his neck and arms. The aircraft landed at Bircham

*'Willie' Tait went on to become CO of No.617 Squadron when they attacked the Tirpitz. He ended the war as Group Captain with the DSO and 3 bars, DFC and bar. He earned the nick-name of *Tirpitz* Tait.

Newton where McNeil was detained in hospital. One No. 77 Squadron aircraft, N1372, was hit by Flak over France en route to the target and was badly damaged. This was the aircraft of Pilot Officer Dunn and crew, the same unfortunate crew who had been involved in the incident on June 5th when the parachute flare had ignited in the aircraft causing a bale-out and forced landing. Again Sergeant Malcolm Lucas was air-observer:

"We were on our way to the target when the starboard engine was damaged by Flak and we were forced to return. I jettisoned the bombs when we were over the Channel. I repeated the procedure to ensure that they all left the aircraft, a trick learned during my training as an armourer.

"When we were over Abingdon the starboard engine caught fire. There was an air raid in progress, but they put the airfield lights on for us. Pilot Officer Dunn gave us the option of baling out but, having done so on the 5th, we all elected to stay. I was in the nose of the aircraft and thought it wise to get to the rear for landing. However, due to the activity in the cockpit, I was unable to do so. On my way back to the nose I saw a row of red lights and thought 'we're not going to make it', so I decided to open the front hatch and chance it. As I lowered myself through the open hatch I was caught around the thighs by some barbed wire and out I went. As I was being pulled out, the aircraft crashed into the bomb dump, the tail wheel ending up just over my head. The Whitley was now on fire and I was seen in the light of the flames by Flight Lieutenant D. E. Cattell (ex-77 Squadron but now stationed at Abingdon) who pulled me out from under as the ammunition exploded around us. I was taken to Station Sick Quarters with the rest of the crew, who also had a miraculous escape. Fortunately none of us were seriously injured and after a few days were discharged and returned to Driffield by train. Before we left we were told that all that remained of N1372 was the tail turret!"

The other Driffield squadron, No. 102, had sent eight aircraft to attack communications in the Abbeville/St Valery area. On this raid Pilot Officer Leonard Cheshire made his debut flying as second pilot.*

Our squadron's targets were communications in the Libremont, Sedan and Neufchateau areas. We were one of the nine crews and took off at 21.30 hours. The North Sea crossing was, as ever, uneventful thanks to our reliable Merlins and we proceeded towards our target, a road/rail junction at Neufchateau on the eastern approaches to Paris. The weather and visibility continued to be helpful and Nipper was able to take us to the target area without too

*Leonard Cheshire was to fly a total of 101 'ops' during the war including numerous night low-level target-marking sorties in a Mustang whilst leading 617 Squadron and a B-29 sortie to Nagasaki acting as observer to the second American A-bomb sortie.

much trouble. Unlike Essen, it was lightly defended - for which we were thankful - and we carried out our attack without distraction from the defences. Our return flight was also uneventful and we were back at base at 03.30 hours. It had been an easy trip, but two on the trot takes its toll and I was glad to get back to my charp!

When we surfaced from our post-flight slumbers on the morning of June 10th we were given the news that Italy had declared war on Britain and France. As Mr Churchill was later to say: "The Italian jackal (Mussolini) is about to start his scavenging." Following the radio announcement anti-Italian feeling ran high in civvy street and Italian ice-cream parlours, as well as fish and chip shops throughout the country were attacked. It was reported that a fish shop proprietor in Scotland, taking advantage of the anti-Italian reaction, displayed a notice which read: 'All Scots - Potatoes, Fish, Dripping, Owner, Assistants and even the Cat!'. Apparently all the Italian restaurants in Soho became 'Continental' overnight!

That night Nos. 10 and 51 Squadrons had the night off which, after raids on consecutive nights, gave us the opportunity to simmer down and catch up with sleep and letters home. Of course some charged off to the local towns to 'whoop it up'. Nos. 58, 77 and 102 Squadrons, however, continued the attacks against communications targets.

The following morning our crew, together with seven others, were woken early and summoned to the Ops Rooms for an early briefing. Here we were joined by seven crews from No. 51 Squadron. We were told that we were going to Guernsey with six crews from No. 58 Squadron, while eight crews from No. 77 Squadron and another seven from No. 102 Squadron would be going to Jersey. The reason for this was that, prior to the Italian Declaration of War, the British and French governments had jointly agreed that in the eventuality of Italy joining forces with Germany against us, the Allies would commence air operations against her. Thus a force of bombers code-named 'Haddock Force' was created, comprising Wellingtons from Nos. 99 and 149 Squadrons of 3 Group. 'Haddock Force' was to be based on the French airfields at Salon and Le Vallon, to which an advance ground party had been despatched on June 7th. On the morning of June 11th, the Wellingtons of No. 99 Squadron arrived at Salon where they were immediately refuelled and bombed-up for a raid on Italian industrial targets that night. However the local French

Air Force commander, backed up by a deputation from local authorities, were aware that the Italians had already bombed Cannes and Nice that morning. They were fearful of possible Italian attacks in retaliation and objected to such a raid. Despite protests from the RAF commander that they had the approval of the French government and the personal intervention of Mr Churchill to the French premier M. Reynaud, the local authorities refused to budge. As the Wellingtons began to taxi out the airfield was blocked by French Army trucks and other vehicles. The French officer informed the RAF that force would be used if necessary to prevent the bombers from taking off. In order to avoid a clash the raid was called off and, to prevent possible sabotage, the Wellingtons were ordered back to England.

While this wrangling had been going on, the RAF had taken out its own insurance against possible opposition to the RAF using French bases. The C in C Bomber Command had ordered our 4 Group Whitleys to the Channel Islands, to which we went following this briefing. That afternoon we were ordered to mount a raid against the Fiat aero-engine and motor works at Turin, with the Ansaldo factories in Genoa as the alternative.

The airfields at Jersey and Guernsey were very small, with a take-off run of approximately eight hundred yards, not the ideal situation for the operation of fully-laden heavy bombers. In order to boost the flagging confidence of our 'drivers, airframe' and crews, Wing Commander 'Kong' Staton demonstrated how it could be done by carrying out a take-off and landing. The raid could now proceed; let battle commence!

Take-off began at 19.30 hours while it was still daylight and our turn came at 20.00 hours. As we taxied out we were slightly, but not fully, reassured when the preceding aircraft got off safely. There had been much bated breath as we had watched them disappear from sight over the cliff edge at the end of the take-off run followed by sighs of relief as they finally reappeared, flying above the waves of the English Channel. However, when our moment of truth arrived nerves went back to the twanging stage and the adrenalin flow reached rip-tide proportions. To say that I was feeling tensed-up as I sat in the tail turret of the Whitley bumping its way along the take-off run was an understatement. I relaxed slightly as the Whitley clawed its way into the air, but my relief was short-lived for the aircraft began to sink towards the waves as we tried to build up speed and climb away. I found out what morbid fascination was as the Whitley skimmed just above the waves for what seemed to be a very, very long time!

Eventually the aircraft began to climb and we settled down to the task of getting over the Alps to Turin. Unfortunately it was not to be, for as we flew over France the weather deteriorated and when we reached the Alps we ran into electrical storms. Lightning flashed constantly around us and ice built up on the leading edges of the wings and tailplane. We were thrown around like a pea in a bucket by the turbulence and as the conditions got progressively worse we were unable to climb to an altitude that allowed us to cross the mountains. Our efforts terminated suddenly when there was a blinding flash and an audible bang which we discovered later had been lightning strike. It resulted in an 'about turn' and we scrambled back to Guernsey after being airborne for six hours.

Of the thirty-six Whitleys stationed in the Channel Islands, two failed to take off, twelve claimed to have bombed the Fiat works and one crew bombed the alternative at Genoa. Twenty crews aborted and one of the No. 77 Squadron crews, Sergeant Songest's in N1362, failed to return. It was later discovered that they had crashed in flames near Le Mans, killing the crew. However the results of the operation were encouraging, as the report submitted by Wing Commander Staton bears out:

"We were warned that over Italy fighter opposition would probably be encountered. The Italian fighters - CR42s, it was pointed out, were biplanes with considerable powers of manouevre and probably better suited to to the task of night interception than the Me109 or Me110. We must be on the look-out for them. Nothing happened till we were over France after refuelling in the Channel Islands. Then we ran into electrical storms of great severity. There was a good deal of lightning. When we emerged from these into a clear patch somewhere near Bourges the lightning continued. This time it was French Flak through which we flew till we ran into heavy weather again and began to climb in order to get over the Alps. I got my heavily laden Whitley up to 17,500 feet flying blind on instruments, but before the climb started in earnest I got a perfect 'fix' of my position from Lac Leman. The town of Geneva at its western end showed bright with many lights. It was ten-tenths cloud over the Alps, but we knew we were crossing them because of the bumps which we felt in the aircraft every time we crossed a peak! Down we went through the murk till I altered course fifteen degrees to starboard so as to find the River Po. I reached it in darkness, but I could make it out by the patches of cultivation along its banks which showed a deeper shade against the prevailing black. I couldn't see the waters of the river.

On I went till I judged we over Turin. Then I let go a flare which lit up the middle of the city. I turned back at once and climbed to 5,000 feet. When I got to that height I loosed off another flare into a cloud which began to glow and shed a soft light over the town including the target. I ran in, dropped two bombs, one of which burst on the Fiat building, the other in the railway sidings beside it.

"The bursting of the bombs seemed to be the signal for the enemy to switch on his searchlights. These couldn't find us, but innumerable flashes of light, constantly renewed, appeared beneath us. It seemed as if the whole of Turin was firing at us. I have never seen anything like it, either before or since. But no shells seemed to be bursting anywhere. We were still at 5,000 feet, but the air about us remained unlit by anything except our flare, though the flashes below winked at us with unabated zeal. I did my second run and hit the north end of the works. There was a large green flash which meant the bombs had fallen on the annealing plant. I knew that if I hit that, the flash would be a green one. Having no more bombs I dropped flares to guide other attacking aircraft and drew off a little to watch the show. The flares lit up everything. I climbed up to 10,000 feet, keeping a sharp look-out for the CR42s. I didn't see any and no-one else did; but we ran into a heavy AA barrage. The shell bursts made a squeaky, gritty noise. It was then I realised what had happened. The Italian gunners who had produced all those flashes I had seen below, had evidently decided that we were flying at 10,000 feet when we bombed. As we were only at 5,000 feet, naturally we saw nothing of the bursts which were about a mile above our heads!"

Subsequently, the 4 Group Whitley squadrons received a signal from Sir Archibald Sinclair, Secretary of State for Air, congratulating them on the success of the raid; another Whitley 'first'. It was rumoured that during the raid, the civilians of Turin had to compete with members of the Italian armed forces to get into the shelters!

As well as the aircraft sent to Italy, a further ten Whitleys attacked German troop movements and communications in the Somme, Abbeville area, losing one of our No. 10 Squadron aircraft, P4954 with Sergeant L. A. Keast and crew on board.

The attacks on communications targets continued, with eight Whitleys attacking targets at Amiens and Aulnoye on the 12th/13th, while next night thirty-four 4 Group bombers were sent to raid similar targets, again without loss.

On June 14th, the Germans entered Paris and that night two of the Whitley squadrons were called upon to use a new weapon against Germany; the 'W' Bomb. These so-called bombs were in fact mines, designed to be dropped in Germany's inland waterways to destroy barges and bridges. The origin of the bomb is somewhat obscure, but it seems that some of the credit (we crews who were called upon to use them would say the 'blame') for its design must apparently go to a manufacturer of pipeless organs!

From the end of 1939, when a plan to attack Germany's inland waterway traffic was devised by the War Cabinet, designs had been submitted and experiments carried out. Despite numerous experimental failures a meeting at the Air Ministry on December 29th, 1939, gave the contract to a firm to produce 10,000 of the 'bombs' and containers - they should have known better!

By April 1940 a supply of the weapons had been sent to eighteen unsuspecting Bomber and eight Coastal Command stations. The 'bomb' was designed to be dropped from aircraft flying at altitudes of between 300 and 1,000 feet at speeds of up to 250 mph. These height and speed restrictions were imposed to minimise the possibility of the bomb shattering on impact. It consisted of a cylindrical casing sixteen inches high by ten in diameter and carrying an explosive charge of twenty pounds of TNT, the total weight being thirty-five pounds. The main body, which had negative bouyancy, was maintained at a pre-determined depth by means of a number of corks attached to it by lines. A contact firing device, which was fitted to the top of the main body, was protected together with the the corks and lines by a lid. On entering the water a soluble plug freed the lid after a lapse of two to three minutes and armed the bomb. The main body sank to a depth of two to three feet at which it was maintained by the floats and was carried downstream by the river current. Impact with the firing device completed an electrical circuit and fired the bomb. A soluble sinking plug was fitted, which operated in six, eighteen or forty-eight hours according to which plug was fitted.

Plans to drop them in the Rivers Rhine, Elbe, Weser, Main and Neckar and the famous Dortmund-Ems and Mitteland canals on the full-moon night of April 22nd were cancelled. However, the use of the bomb was resurrected when in June 1940 oil targets moved up the list of priorities and it was envisaged as the most suitable weapon with which to attack oil barges en route from Rumania to Germany by way of the River Rhine. The Whitley squadrons were lumbered with this unenviable task on the night of June 14th/15th, 1940.

Seven Whitleys of No. 10 Squadron, together with five of No. 51 Squadron, were detailed to carry out this initial operation, but unfortunately it was a dismal failure. Of the twelve crews ten got off, but only two claimed to have dropped their bombs in the Rhine as briefed. The odds against their success were far too high. Having to stooge around Germany at 1,000 to 2,000 feet at night in far from ideal weather conditions, having to rely on DR navigation and with the possibility of blundering into heavily defended areas made it a difficult if not impossible task. It made one think that the 'Whitehall Warriors' and the chairborne 'Mahogany Bomber Pilots' engaged in strategic planning had little idea of what such an operation actually entailed.

The same night other aircraft of 4 Group, including five from No. 10 Squadron, attacked road and rail communications in France and Germany. They encountered heavy opposition which damaged one the aircraft.

On June 15th the French government sued for an armistice and what was left of the AASF squadrons were ordered back to England. That night was the only one in June when no Whitleys operated. The taverns in the group's area, 'Betty's' in York, 'The Unicorn' in Ripon, 'The Prospect' in Harrogate and 'The Stag' in Driffield must have done a roaring trade. Harrogate was now on our list of stamping grounds, especially now that most of the civilian residents had modified their pre-war attitude towards servicemen. 'Other ranks' had not been welcomed, but now some of us were even getting our feet under the table. There was one establishment where we had always been welcome; the 'Yorkshire Cafe' in James Street. Mrs Robinson, the owner, had a soft spot for boys in air force blue and even now managed to produce something tasty in spite of rationing. Her establishment had another attraction in that some of her other customers were nurses from the local hospital. The 'Yorkshire' was the rendezvous for many a romantic assignation!

Nine crews of No. 102 Squadron sent to attack Gelsenkirchen was the effort for 4 Group on June 16th/17th. The next night they were given the night off while Nos. 10, 51, 58 and 77 Squadrons were back on the job flying against the oil targets again, the main objective being Gelsenkirchen to which twenty-nine aircraft were detailed. One Whitley of No. 58 Squadron, N1463 captained by Flight Sergeant C. L. Ford, failed to return. This aircraft fell at Culemborg, Holland. Another attempt was made to drop the 'W' Bombs for which task eleven aircraft were selected, seven from No. 10 squadron and four from No. 51 Squadron. Ours was one of the crews detailed and we were airborne at 20.35 hours. The weather was cloudy with intermittent rain falling as we set course. After an uneventful sea crossing we entered German territory and set about the task of flying down the Rhine valley to locate our dropping point which was Bingen to the south of Mannheim. As we continued on our way the cloud base was generally 2,500 to 4,000 feet and the visibility below was restricted by rain and haze.

We flew just below the cloud base trying to locate the Rhine, but were hampered by the weather conditions. After a while Nipper, who was in the nose attempting to map-read, called over the intercom that he had spotted it and directed the skipper which way to fly. We were still flying at 2,000 feet, just under the cloud base when the skipper altered course. It was then that all hell broke loose; we had blundered into the defences protecting Mannheim. The Flak came at us from all directions, tracers and incendiaries criss-crossing above and below the aircraft - mostly, in my estimation, in close proximity to my rear turret!

Once again in times such as this I had the compensation of being able to retaliate. I belted away with my four Brownings, firing in the general direction of the ground fire and I like to think that I might have put some of the Flak gunners off their aim. In any case, it took my mind off our immediate predicament. The skipper lost no time in turning and climbing the aircraft into the cloud, but even then the Flak seemed to follow us and the flashes were magnified making it more frightening. Eventually we escaped into the darkness, but by this time we were well away from the river and in cloud.

After collecting our somewhat scattered wits, and summoning up our courage, we turned back to have another go. When it was calculated that we were again within range the skipper put the aircraft into a slow descent. However, when we broke cloud the fireworks started all over again so it was a smart about turn back into cloud to get out of the Flak. All in all we spent about thirty minutes trying to get below the dropping restriction height of 1,000 feet, but we were frustrated by the low cloud and the defences. We eventually gave it up as a bad job and scuttled back to land safely, and thankfully, at Feltwell to where we had been diverted because of adverse weather back at base.

Out of the eleven aircraft only four crews claimed to have dropped their 'W' bombs in the Rhine. The concensus of the crews given the onerous task of dropping these weapons was that whoever had dreamed it up needed his bumps read! Amazingly, all the aircraft got back safely even though some sustained Flak damage. As it turned out this was my last trip as 'Tail-end Charlie'.*

*At the beginning of June the 4 Group squadrons began receiving Volunteer Reserve aircrew (pilots, navigators and WOP/AGs) who had now completed their operational training at No. 10 (Whitley) OTU, RAF Abingdon. With the increase in squadron strength, new crews were formed. The all-regular crews formed at the beginning of the war were split up, the original second pilots being promoted to first pilot and captain and the WOP/AGs like myself who had been flying as tail-gunner were made first WOP/AGs, our places being taken by the VRs. This meant that with these reinforcements from the OTU, more crews were formed.

On June 21st, I was crewed with Flying Officer W. H. Nelson DFC as his first WOP/AG. The other members of the crew were Flying Officer P. G. Whitby, second pilot, Pilot Officer J. N. Forrest, air-observer, and Sergeant M. L. Sharpe, WOP/AG tail-gunner. This turned out to be a paper exercise only, because Flying Officer Nelson was posted shortly afterwards and I found myself on the 'Spare crew list'.

While I went 'spare', the rest got on with the war. On June 18th/19th, marshalling yards, oil plants, industrial targets and communications were the objectives assigned to 4 Group. Thirty-seven Whitleys were sent out, meeting heavy opposition. Four out of five crews from No. 58 Squadron sent to attack communications around Castrop-Rauxel attacked as briefed. The fifth crew, that of Flying Officer J. T. McInnes in N1460, failed to return. No. 102 Squadron also lost a crew when N1499, captained by Sergeant S. E. Masham went down. This was one of seven crews briefed to bomb the oil plants at Bottrop and Sterkade.

There was some good news for the Whitley squadrons on June 19th when it was announced that no further raids using the dreaded 'W' bomb were envisaged. Could it be that the 'higher-paid help' was beginning to see the light of reason?

Our squadron despatched five aircraft that night with industrial plants at Mannheim and Coblenz as their objectives. One crew, that of Flying Officer H. V. Smith in P4960, suffered generator failure. It was decided to abandon the primary target and attack the alternative of Schipol airfield near Amsterdam instead. While they were preparing for their run-in to the secondary target the starboard engine caught fire. They set course for home and, after a hazardous sea crossing during which the aircraft lost height, a landing was attempted at RAF Honington. Unfortunately there was an air raid warning in the area and the airfield was blacked-out. There was little alternative to attempting a landing, but they didn't make it. During the approach the Whitley hit trees in Ampton Park, crashed and burst into flames. Flying Officer Smith was killed and two of his crew suffered burns.

The other squadrons had sent sixteen Whitleys out. Two from No. 77 Squadron had a particularly rough time on their sorties to the Wanne-Eickel marshalling yards. One aircraft was badly damaged by Flak, but got back without casualties. The other, N1476 captained by Pilot Officer A. W. Dunn, was attacked by two Bf109s during the bomb-run. In the first fighter attack the Whitley was hit many times and the air- observer and front-gunner were wounded. It was bright moonlight and during the second fighter attack Dunn's tail-gunner got in a good burst from his four Brownings which sent one of the Bf109s plunging to the earth in an inverted dive. The crew then pressed on with their bombing attack at 8,000 feet, observing hits on a blast- furnace. On the return flight their problems continued. The port engine caught fire, was extinguished, flared up again, but was finally put out and the engine shut down. The aircraft gradually lost height during the sea crossing and was successfully ditched. All the crew were rescued. In the face of overwhelming odds the crew had carried out their task and had made a valiant attempt to get their crippled bomber back to England. Although the Whitley could absorb punishment you were generally on a hiding to nothing if you lost an engine.

On the morning of June 20th, HRH Group Captain, The Duke of Kent visited RAF Dishforth and personnel from both squadrons were presented to him. I wasn't afforded that honour, but I was to have that privilege at Middleton-St-George during my second bomber tour in 1941-42.*

Marshalling yards and industrial plants were the targets for the Whitley squadrons on June 20th/21st. Thirty-nine crews were sent out, all reporting severe opposition. One unidentified aircraft was seen shot down over Hamm and a No. 58 Squadron Whitley, N1442

---

*Also in October 1942 I was at Invergordon on a conversion course onto Sunderland flying boats when HRH took off from there on what was to be his last flight. The Duke's Sunderland crashed at Eagle's Rock, near Dunbeath, Scotland, en route to Iceland. The only survivor was the tail-gunner Flight Sergeant Andrew Jack.

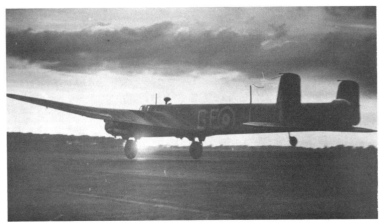

A Whitley of No.58 Squadron, wearing the code 'GE' takes off from Linton-on-Ouse.

flown by Flying Officer G. E. Walker was reported missing from Essen. Over the past four nights the squadron had been hit hard, losing three aircraft. One aircraft of No. 102 Squadron had an engine put out of action over Ludwigshaven, but the crew managed to scramble back and put down safely at Manston.

Twenty-two Whitleys went to Salzbergen, Bochum and Hamm on June 21st/22nd. One aircraft from No. 10 Squadron was attacked by a nightfighter, but escaped undamaged, while crews from No. 77 Squadron attacking the Hamm marshalling yards sighted three enemy fighters which did not attack them.

During the morning of June 22nd there was a tragic sequel to the 'W' bombs debacle. An explosion occurred in the bomb dump at Dishforth resulting in two airmen being killed and three injured. Defective 'W' bombs was one of the suspected causes as they were being defused at the time.

Volume I of the Air Historical Branch monograph 'Armament, 'W' Bomb' produced after the war states:

"The 'W' bomb is an example of a weapon conceived in great haste and developed so rapidly that weak points in design were inevitable. Its outstanding disadvantage lay in the fact that it could not be stored. Small batteries and soluble plugs deteriorated rapidly and were intended for immediate use. The bomb, too, was never completely safe. Dissolution of soluble plugs which formed part of the safety device and the possibility of electrical 'shorts' made it a constant source of danger during carriage, storage or under preparation."

Now, they tell us!

On June 22nd/23rd, No. 102 Squadron operated on their own when six aircraft attacked industrial targets at Wendau/Cologne. Next morning 4 Group Headquarters issued an order to the effect that crews would, in future, operate on a one night on, one night off roster - thank the Lord for small mercies!

The first raids under the new system took place that night with twenty-six Whitleys operating. Nos. 10 and 51 Squadrons ran the gauntlet of the defences in 'Happy Valley' to attack industrial targets in the Ruhr, while No. 58 Squadron attacked similar targets at Lunen. There were no losses, but the crews were finding that the Ruhr defences were now something to be reckoned with.

It was the turn of the Driffield squadrons the following night to send sixteen Whitleys to attack Ludwigshaven. Fourteen crews attacked as briefed in the face of atrocious weather conditions.

The French government accepted the German and Italian surrender terms and an armistice became effective at 01.35 hours on June 25th, 1940. France had fallen and we were now on our own. That night our squadron sent six aircraft to attack the Focke-Wulf factory at Bremen, while six crews from No. 51 went to bomb industrial targets in the Ruhr, all without loss. On June 26th/27th twenty Whitleys were despatched to an aluminium factory at Ichendorf and industrial targets at Ludwigshaven. One crew from No. 77 Squadron returned early on one engine and landed successfully at Bircham Newton after two of the crew elected to bale out over the airfield.

Twenty-one Whitleys were sent to Duisburg in the Ruhr on June 27th/28th. Only one No. 51 Squadron aircraft was damaged, despite the heavy Flak defences. Targets were again switched the following night to include ammunition factories at Frankfurt and Moorst. Twenty bombers were despatched on that occasion. We were beginning to suspect that target selection was being done by someone blindfolded and wielding a pin!

Two of our No. 10 Squadron aircraft were damaged by Flak over Frankfurt and one crew sighted an enemy aircraft which fortunately did not attack. A Whitley crew of No. 58 Squadron targetted to Moorst, Flying Officer W. C. Espley and crew in N1469, was attacked by a nightfighter over Eindhoven, but the tail-gunner got in some good bursts of gunfire and claimed to have damaged the fighter which broke off the attack. A second crew from No. 58 Squadron,

---

*A regular officer who had tried to break his neck racing cars pre war on the Brooklands circuit. He later became a Group Captain with the DFC.

P4951 flown by Flight Lieutenant Frank Aitken,* bombed from 2,000 feet causing an explosion and a resulting fire which could be seen from fifty miles away. That wasn't the end of their adventures because on return they became slightly uncertain of their position (lost!) and blundered over Newcastle-upon-Tyne where they were fired on by our anti-aircraft batteries and then followed by Spitfires. After firing the correct 'colours of the day' with their Verey pistol, the AA gunfire ceased, but their troubles weren't over. When they reached the Middlesborough area, they were attacked by three Spitfires and a fighter Blenheim and were forced down at RAF Thornaby-on-Tees. The fighters continued to fire on the Whitley even though the undercarriage was being lowered, the recognised international sign of aircraft surrender. Luckily no hits were sustained and they were able to land safely.

It was rumoured by the Whitley crews after this incident that Wing Commander Richard 'Batchy' Atcherley's fighter boys at Catterick were subjected to extra sessions at the air firing range and given additional training in aircraft recognition. It was also ironic that when he came to Dishforth to give a talk to the Whitley crews on UK fighter defence procedure, he was most emphatic with his advice to us not to fly over any of the fishing trawlers operating out of Hull (apparently they were being armed and were very trigger-happy). I believe his actual words were: "The buggers don't know the difference between a Spitfire and a Sunderland!"

On June 29th/30th nineteen Whitleys were sent to a petroleum plant at Bremen and an explosives factory at Frankfurt. One enemy aircraft was sighted by a No. 51 Squadron crew, but this made no attempt to attack. One of the No. 77 Squadron aircraft, P4948 flown by Squadron Leader Mark Hastings, did not return from Frankfurt.

On the last night of the month, June 30th/July 1st, No.10 Squadron sent nine crews to bomb the Hamm marshalling yards while ten of No. 102 Squadron were detailed to attack Frankfurt. For No. 10

squadron the searchlight and Flak opposition was, as usual, severe. Hamm was becoming quite a 'hot' one.

Summary of operations by 4 Group
1st - 30th June 1940

1st-2nd - Bombing - Oil Plants and Marshalling Yards - Hamburg, Osnabruck and Hamm.

10 Sqn. Eight a/c to Hamburg. Weather filthy, primary not attacked. Two a/c bombed alternatives.

51 Sqn. Twelve a/c to Osnabruck. Bad weather, only one bombed.

58 Sqn. Eight a/c to Hamm. Bad weather, four bombed.

2nd-3rd. - Bombing - Oil Plant at Hamburg - Marshalling Yards - Osnabruck and Hamm.

10 Sqn. Six a/c to Hamburg. All bombed, one gunner wounded 51 Sqn. Six a/c to Hamburg. All bombed.

58 Sqn. Four a/c to Osnabruck. All bombed.

77 Sqn. Eight a/c to Hamm. All bombed, two aircrew wounded.

3rd-4th - Bombing - Oil Plants at Hamburg and Gelsenkirchen.

10 Sqn. Eight a/c to Hamburg. Heavy opposition. All bombed, one crashed on return.

51 Sqn. Eight a/c to Hamburg. All bombed.

58 Sqn. Eight a/c to Kamen. Four bombed primary, four bombed alternatives.

77 Sqn. Eleven a/c to Gelsenkirchen. All bombed, one crashed on return.

102 Sqn. Eleven a/c to Gelsenkirchen. Two returned early, nine bombed.

4th-5th - Bombing - Oil Plants at Kamen-Buer and Gelsenkirchen

58 Sqn. Seven a/c to Kamen-Buer. All bombed.

77 Sqn. Four a/c to Gelsenkirchen. Three bombed, 1 FTR.

102 Sqn. Six a/c to Gelsenkirchen. all bombed.

5th-6th - Bombing - Troops and Transport, France.

10 Sqn. Five a/c to Doullens, all bombed.

51 Sqn. Six a/c to Doullens, all bombed.

77 Sqn. Five a/c to Bapaume. Four bombed, one force landed at Finningley.

102 Sqn. Six a/c to Somme/Aisne. All bombed.

6th-7th - Bombing - Marshalling Yards at Rheydt and Euskirchen - Troops and Transport at Doullens.

10 sqn. Nine a/c to Rheydt and Euskirchen. Eight bombed.
51 Sqn. Eight a/c to Doullens. All bombed.

7th-8th - Bombing - Railway Communications at Hirson.
58 Sqn. Six a/c. One returned early, five bombed.

8th-9th - Bombing - Arms Dumps and Communications in France - Marshalling Yards in Germany.
10 Sqn. Ten a/c to Rheydt, Wedan and Essen marshalling yards. One crashed on take-off (two injured), one returned early, eight bombed.
51 Sqn. Nine a/c to arms dumps in France. All bombed.
58 Sqn. Six a/c to road/rail comms Avesnes and Aulnoye. All bombed.
77 Sqn. Nine a/c to road/rail comms Hirson and Charleville. All bombed.
102 Sqn. Nine a/c to road/rail comms Sedan. One returned early, eight bombed, one damaged by Flak.

9th-10th - Bombing Road and Rail Communications in France.
10 Sqn. Nine a/c to Libremont, Sedan and Neufchateau. All bombed.
51 Sqn. Eleven a/c. All bombed. One damaged by Flak, tail-gunner wounded.
58 Sqn. Six a/c to Amiens. All bombed.
77 Sqn. Seven a/c to Somme bridges. Six bombed. One hit by Flak and crashed at Abingdon on return.
102 Sqn. Eight a/c to Abbeville and St Valery. All bombed.

10th-11th - Bombing Road and Rail Communications in France.
58 Sqn. Six a/c to Forges and Dumale. One returned early, five bombed.
77 Sqn. Three a/c to Fleury and Gournay. All bombed.
102 Sqn. Seven a/c to Abbeville. All bombed.

11th-12th - Bombing - Aero-engine Works at Turin and Genoa, Italy - Road and Rail Communications in France.
10 Sqn. Eight a/c to Turin. Five aborted, three bombed. Five a/c to Somme/Abbeville. Four bombed, one FTR.
51 Sqn. Seven a/c to Turin. One aborted, six bombed. Four a/c to Somme/Abbeville. One returned early, three bombed.
58 Sqn. Six a/c to Turin. Five aborted, one bombed.
77 Sqn. Eight a/c to Turin. Six aborted, one bombed, one FTR. 102 Sqn.
Seven a/c to Turin. Five took off, three aborted, one bombed Turin, one bombed Genoa. One a/c to Somme/Abbeville, successful.

12th-13th - Bombing - Road and Rail Communications in France.
58 Sqn. Four a/c to Amiens. Two bombed, one damaged by Flak.

149

102 Sqn. Four a/c to Aulnoye. One returned early, two bombed.

13th-14th -Bombing -Road and Rail Communications in France.
10 Sqn. Five a/c. One returned early, four bombed.
51 Sqn. Five a/c, all bombed.
58 Sqn. Six a/c to Laon. All bombed.
77 Sqn. Eight a/c, all bombed.
102 Sqn. Ten a/c to Charleville/Dormans. Nine bombed.

14th-15th -Bombing -Road and Rail Communications in France -Marshalling Yards in Germany -Mining River Rhine.
10 Sqn. Seven a/c, 'W' bombs in Rhine. Five got off, two bombed. Five a/c road/rail communications. Three recalled, two bombed.
51 Sqn. Five a/c, 'W' bombs in Rhine. None bombed. One a/c road/rail communications. Successful.
58 Sqn. Ten a/c to Laon, Vernon and Soissons. Seven recalled, two bombed.
77 Sqn. Eight a/c to Euskirchen, Fagiers and Hirson. All bombed. One damaged by Flak.
102 Sqn. Eight a/c to Oberhausen and Cologne. All bombed, one damaged.

16th-17th -Bombing -Oil Plant at Gelsenkirchen.
102 Sqn. Nine a/c, all bombed.

17th-18th -Bombing -Oil Plant at Gelsenkirchen -Mining River Rhine.
10 Sqn. Seven a/c 'W' bombs in Rhine. Four aborted, three bombed. Three a/c to Gelsenkirchen. Flak intense. All bombed.
51 Sqn. Seven a/c to Gelsenkirchen. Flak intense. All bombed. Four a/c 'W' bombs in Rhine. Three aborted, one bombed.
58 Sqn. Ten a/c to Gelsenkirchen. Nine bombed, one FTR.
77 Sqn. Nine a/c to Gelsenkirchen. Two returned early, seven bombed.

18th-19th -Bombing -Oil Plants -Industrial Works -Marshalling Yards -Communications.
10 Sqn. Four a/c to Soest marshalling Yards. All bombed.
51 Sqn. Nine a/c to oil plant Frankfurt. All bombed.
58 Sqn. Five a/c to Dusseldorf. All bombed. Five a/c to Castrop-Rauxel. Four bombed, one FTR.
77 Sqn. Seven a/c to oil plants Hanover and Sterkrade. All bombed.

102 Sqn. Seven a/c to oil plants Sterkrade and Bottrop. Five bombed, one FTR.

19th-20th - Bombing - Industrial Works - Marshalling Yards.

10 Sqn. Five a/c to industrial plants Mannheim and Coblenz. One returned early, three bombed, one crashed on return.

51 Sqn. Three a/c to Marshalling Yards Mannheim. All bombed.

58 Sqn. Three a/c to industrial plant Ludwigshaven. All bombed.

77 Sqn. Five a/c to Marshalling Yards Wanne-Eickel. All bombed. One damaged by Flak, one damaged by two Bf109s (two wounded) and ditched off Hastings Pier.

102 Sqn. Eight a/c to marshalling yards at Schwerte. All bombed.

20th-21st - Bombing - Industrial Works - Marshalling Yards.

10 Sqn. Eight a/c to marshalling yards Hamm. Seven bombed.

51 Sqn. Nine a/c to marshalling yards Hamm. Eight got off, seven bombed.

58 Sqn. Seven a/c to industrial plant Essen. Six bombed; explosion and fires in target area. One FTR.

77 Sqn. Seven a/c to industrial plant Ludwigshaven. One returned early, Six bombed. Opposition severe.

102 Sqn. Eight a/c to industrial plant Ludwigshaven. Two returned early, one damaged by Flak and force landed at Manston.

21st-22nd - Bombing Oil Plants - Marshalling Yards.

10 Sqn. Seven a/c to oil plant Salzbergen. One returned early, six bombed. One attacked by fighter but not damaged.

51 Sqn. Nine a/c to oil plant Salzbergen. All bombed. Two a/c to oil plant Bochum. Both bombed. Opposition severe.

77 Sqn. Six a/c to Marshalling yards Hamm. All bombed. Three enemy aircraft sighted, but these did not attack.

22nd-23rd - Bombing - Industrial Works at Wedau/Cologne.

102 Sqn. Six a/c. All bombed. Opposition moderate.

23rd-24th. - Bombing - Industrial Works.

10 Sqn. Eight a/c to Aluminium works Ichendorf. All bombed. Opposition severe

51 Sqn. Ten a/c to Aluminium works Ichendorf. All bombed. Opposition severe

58 Sqn. Eight a/c to industrial works Lunen and Ludwigshaven. Two

returned early, six bombed.

24th-25th. - Bombing - Aluminium Works.
77 Sqn. Eight a/c to aluminium works Ludwigshaven. Weather filthy. Seven bombed.
102 Sqn. Eight a/c to aluminium works Ludwigshaven. Two returned early, six bombed.

25th-26th - Bombing - Aircraft Factory and Industrial Works.
10 Sqn. Six a/c to aircraft factory Bremen. Five bombed.
51 Sqn. Six a/c to industrial works Ruhr. All bombed.

26th-27th - Bombing - Aluminium Works.
58 Sqn. Ten a/c to Ichendorf. Four bombed primary, four bombed alternatives.
77 Sqn. Five a/c to Ludwigshaven. One returned early and landed at Bircham Newton after two aircrew baled out. Four bombed.
102 Sqn. Five a/c to Ludwigshaven. Two returned early, one bombed primary, one bombed alternative.

27th-28th - Bombing - Duisburg Docks and Marshalling Yards.
10 Sqn. Five a/c, all bombed.
51 Sqn. Six a/c, all bombed. One damaged by Flak.
77 Sqn. Three a/c to marshalling yards. One returned early, two bombed.
102 Sqn. Six a/c to marshalling yards. All bombed.

28th-29th - Bombing - Explosives and Industrial Works.
10 Sqn. Four a/c to explosives factory Frankfurt. All bombed. Two damaged by Flak. Enemy aircraft sighted.
51 Sqn. Six a/c to explosives factory Frankfurt. Five bombed. 58 Sqn. Ten a/c to industrial works Moorst. One returned early, seven bombed primary. One attacked by fighter (claimed as damaged), one forced down by friendly fighters on return.

29th-30th - Bombing - Petrol Plant and Explosives Factory.
51 Sqn. Eleven a/c to petrol plant Bremen. One returned early, ten bombed. Enemy aircraft sighted, but no attack.
77 Sqn. Eight a/c to explosives factory Frankfurt. None bombed primary, six bombed alternatives. One FTR.

30th-1st - Bombing - Marshalling Yards and Industrial Works.
10 Sqn. Nine a/c to marshalling yards Hamm. All bombed. Opposition severe.
102 Sqn. Ten a/c to industrial works Frankfurt. Three bombed primary,

Chapter Seven

Britain Versus the Third Reich

The evacuation of the remnants of the British Expeditionary Force from Dunkirk and the departure from France of the Advanced Air Striking Force heralded the capitulation of France and the Low Countries. Britain was left alone to face the might of the all conquering Nazi war machine. It seemed inevitable that it was only time until the full weight of the Luftwaffe would be turned against our besieged isle. Sure enough the attacks came. On July 3rd, 1940, the Luftwaffe made its first tentative strike from its new French bases and began a series of raids against shipping and channel ports. The 4 Group Whitley squadrons had their part in the RAF's grand 'Anti Invasion' strategy and each was instructed to have crews available on standby as of July 2nd.

In the meantime crews continued to make their nightly sorties over Europe to attack a multiplicity of targets including docks, ports, battleships in harbour, marshalling yards, aircraft factories, aircraft parks, oil installations and so on. This haphazard selection of targets was spreading the available bomber force too thinly. This was duly recognized for, on July 24th, an Air Staff Directive was issued to Air Marshal Sir Charles Portal, the Commander-in-Chief Bomber Command, instructing him to concentrate the heavy bomber force against fifteen selected targets: five aircraft storage depots; five airframe assembly factories and five oil installations. Attacks on communications targets were also to continue, although only on a limited scale. From now until the invasion of Europe, Bomber Command would be the only means of carrying the fight to Germany proper, a task which would be carried out with increasing vigour and determination.

On the first night of July the crews from two Whitley squadrons were on operations. Five crews from No. 58 Squadron were sent out to attack the battleship *Scharnhorst* in the naval base at Kiel where they encountered heavy defences. Flight Lieutenant Frank Aitken, who had gained the reputation of being slightly 'Flak Happy' made a diving attack from 10,000 feet to just 800 feet, scoring direct hits as he streaked over the target at 1,500 feet. One crew failed to return, that of Pilot Officer C. J. T. Jones, whose aircraft (N1461) was shot down by Flak over Hamburg. Eight crews from No. 102 Squadron made a successful sortie to the usually well defended railway yards at Hamm and, finding hardly any anti-aircraft fire there to welcome them, all returned safely.

I was on the spare crew list the following night, 2nd/3rd July, and was put on the first 'anti invasion standby' which meant that I had to spend the night on the base and keep the SPs. in the guardroom aware of my location at all times just in case I was needed. Meanwhile the rest of the crews carried on with the real war. Crews from three Whitley squadrons were scheduled for ops that night and thankfully all returned safely, though one was fortunate to do so. It was one of the three crews sent out by No. 51 Squadron which was over the target when, to the pilot's horror, the dark shape of another bomber appeared out of nowhere dead in front and on a collision course. Pulling back on the control column he just managed to avoid disaster. The nose reared up, air speed fell away and then came the inevitable stall. One wing went down and an incipient spin developed from which there seemed to be no recovery. The skipper gave the order to bale out and in two shakes the second pilot had gone. For reasons unknown the good old Whitley then pulled itself together and came out of the spin, but it was too late for the second pilot who was already hanging under his parachute somewhere below. The rest of the crew were recalled to their positions and a safe return made to base. We all heard stories of how the embarrassed pilot explained the disappearance of his crew-man to his commanding officer. 'Well Sir', went one story, 'all I said was bale ..... and there he was, gone!' Another told how his fellow skippers briefed the replacement second pilot. 'You had better watch out, if Butch doesn't like you he'll dump you over the target'. During August there was to be a wry sequel to this incident.

Bad weather continued to affect operations on July 3rd/4th, only five of the twelve operating Whitleys managing to hit their assigned airfield targets, but the next night, when the Driffield squadrons went to Hamburg, eleven of the twelve Whitleys braved the heavy defences and bombed successfully. While they were away, a solitary German aircraft bombed their base causing slight damage and light casualties.

On July 5th/6th, when we and No. 51 Squadron sent six Whitleys to attack Merville airfield, weather again hampered operations and none of the bombers found their target. Further north, five out of six

No. 58 Squadron Whitleys managed to deliver attacks against naval targets at Wilhelmshaven against severe opposition.

On the morning of July 6th, an advanced party from No. 10 Squadron left Dishforth for our new base of Leeming, just to the south of Catterick. That night the German battleship *Scharnhorst* at Kiel was again the main target for ten Whitleys, but only three attacked and another, N1523 of No. 102 Squadron flown by Pilot Officer J. M. Lewis, was shot down by Flak over Kiel.

Raids to Ludwigshaven and Hamm on July 7th/8th were again hindered by weather when five out of twelve Whitleys hit their primary targets.

Next morning, July 8th, all the personnel and aircraft not required for operations that night left for the new base at Leeming. The five crews that remained carried out our 'swansong' from Dishforth joining three crews from Nos. 58 and 51 Squadrons in another raid on the Kiel dockyards. The Flak which greeted our crews was indeed severe. Squadron Leader 'Charles' Whitworth's aircraft, P4109, was hit just south of Eckenforde and a piece of shrapnel ricocheted off his parachute harness hitting him under his left eye. More shrapnel severed the rudder control cables and smashed the fixed aerial. Finally a piece hit the IFF equipment and detonated its self destruct device which was fitted to prevent the enemy capturing it intact and learning its secrets. Despite the damage and his injuries Whitworth brought his aircraft back, but Flight Lieutenant Ffrench-Mullen and his crew were never to see Leeming for they did not come back. They had become one of the earliest victims to nightfighters when Feldwebel Forster of III *Gruppe Nachtjagdgeschwader* 1, flying a Bf109E, shot them down near Heligoland. An attack on Brussels/Evere airfield by four crews from No. 58 Squadron was successful, although one was hit by Flak.

Bad weather prevented us carrying out any operations for the next two nights and this respite gave us a chance to settle in at Leeming. Although it was a brand new station, and had the luxury of concrete runways, most of us were sorry to leave Dishforth. Some, who had been there for a long time, had befriended locals and not a few romances had blossomed. Our new station commander was our old squadron commander, W. E. Staton* DSO, MC, DFC now promoted to the rank of Group Captain. He was replaced in No. 10 Squadron

*Later Air-Vice Marshal CB DSO MC DFC.

by Wing Commander Sidney Bufton*. The accommodation offered little improvement to we lower ranks for, being built to peacetime specifications, single rooms were in short supply and the few that were available were allotted in accordance with rank and status. Thus I ended up with my fellow air gunners in a barrack block dormitory sleeping six to a room, the only bright spot was that we were all aircrew and thus went on ops together and, more importantly, slept at the same odd hours. Up until this time no limit had been laid down for the number of operations a man could be expected to fly before being rested (what would later be called a tour) but now the process of screening came into being. In No. 10 Squadron several experienced and long serving aircrew were sent off to become instructors at Whitley Operational Training Units, Nos. 10 or 19 OTU at Abingdon or Kinloss respectively, to impart some of their hard won knowledge to the new up and coming crews. My old skipper, Squadron Leader 'Bick' Bickford, air-observer Sergeant Arthur 'Nipper' Knapper and WOP/AG Sergeant Johnny 'Fletch' Fletcher† were among the first to go. I was granted some leave, which I must admit I considered to have been well earned, and took myself off home, leaving the war behind me. When I entered my remote village I realized that there was no escaping the effects of this war for Mr Churchill's 'We'll fight them on the beaches', rallying call had been heeded even here. Tank traps and concrete block houses had sprung up where sheep and cows once were and many of the population, including veterans of World War One, were wearing the arm bands of the Local Defence Volunteers. For my part, I was glad for the opportunity to be with my parents and tried to reassure them that things were not as bad, or as dangerous, as the media made them out to be. Unfortunately my parents remembered well the carnage of the Great War and I believe that my assertions fell on deaf ears for they had almost reconciled themselves to hearing the dreaded knock on the door and receiving the telegram which would inform them that their son had gone missing.

I returned to Leeming and caught up on the news. On July 11th/12th No. 58 Squadron had attacked Leverkusen and lost Sergeant F. F. Young and his crew in N1424, which was hit by Flak and crashed at Schoonselhoof, Holland. Our squadron had sent out six crews to the Krupps works at Kiel on the night of July 12th and

*Later Air-Vice Marshal CB DFC.
†'Fletch' was tragically killed in a flying accident with No.10 OTU on October 11th, 1940.

all had come back, I was also told the story of Sergeant Langton's No. 102 Squadron crew who had gone to Emden that night. They had been hit by Flak over the target and the port engine was put out of action, but the Whitley kept on going and brought them back a fair way. One of the problems with the Whitley was that it could not maintain height on one engine, thus it had to be kept in a shallow dive to maintain flying speed. Thirty-eight miles from Cromer their height ran out. The wireless operator had time to send one last SOS and enable a radio location fix to be made before they were forced to ditch in the North Sea, a difficult task which was accomplished successfully. The crew scrambled out of their bomber and released the dinghy which, following Sod's Law, had inflated upside down which meant that they had to right it in the cold and turbulent sea. Fortunately they did not have long to wait for rescue and about an hour later they were picked up by a trawler and taken to Yarmouth. A point which made our ears prick up when we heard the tale was that the Whitley had stayed afloat for around twenty minutes before sinking. This was good news, for up to now it had generally been assumed that the Whitley had all the propensity for floating of a house brick!

Industrial targets and oil plants were the objectives on the night of 13th/14th July. Nos. 10 and 51 Squadrons each sent three aircraft to Mannheim which was bombed successfully by all but one of the No. 51 Squadron crews. All six crews got back safely, but Flying Officer G. A. Lane's aircraft (P4969 of No. 51 Squadron) was badly damaged by flak and had to put down at Honington on return. Also on this night No. 58 Squadron sent crews to Leverkusen and Gravenbroich, while No. 77 Squadron sent seven Whitleys to an oil plant near Mannheim. Two of these crews had narrow escapes when their aircraft were hit by flak over the target. Flying Officer J. A. Piddington's Whitley (N1365) had an engine damaged which finally seized up over Holland. After struggling across the North Sea on one engine Piddington ordered his air observer, rear-gunner and wireless-operator to bale out. All three landed safely and Piddington, assisted by his second pilot, successfully put the bomber down at Martlesham Heath. Pilot Officer R. B. McGregor, flying N1521, was coned by searchlights over the target and badly shot up. The bombs were jettisoned and an escape made back to Duxford where a successful landing was made.

On July 14th/15th, twenty-two Whitleys attacked aircraft parks at Paderborn and Diepholz. Three enemy aircraft were sighted, but didn't attack, and the crews returned reporting the opposition as light. Lucky for them!

Because of the adverse weather, there were no operations for four nights and it was at this time I returned from leave to discover that I'd been re-crewed with 'Enery' (Flying Officer Henry) as first WOP/AG, Fletch having gone to Abingdon on rest. Flying Officer P. W. F. Landale, was second pilot, Sergeant J. 'GBS' Shaw was air-observer and Sergeant George Dove was tail-gunner. We were all old hands except for Landale who was one of the New boys. I had enjoyed my bash at being tail-gunner, but it would make a nice change to get back to full-time key-bashing as wireless-operator.

No. 78 Squadron, which had until now been the 4 Group reserve unit, was now elevated to operational status and made its debut from my old station at Dishforth on the night of July 19th/20th. Four crews were sent to attack marshalling yards in the Ruhr complex where they received their baptism of fire courtesy of the gunners. One aircraft was attacked by two enemy fighters, but escaped without a scratch. Of the twenty-five other Whitleys despatched to Gelsenkirchen, Kassel and Bremen, one of No. 51 Squadron, P5007 flown by Flight Lieutenant S. E. F. Curry, failed to return, crashing near Bremen due to Flak damage. N1384 of No. 77 Squadron flown by Flight Lieutenant D. D. Pryde was hit by Flak and one engine was disabled, forcing them to jettison the bombs. They succeeded in returning on one engine to land safely at Duxford while one of No. 102 Squadron, shot-up by Flak over Bremen, force landed at Bircham Newton.

No. 10 Squadron got back into the fray on July 20th/21st by sending nine aircraft to join others from Nos. 51, 58 and 78 Squadrons attacking industrial targets and aircraft factories. The following night, during attacks on Hamm, Soest and Kassel by twenty-seven Whitleys, N1487 of No. 78 Squadron piloted by Sergeant V. C. Monkhouse was lost, the squadron's first operational casualty of the war. This crew had fallen victim to a Bf110 of I *Gruppe, Nachtjagdgeschwader* 1, flown by Oberleutnant Werner Streib. It crashed in flames near Munster at 01.00 hours.*

---

*Werner Streib was to become recognised at the "Father of the Luftwaffe Nightfighter Force" and would survive the war with the rank of Oberst (Colonel) and was credited with sixty-six victories, all but one at night.

Another Whitley went down next night during attacks on Bremen and the Ruhr. Returning crews reported the Flak defences as heavy, which accounted for the loss of N1472 of No. 58 Squadron. The Whitley, flown by Sergeant J. B. Jones crashed at Bad Lippspringe.

Targets were varied on July 23rd/24th; twenty-three aircraft raided the aircraft factory at Kassel, road and rail communications, and the Docks at Hamburg. One crew from No. 77 Squadron flying in N1371 attacked Kassel from 6,000 feet and was hit by Flak which put the starboard engine out of action. Flying Officer J. A. Piddington managed to fly the Whitley back on one engine and put down safely at Bircham Newton. This was the second 'shaky do' for this crew in a fortnight.

The first trip with my new crew came on the night of July 24th, when we were detailed to send eight aircraft to attack the port of Hamburg where the battleship *Bismarck* and the liners *Bremen* and *Europa* were believed to be, our aircraft joining five of No. 58 Squadron. I was most meticulous with my checks of the W/T equipment, even going to the extent of re-calibrating all the frequencies I would require. At briefing the met. man was far from optimistic about the weather for the night, but no cancellation came and the game was on. We got off at 21.30 hours and set course, keeping radio silence all the way so as not to alert any enemy listening stations. I kept a listening watch for any messages from our control as it was still possible that we could be recalled. To help with the navigation on this foul night I tuned my R1082 receiver to search for any enemy radio beacons which might help us as we now had a list of their frequencies and could use them just as well as the Germans! The Texel beacon came up loud and clear and I got a good bearing on it. The weather really was filthy and getting worse, just as predicted by our 'corns and cones merchant' as we called the met. man. By the time we arrived over the target, or what we believed to be target, it was 'Harry Clampers' * and the clag† was thick at all levels so we stooged around for some time in an effort to find a hole in the cloud to go down through. We were out of luck and reluctantly had to set off back to base with our bombs still in place. As we churned our way back through solid cloud I tried again to tune into the German beacons and found two, perfect for a cross bearing to pin-point our position. I passed our fix to GBS who was delighted, and I think I converted him to radio navigation because

*Cloud obscured. †Heavy cloud.

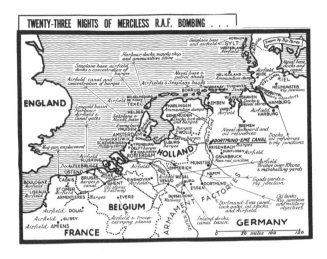

A map published on July 20th, 1940, showing RAF bombing attacks.

dead reckoning navigation was next to useless that night. I kept up the fixes all the way back until we could get a reliable M/F D/F fix and a QDM (home bearing). The sortie had been an abortive one, but a good debut from my point of view and I was quite pleased with my performance. The squadron Operational Record Book keeper recorded, 'A number of loop fixes brought this aircraft back with remarkable navigational accuracy'.

On July 25th/26th attacks were carried against an oil plant and factories in the Ruhr by twenty-four Whitleys. One of No. 77 squadron, P4992 flown by Flight Lieutenant D. D. Pryde, was hit by Flak shortly after leaving their target at Bottrop and one engine set ablaze. They were able to put the fire out and struggle back on one engine to force land at Bircham Newton - for the second time in a week! Only No. 102 Squadron was operating the following night when nine Whitleys raided the Hamm and Mannheim marshalling yards. N1377 failed to return, its crew led by Pilot Officer R. F. Beauclair being captured when their bomber crashed near Amsterdam.

There were no operations scheduled for July 27th, due to bad weather, so we had the night off. By now we had reconnoitred the Leeming area and the squadron had adopted the 'Green Dragon' in the nearby village of Bedale as its local. That night, as on others when there was a stand down, the Green Dragon's trade improved considerably.

Although the weather was far from ideal on July 28th/29th, fourteen Whitleys were sent out to bomb an aircraft factory at Wismar. They all got back, some crews reporting that enemy aircraft had dropped flares over the target in an attempt to illuminate them on their bomb-runs. The following night was the last of the month when the 4 Group squadrons were able to operate, flying sixteen aircraft out to raid Hamm and Düsseldorf without loss, despite heavy opposition.

There had been quite a bit to celebrate in July including the award of a clutch of medals to No. 10 Squadron pilots. I say pilots for during the whole of the first year of war not a single airman other than a pilot received a medal of any kind in our squadron. That July my skipper 'Enery' received a DFC. He was supported by a first class crew!*. Pilot Officer E. I. 'Pip' Parsons also got the DFC, Sergeant A. S. 'Johnny' Johnson got a bar to his DFM, while Sergeant J. G. McCoubrey and Sergeant W. S. Hillary received DFMs - yes, they were all pilots.

Summary of operations by 4 Group
July 1940

1st-2nd. Bombing - German battleship *Scharnhorst* at Kiel. Marshalling yards at Hamm.

58 Sqn. Five a/c to bomb *Scharnhorst* - direct hits claimed. Opposition heavy. One FTR.

102 Sqn. Eight a/c to Hamm. All bombed successfully. Opposition light.

2nd-3rd. Bombing - Marshalling yards at Hamm. Evere (Brussels) Airfield.

10 Sqn. Three a/c to Hamm. All bombed successfully. One aircraft damaged by Flak. Opposition heavy.

51 Sqn. Three a/c to Hamm. All bombed successfully. One man baled out over target. Opposition heavy.

77 Sqn. Ten a/c to Evere. Only six bombed due to bad weather.

*Author's comment!

3rd-4th. Bombing - Occupied airfields at Merville and Rotterdam.

51 Sqn. Four a/c to Merville. Three bombed successfully, one returned early.

58 Sqn. Eight aircraft to Rotterdam. Only two bombed, weather very bad.

4th-5th. Bombing - Aircraft factory at Hamburg.

77 Sqn. Six a/c sent, all bombed. Opposition intense.

102 Sqn. Six a/c sent, five bombed, one returned early. Opposition heavy.

5th-6th. Bombing - Occupied airfield at Merville. Naval targets at Wilhelmshaven.

10 Sqn. Three a/c to Merville. None bombed, weather atrocious.

51 Sqn. Three a/c to Merville. None bombed, weather atrocious.

58 Sqn. Six a/c to Wilhelmshaven. Five bombed, one returned early. Opposition severe.

6th-7th. Bombing - German battleship at Kiel.

51 Sqn. Four a/c sent, only one bombed, adverse weather. Two enemy aircraft seen, no attacks.

102 Sqn. Six a/c sent, only two bombed, bad weather. One FTR.

7th-8th. Bombing - Ludwigshaven. Marshalling yards at Hamm.

58 Sqn. Eight a/c to Ludwigshaven. Only two bombed, two more bombed alternative targets.

77 Sqn. Four a/c to Hamm. Three bombed, one iced up and returned early.

8th-9th. Bombing - Dockyards at Kiel. Evere Airfield.

10 Sqn. Five a/c to Kiel. Two bombed, one damaged by flak. One FTR.

58 Sqn. Two a/c to Kiel. Both bombed and started fires.

51 Sqn. One a/c to Kiel. Four a/c to Evere. All bombed, one hit by flak. Opposition severe.

9th-11th. Operations cancelled due to weather conditions.

11th-12th. Bombing - Leverkusen.

58 Sqn. Eight a/c sent, one bombed primary and remainder attacked alternative targets. One FTR.

12th-13th. Bombing - Krupps Works, Kiel and Fuel Targets at Emden.

10 Sqn. Six a/c. Bad weather. One returned early, two bombed.

51 Sqn. Six a/c. Bad weather. Two bombed.

102 Sqn. Ten a/c to Emden. All bombed. Opposition heavy. One hit by Flak and ditched 38 miles from Cromer, crew rescued.

13th-14th. Bombing - Industrial Targets at Mannheim, Leverkusen and Gravensbruk.

10 Sqn. Three a/c to Mannheim. All bombed.

51 Sqn. Three a/c to Mannheim. Two bombed. One hit by Flak, landed Honington.

58 Sqn. Ten a/c to Leverkusen and Gravensbruk. Eight bombed.

77 Sqn. Seven a/c to Mannheim. Six bombed, two hit by Flak. One landed at Martlesham Heath and one at Duxford.

14th-15th, Bombing - Aircraft Parks at Paderborn and Diepholz.

10 Sqn. Four a/c to Diepholz. All bombed. Opposition severe.

51 Sqn. Eight a/c to Diepholz. All bombed. Opposition severe.

102 Sqn. Ten a/c to Paderborn. One returned early, nine bombed.

15th-16th. No ops due to bad weather.

16th-17th. No ops due to bad weather.

17th-18th. No ops due to bad weather.

18th-19th. No ops due to bad weather.

19th-20th. Bombing - Industrial Targets and Bremen and The Ruhr.

51 Sqn. Seven a/c to Gelsenkirchen. One FTR.

77 Sqn. Nine a/c to Kassel. Two returned early, six bombed. One hit by Flak and landed at Duxford.

78 Sqn. Sqn's first raid of the war. Four a/c to the Ruhr. All bombed. Opposition severe. One attacked by a fighter but not damaged.

102 Sqn. Nine a/c to oil plant Bremen. All bombed. Opposition severe, one hit by Flak and landed at Bircham Newton.

20th-21st. Bombing - Industrial Plant at Düsseldorf and Dornier Factory at Wismar.

10 Sqn. Nine a/c to Düsseldorf. Eight bombed. Opposition severe. One hit by Flak.

51 Sqn. Three a/c to Wismar. All bombed. Opposition severe.

58 Sqn. Eight a/c to Wismar. Six got off, one returned early, four bombed primary, one bombed alternate. Two hit by Flak.

78 Sqn. One a/c to Wismar. Bombed, but hit by Flak.

21st-22nd. Bombing Marshalling Yards at Hamm and Soest and Aircraft Factory at Kassel.

51 Sqn. Three a/c to Hamm. One bombed - direct hits. Opposition heavy.

77 Sqn. Ten a/c to Kassel. Nine bombed. Eight fighters sighted but none attacked.

78 Sqn. Five a/c to Hamm and Soest. Four bombed, one FTR.
102 Sqn. Ten a/c to Kassel. One returned early, nine bombed. Two fighters seen but none attacked.

22nd-23rd. Bombing - Aircraft factory at Bremen and Industrial Targets Ruhr.
10 Sqn. Eight a/c to Bremen. All bombed.
51 Sqn. Seven a/c to the Ruhr. Three bombed.
58 Sqn. Eight a/c to Bremen. Two returned early, two bombed primary, three bombed alternative targets. One FTR.

23rd-24th. Bombing. Road and Rail Communications at Osnabruck, Hamburg Docks and an Aircraft factory at Kassel.
77 Sqn. Ten a/c to Kassel. Nine bombed. One hit by Flak and landed at Bircham Newton.
78 Sqn. Three a/c to Osnabruck. One returned early, one bombed primary, one bombed alternate.
102 Sqn. Ten a/c to Hamburg. Seven bombed.

24th-25th. Bombing - Naval and Merchant Shipping at Hamburg.
10 Sqn. Eight a/c. Weather bad. Two bombed.
58 Sqn. Five a/c. Two returned early, one bombed.

25th-26th. Bombing - Industrial Targets Ruhr.
51 Sqn. Nine a/c to Sterkrade-Holten. Five bombed. Opposition heavy.
77 Sqn. Ten a/c to Bottrop. Opposition severe. One hit by Flak and landed at Bircham Newton.
78 Sqn. Five a/c to the Ruhr. One returned early, four bombed. One fighter seen.

26th-27th. Bombing - Marshalling Yards at Mannheim and Hamm.
102 Sqn. Nine a/c. One returned early, three bombed, one FTR.

27th-28th. No ops due to bad weather.

28th-29th. Bombing - Dornier Factory at Wismar.
77 Sqn. Ten a/c, all bombed. Weather bad, opposition heavy. Flares dropped by enemy aircraft during bomb-runs.
78 Sqn. Four a/c. One returned early, three bombed. Five fighters seen, but none attacked.

29th-30th. Bombing - Marshalling yards at Hamm and Oil Plant at Düsseldorf.
58 Sqn. Eight a/c to Hamm. Weather bad. One bombed primary, seven bombed alternative targets.

164

102 Sqn. Eight a/c to Düsseldorf. Weather bad and opposition heavy. Five bombed.

30th-31st. No ops due to bad weather.

Chapter Eight

Bombs to Berlin

The Luftwaffe air attacks against our shipping in the English Channel and offensive reconnaissance sorties over the mainland increased at the beginning of August. On August 12th the Luftwaffe attack began in earnest with the intention of knocking out Fighter Command.

While our fighter boys took on the Germans by day, we in Bomber Command pursued the new strategic offensive with nightly attacks against German and Italian targets. It's easy to fall into the 'hindsight trap', but in retrospect it intrigues me why our powers-that-be insisted on committing our night bombing force to strategic targets, except of course for attacks against the German invasion fleet building up in the Channel ports, instead of attacking the Luftwaffe air bases in France and the Low Countries during those crucial months of the Battle of Britain. I know from experience that locating and attacking airfields and dispersed aircraft at night is very difficult without special navigation and bombing aids such as 'GEE', 'H$_2$S' and 'OBOE', which we got later on in the war, but in my opinion it would have been worth a try. Let's face it; at that time we were in the 'fertiliser' up to our necks.

We could have used advanced bases in the southern counties from where we could have carried out interdiction raids, possibly two each night because of the short distances involved, and we would always have been within range of the southern and eastern M/F D/F Fixing stations which could have given us fixes and bearings to improve our navigational accuracy. In addition to destroying German installations and aircraft, there would have been the added bonus of keeping the enemy in a constant state of air-raid alert every night, thus depriving the Luftwaffe aircrews of their much-needed rest. This could have impaired their operational efficiency and morale, making it easier for our fighter boys to hack them down. With hindsight, we can all be Napoleons!

Also during August the 'Boffins' inflicted their latest secret weapon, code-named 'RAZZLE' on we unsuspecting Bomber Command aircrews. This was an incendiary device; pills of phosphorus covered with gauze and inserted between square pieces of celluloid. They were carried in sealed cans containing water which kept them from drying out and becoming combustible and the idea was to scatter these incendiary 'leaves' over areas of the Black Forest where, it was believed, arms and other military stores were being concealed. After fluttering to earth they would dry out, instantaneous combustion would take place and 'Pouf' up would go the arms dumps. During the first use of 'RAZZLE' the aircraft, after first bombing their primary target, proceeded to the Black Forest area where the first WOP/AG (who else?) opened the cans and poured the contents down the flare chute. However not all the leaves fluttered to earth. Some of them, caught in the aircraft's slipstream, were blown onto the tailplane, elevators and even the tailwheel. Consequently when they dried out they burnt whichever surface they had stuck to. The safety device supplied to us for use in such an emergency was - you'd better believe it - a garden water syringe!

What with 'W' bombs and 'RAZZLES', the Boffins were playing a blinder. In 4 Group they were about as popular as a fart in a flying suit. The only damage caused by these 'RAZZLES' was to unsuspecting German souvenir hunters who put the leaves in their trouser pockets and had more than their fingers burned when they dried out!

During August, long-range H/F D/F became available to us when three new D/F stations were established at Butser Hill, near Petersfield, Hampshire, Acklington in Northumberland and Dyce, near Aberdeen. Butser Hill acted as control with Acklington and Dyce as 'slaves', operating on a frequency of 4077 kcs. This system now gave us bearings and fixes when we were deep over Germany. Although the weather over England was fairly good in August, it was not so over Germany and the new facility helped reduce some of the consequent difficulties and fallibility of DR navigation. Another improvement was the extension of the Group W/T system. In addition to its use to pass instructions and diversion information it was now to be used for raid reporting, each aircraft sending a 'bombs gone' signal which also let crews know how their 'oppos' on the squadron were faring.

My transition from tail-gunner to first WOP/AG now meant that I was up at the sharp end with the pilots and air-observer. I could now see where we were going rather than where we'd been, but it had its drawbacks. As we approached the target I now got a preview of the Flak batteries throwing up their barrage through which we would have to fly on the bomb-run. Also, the first WOP/AG was the

'Bombs for Berlin'

official flare dropper so this meant that it was my task to drop parachute flares as and when required. This was generally when we were endeavouring to illuminate the target prior to bombing and, following 'bombs gone', to indicate the target to following aircraft. This meant going aft to the flare chute in the fuselage where the claustrophobic darkness was only relieved by the bursting Flak and when the aircraft was caught in a searchlight beam. There would be times when I wished I was back in the tail from where I could retaliate with my four Brownings. However I found another way to dispel the surges of apprehension ('twitter') during my lonely sessions in the fuselage when we were receiving the unwelcome attentions of the German defences.

In the fuselage we carried a box of twenty, four-and-a-half pound incendiary bombs which were supposed to be used for drift assessment as follows; with the aircraft flying straight and level the wireless operator launched one down the flare chute, announcing the fact over the intercom. As the bomb ignited on ground below the tail-gunner centred it in his gunsight and kept it there until the air-observer asked for a drift reading from the Drift Scale in the rear turret. On receipt of the readings the air-observer could assess the aircraft's drift from the required track and adjusted his plot accordingly. A sound idea, but difficult in practice so there were always a lot of unused incendiaries going begging - the answer to an apprehensive, blood-thirsty wireless operator's prayer. In the target area during my vigils by the flare chute I launched the incendiaries, at first singly, but as I became more adept in salvoes of four. Thus the supposed aid to navigation enabled me to wage my personal war against the infamous Third Reich!

Following raids by fifteen Whitleys of Nos. 58 and 102 Squadrons against oil targets on August 1st/2nd our squadron assigned seven Whitley crews, including ours, to join eight of No. 51 Squadron to attack the refinery at Salzbergen on 2nd/3rd. We were airborne in P4953 'F for Freddie' at 22.05 hours. At briefing we had been told that the weather in the target area would be fine and hazy, however, to get there we had to fly through some real 'clag'. The D/F loop came in handy again. As we approached Osnabruck the weather improved and when we neared the target area GB was able to get a good pin-point and take us in to the target. We came under heavy fire during the bomb-run. I was in the fuselage by the flare chute and although I couldn't see much it was evident from the way that the aircraft lurched from time to time, and the muffled thuds, that some of the heavy stuff was bursting quite close. I was more than pleased to hear 'Bombs gone!' and was able to drop a flare and get back up front where I could at least see what was going on.

On the way home the weather deteriorated, so it was no surprise to receive a signal from Group diverting us to Driffield. In such weather conditions fixes were at a premium and all the returning aircraft were literally queuing up on the frequencies. I eventually squeezed in and got a couple of fixes which GB used to keep us on track until we got within homing range of Driffield, from whom we got QDM's which enabled us to get in before the weather really closed in.

Next night, August 3rd/4th, eleven aircraft from Nos. 77 and 78 Squadrons attacked oil installations at Düsseldorf and Mannheim. They all got back, but two of the three No. 78 Squadron Whitleys had to carry out forced landings. One landed without mishap at Market Weighton, but the other, P4941 flown by Flying Officer D. S. Robertson, was badly damaged when it came down near Pickering - fortunately without casualties.

Only No. 58 Squadron operated on August 4th/5th, attacking the Sterkrade oil plant, where a single German fighter was sighted. This target was raided again next night by six of the twenty-one Whitleys operating. The rest, including our crew, attacked the Dornier factory at Wismar against severe opposition which damaged three aircraft without causing casualties.

The weather for a change wasn't too bad and we crossed the enemy coast heading for Wismar, situated on the Baltic coast about thirty-fives east of Lubeck. Since the beginning of the war my geographic knowledge of Europe had increased considerably - another instance of learning the hard way.

Although visibility was affected by haze we were able to recognise and avoid the heavily defended naval base at Kiel and shortly afterwards passed to the north of Lubeck, following the coast towards Wismar. GB went to the bomb-aimer's position and map-read the aircraft in to the target. As we approached we could see considerable searchlight and Flak activity; obviously some of the early birds were stirring it up.

With everything set up for the bomb-run, I went back to stand by for flare dropping and during the bomb-run gave the Hun my 'four-penn'orth' of loose incendiaries down the flare chute. We had to run the usual gauntlet of searchlights and Flak and the aircraft juddered as it was buffetted by explosions from the heavy stuff. Escaping unscathed we lost no time in leaving the area and setting course for home.

I returned to my W/T position, transmitted 'Bombs gone', and then retuned to the long-range D/F to obtain bearings from Butser Hill. Keeping well away from defended areas it wasn't long before we crossed the coast and headed out over the North Sea. When we got within M/F fixing range I joined the queue of wireless operators of the other returning aircraft.* This was the time when, because of the inadequacy of the T1083/R1082 transmitter/receiver combination, you had to clamp the earphones tightly over your ears and strain to hear the faint 'cheepings' of the ground station Morse signals through the cacophony of interference, thus explaining why most surviving 'key-bashers' are as deaf as posts and sport cauliflower ears!

*In an attempt to relieve the congestion on the W/T frequencies, all of the Bomber Groups were assigned their individual M/F D/F Sections for navigational assistance, identification and security. 4 Group was given two sections: (a) Section 'F' - Sealand (control) with Andover No 1 and Leuchars as slaves operating at 340 kcs and (b) Section 'G' - Bircham Newton (control) with Lympne No 2 and Newcastle No 2 as slaves and operating at 326 kcs.

We were supposed to listen out before transmitting to avoid interfering with transmissions from other aircraft. Unfortunately there were times when this was ignored. This could happen when an impatient navigator whose plot wasn't working out as it should (and there were plenty of them about), put pressure on the wireless operator to get him a fix. I recall one such navigator being informed by his exasperated wireless operator, "This is a wireless set I'm operating, not a bloody slot machine!" I think he got the message. Eventually I managed to attract the attention of the D/F station operator and obtained the fixes which GB required to confirm his plot and get him off my back. We landed at base at 04.35 hours.

Because of adverse weather the 4 Group squadrons did not operate again until August 9th/10th when fourteen Whitleys were sent to attack the Ludwigshaven aluminium works. One aircraft from No. 78 Squadron was damaged and a fighter was seen, but all returned safely. No. 58 Squadron, operating alone again on August 10th/11th, sent ten crews to bomb an industrial target at Frankfurt-am-Main. Again there were no losses, but Pilot Officer L. Crooks, his aircraft running short of fuel and with battery problems, crashed N1346 at Hemswell, luckily without casualties.

Oil was again the priority on August 11th/12th when twenty-six Whitleys set out for Gelsenkirchen and Frankfurt also carrying the new secret weapon - 'RAZZLE'. Moderate opposition was reported over Frankfurt by No. 102 Squadron crews, but it was slightly worse for us at Gelsenkirchen. We had been detailed to attack this target then to proceed to the Black Forest to drop 'RAZZLE'. As this was to be the first use in action and we were one of the 'guinea pig' crew, I made it my business to find out what it was all about from our armament Chiefy, especially as it would be my task to off-load it. The aircraft had been fitted with wooden racks inside the fuselage containing forty-eight of the sealed cans. The method of despatch was simple; rip off the tin-foil seal on top of the can and pour the contents down the flare chute. We were warned to ensure that all the leaves left the aircraft and, in the event of any remaining, we were instructed to use the DIY fire prevention kit - the garden syringe.

This turned out to be a slightly 'hairy' trip in more ways than one. We got airborne in P4953 at 21.00 hours from Leeming and found the weather not too bad. After crossing the enemy coast we proceeded down Happy Valley and were picked up by searchlights.

The associated Flak batteries tried to give us a pasting, but we managed to escape into the darkness before they could nail us. We got the same reception going in over the target, but again our luck held. We dropped our bombs and got away unscathed then proceeded towards the 'RAZZLE' dropping area. The aircraft stooged around unmolested while I diligently poured the leaves down the flare chute and after the last can had been emptied I used my shaded hand torch to ensure that none of the 'RAZZLES' remained in the aircraft before returning to the cockpit to resume my wireless operating.

We landed back at base at 05.25 hours and taxied back to dispersal basking in the relief that we'd made it once again. Our complacency was rudely shattered by a call from George Dove in the tail turret reporting that the fabric on the elevators was burning! We lost no time in getting to dispersal where our ground crew extinguished the fire. Some of the 'RAZZLE' pellets had lodged in the the control hinges and had dried out during the return flight, thus causing the fire. 'Boffin' was fast becoming a dirty word in the 4 Group aircrew vocabulary! Ours was one of the six affected in our squadron and we learned that our friends in No. 51 Squadron had met the same problem in addition to a combat loss. P4983 flown by Sergeant J. M. Kearney did not return, having been shot down by Flak near Jever on the north German coast.

Although the weather over Britain was fairly good on August 12th/13th it was filthy over Germany, yet fifteen aircraft attacked Heringen and the Ruhr with only one aircraft suffering Flak damage. The bad weather over the continent persisted, thus attacks were switched to Italian targets on August 13th/14th. We were to use advanced bases to increase our range, thus Nos. 10 and 51 Squadrons, detailed to bomb the Fiat works at Turin, sent twenty aircraft to Abingdon during the day while No. 58 Sqn positioned their ten aircraft at Harwell.

We took off from Abingdon at 20.00 hours, crossed the sea, and proceeded across France towards the Alps. As we were climbing to clear the mountains a problem developed in one of the engines and we couldn't make it. I remember seeing the lights of Geneva before we turned back and, as this was my second abortive attempt to reach Italy, I was getting that jinxed feeling. We got back on the one good engine and landed safely at 02.00 hours - a six-hour flog for nothing.

173

Most other No. 10 Squadron crews got to the target, but P4965 flown by Pilot Officer E. I. 'Pip' Parsons, was attacked and damaged by an Italian nightfighter after completing the bomb-run. They struggled back across the Alps but were unable to maintain height whilst crossing France. They eventually attempted to ditch one mile from Hythe on the south coast, but the aircraft crashed, killing the two pilots. The other three crew members survived and were thrown clear, but without their dinghy. Inflating their Mae Wests they attempted to reach the shore, but drifted apart.

The crash had been witnessed from shore by two fishermen (one a former lifeboat Coxwain) and also by Miss Peggy Prince, a young physical training instructress. The fishermen launched their boat and rowed out to rescue Sergeants W. Chamberlain (air-observer) and M. L. Sharpe (tail-gunner). Miss Prince, wearing only pyjamas, paddled out into the Channel in her frail river canoe to pick up Sergeant J. R. Marshall (WOP/AG), a feat for which she was subsequently awarded the British Empire Medal. When Jimmy Marshall got back to the squadron he got the usual treatment from his 'oppos' in the W/T Section: 'Trust you to get picked up by a bint wearing pyjamas!'.

During this sortie a No. 51 Squadron aircraft, P4987 flown by Flight Lieutenant T. P. Bradley, was hit by Flak over Dunkirk and turned back. Only one crew of No. 58 Squadron, that of Pilot Officer N. O. Clements in N1446, managed to hit their primary target which was the Caproni factory at Milan.

Oil targets in France and the Caproni works in Milan (again) were the targets for thirty-one Whitleys on August 14th/15th. All returned to the U.K., but tragically two aircraft fell victim to balloon barrages. P4982 of No. 51 Squadron, flown by Flying Officer S. P. Swenson, was returning from Bordeaux when it hit a cable near Slough and crashed, killing the crew. N1453 from No. 77 Squadron struck a balloon cable at Southampton when coming back from St Nazaire. Flying Officer W. A. Stenhouse and his entire crew died in the crash. Little did the crews of Nos. 77 and 102 Squadrons suspect that their post-flight relaxation would be drastically interrupted later in the day when Driffield was attacked by the Luftwaffe.

Since August 12th the Luftwaffe had begun to direct increasingly severe attacks against radar stations and Fighter Command airfields in the south, but thus far had been frustrated by the heroic defence put up by Fighter Command pilots. On August 15th the Germans,

The bombing of Driffield on August 15th, 1940, as photographed by Jim Verran of 102 Squadron.

Damage to the Officer's 'Transport'.

Wrecked Whitleys.

under the mistaken impression that all of the fighter squadrons had been committed to the defence of the southern airfields, despatched a strong force of bombers from Scandinavia to attack targets in the north-east. Some fifty Ju88s of Kampfgeschwader 30 set out from Aalborg in Denmark to attack Driffield. Further north sixty He111s of *Kampfgeschwader* 26, escorted by Bf110s of *Zerstorergeschwader* 76, departed from Stavanger in Norway to attack other targets. The northern force was engaged by Spitfires of Nos. 72 and 41 Squadrons and by Hurricanes of Nos. 605 and 79 Squadrons. These fighters caused many losses and rendered the attacks largely unsuccessful. Meanwhile at approximately 13.00 hours a radar station near Bridlington had picked up the Ju88s, to which Spitfires of No. 616 and Hurricanes of No. 73 Squadron were directed, catching the bombers as they were crossing in near Bridlington Bay. Although seven bombers were shot down, about twenty more got through and really clobbered Driffield.

At this time, although there were batteries of heavy anti-aircraft guns in the area, defences against low-level attacks were woefully lacking. At our airfields the defences comprised a few ancient Lewis guns, so the Ju88s were able to sweep across Driffield with impunity, dropping their bombs and raking the hangars and dispersed Whitleys with gunfire. Four hangars were hit, three being burnt out. Installations including two airmen's barrack blocks, one wing of the Officer's Mess and the hutted Sergeant's Mess were destroyed. Ten Whitleys were destroyed, five each from Nos. 77 and 102 Squadrons. The casualties were fortunately light; fifteen killed and twenty-six wounded.

Squadron Leader Jim Verran, DFC and Bar, a New Zealander, was a Pilot Officer at that time. Another of the adventurous air-minded young men from the Dominions, he had joined the RAF on a short-service commission in August 1939 and had been posted to No. 102 Squadron at the end of June, 1940. Two of his fellow officers at that time were Pilot Officers Leonard Cheshire and H. M. 'Dinghy' Young, both beginning what would prove to be illustrious careers as bomber pilots.

Jim Verran recalls that day:

"I had returned to Driffield during the middle of the night after taking part in the Milan raid. After sleeping it off I surfaced and went to the Mess for lunch, after which I went into the ante-room to read the papers and relax. It was then that the air-raid siren sounded. As usual the reaction was lethargic, that is until the bombs

*See Epilogue.

Jim Verran (right) with a fellow No.102 Squadron Officer.
(Jim Verran)

started exploding, then pandemonium reigned as everyone rushed to the shelter adjacent to the Mess. I made it OK, but one fellow officer was blown into the shelter with a wooden window frame around his neck - the result of a 500 kg bomb which exploded when it hit the wing of the Officer's Mess near the shelter just after we'd left it. Although I had no external injuries it was subsequently discovered that the blast has impressed a uniform button through my clothing to cause internal injury to my chest."*

Another survivor was Sergeant Arthur 'Stokey' Stokes, later first wireless operator to Leonard Cheshire:

"It was about one-thirty pm on the 15th when my roommate in the Sergeant's Mess looked out of the window and said, 'What the Hell are all those Blenheims doing flying around here?' then the bombs started exploding. I left my bed in hurry - I'd been on the Milan raid and was having a bit of a lie-in. Our room was on the first floor, but without hesitation I opened the window and leapt out, landing in a heap on the grass below. I picked myself up, streaked across the grass and flung myself into a nearby air-raid shelter."

Inside the shelter he discovered that he was wearing only a shirt. He had literally 'streaked' across the grass!

Further south, the Luftwaffe dealt Bomber Command another blow by raiding the Short Brothers and Pobjoy factories, builders of Britain's newest bomber, the four-engined Short Stirling. Because of the damage caused to the production lines and the damage to already completed airframes the first unit to be equipped (No. 7 Squadron with us at Leeming) was unable to begin operations until February 10th/11th 1941.

Our squadron was the only 4 Group unit to operate on August 15th/16th, four Whitleys attacking factories at Milan and Turin. N1497 did not return. Sergeant D. W. 'Mitzi' Green's aircraft had been hit by Flak over Turin and Green ordered his crew to bale out over the Alps. The aircraft had received a direct hit, setting it on fire. It crashed in flames at Ceresola d'Alba. 'Mitzi' Green and three of the crew, including my ex-crew colleague Sergeant Arthur 'Lofty' Millington, were captured. Flying Officer Higson perished and was buried by the Italians with full military honours.

The targets for the following night (August 16th/17th) were factories at Jena, Augsburg and the Bohlen power station. Our squadron was briefed to bomb the Zeiss optical works at Jena and we were one of the nine crews despatched. We took off from Leeming at 20.35 hours and were fortunate to proceed to our target area unmolested. On the way I used the new D/F station at Butser Hill to obtain fixes and bearings When we arrived at Jena we found only slight opposition. We carried out four bomb-runs at 5,000 feet and estimated that the bombs had fallen in the target area, including my incendiaries I hoped. The return flight was easy and we landed at Leeming at 05.20 hours.

This nine-hour trip had been my thirty-first raid, the last three within six days, and though I might not have realised it at the time, I suppose that some of the effects were beginning to bite. Looking back I recall how, after every successful return, when I left the aircraft I lit up the dreaded 'weed'. How those first inhalations helped me to relax! From being a non-smoker at the beginning of war, I had become a twenty-a-day man. Smoking may be detrimental physically, but I can personally vouch for its mental therapy. I also remember that as we sat by our aircraft awaiting transport to de-briefing there was little conversation, if any. We would have been loth to to admit it, but I suppose we were trying to reconcile the tranquility of the dawn with the fact that just a few hours previously we had been six hundred miles away with our lives hanging in the balance.

Of our other squadron aircraft P4993, flown by Flight Lieutenant G. L. Raphael, was attacked by a Bf110 just before reaching Jena. Leading Aircraftsman A. Cowie (whose promotion to Sergeant was snarled up in the administration pipeline) got in three good bursts from his quadruple Brownings and claimed it as a 'possible'. Flying Officer G. W.'Pinpoint' Prior and his crew had actually seen this Messerschmitt taking off from Weimar, west of Jena, but didn't witness the combat.

Flying Officer W. M.'Max' Nixon's crew weren't so lucky. An SOS was received from P4955 at 00.30 hours reporting engine trouble, but then five minutes later they reported that their bomb-load had been dropped on target. Nothing further was heard until 03.24 hours when they were 'fixed' some twenty miles from Zeugenbergen in Holland. Then there was silence. During the midnight news on 17th August the BBC announced that the Germans were offering a reward for the capture of aircrew from a British aircraft that had crashed near Zeugenbergen and it was subsequently revealed that Max Nixon and his crew had been taken prisoner after evading capture for some considerable time.

A further thirty-five from the other squadrons, including five from No. 77 Squadron, were also on operations that night. N1466 of No. 58 Squadron, captained by Pilot Officer V. F. B. Pike, had to abort after being damaged by our own AA defences near Norwich. Several other crews delivered attacks on the primary target, including Pilot Officer N. O. Clements in P5002 and Sergeant H. Cornish in N1434. Both descended to low level, 1,500 and 2,000 feet respectively, to machine-gun the factory after bombing. From No. 51 Squadron P4974 flown by Flying Officer Barclay force landed at Nuneaton on return, but Flight Lieutenant J. S. Scott's P4986 was lost. Like Max Nixon's No. 10 Squadron aircraft, it was claimed by Luftwaffe Flak gunners.

On the following night, August 18th/19th, four aircraft revisited Milan and twenty bombed the aluminium factory at Rheinfelden. Flying Officer J. A. Piddington of No. 77 Squadron, flying N1365, bombed the Caproni factory from 2,000 feet. His bombs caused fires and a large explosion, but he was soon attacked by a nightfighter which was promptly claimed destroyed by the tail-gunner.

We were one of the crews detailed for Rheinfelden, getting airborne from Leeming at 23.00 hours. After crossing the enemy coast the weather deteriorated and I could tell from the radio interference that there was heavy cloud about. From time to time the darkness was illuminated by brilliant flashes of lightning from the towering cumulo-nimbus clouds. As we avoided these we seemed also to be steering clear of the heavily defended areas and were thus able to proceed to the target area unhindered. The weather worsened and when the estimated time of arrival over target was reached we were flying in cloud. I was sent back to prepare flares for when we found a break in the cloud while we flew back and forth trying to find one. It wasn't our night. After spending as much time as we could seeking the primary target we gave it up and set course for our alternate. I returned to the cockpit and my W/T duties, finding that reception was extremely bad.

Our bad luck continued and because of the filthy weather we were unable to find the alternate, even though we spent time that we could ill-afford searching for it. We set course for home, hoping to find a target of opportunity on the way, but were again out of luck. To make matters worse the generator supplying H/T to my W/T transmitter packed in, and all I was left with was my receiver. While we were still within range I used the German radio beacons to obtain loop bearings, but even these were affected by electrical interference. Once out of range GB had to rely on his DR only. Fortunately he was on the ball, the weather improved as we crossed the North Sea and this enabled him to get a pin- point when we crossed the coast. We landed back at base at 08.00 hours, still with the bombs aboard, having spent nine frustrating hours airborne, mostly over enemy territory.

Then it was back to the Operations Room where we told our tale of woe to the duty 'Spy' (Intelligence Officer) and made out the Sortie Report. If I recall correctly the IO that morning was David 'H', a fairly well-known film actor who had forsaken the silver screen to do his bit - or anything else he could get, according to rumour! By the time we had finished the de-brief and had our post-flight meal the sun was climbing high into the sky. I was fast coming to the conclusion that this was an arduous way of earning bacon and eggs.

On August 19th/20th sixteen Whitleys took off to bomb the Schornewitz power station, losing P4968 of No. 51 Squadron flown by Flying Officer P. G. 'Butch' Brodie. This aircraft, badly damaged after bombing the target, was crash landed in Holland where the crew were captured unhurt. 'Butch' had been the skipper involved in the incident of July 2nd, when he returned minus his second pilot. One can assume they renewed their acquaintance in Stalag Luft III. No record is available of their reunion, but the betting is that it was 'interesting'!*

Because of the bad weather prevailing over the continent no operations were possible for the next four nights, although the Luftwaffe attacked Driffield again on August 20th/21st without causing damage or casualties. Operations were resumed on August 24th/25th when ten aircraft of our squadron attacked Milan and nineteen more went to the Messerschmitt factory at Augsburg and the Daimler-Benz motor works at Stuttgart. Our crew was detailed and after briefing we flew down to Abingdon which was again being used as an advanced base for raids on Italy. The weather was fine and after the aircraft had been topped up with fuel we spent the time before take-off lying on the grass beside it, relaxing and enjoying the evening sun. Lounging there it all seemed so peaceful until suddenly you remembered what you were there for. The old phrase comes to mind, 'If you can't take a joke, you shouldn't have joined. Besides, if you want the 'glamour' of wearing a brevet, you must be prepared to pay the price' - some of us thought it was worth it.

Enery, our skipper, reminded me that this would be our third attempt to reach Italy together and this time we'd get there, even if we had to get out and push. This would also be the very last time that we would fly together because earlier in the day he had been informed that he and Sergeant Donald Witt**, one of the squadron's SNCO captains, were to be posted with effect from September 4th. Thus he was determined to end his tour on a high note.

That night we were lucky. After climbing away from Abingdon at 20.00 hours we set course, climbing steadily across France. As we approached the Alps we could see the lights of Geneva to the north.

---

*In 1947, I was on a pilot refresher course at RAF Moreton-in-the-Marsh together with 'Butch', Max Nixon and several other ex-PoWs, but as he was a Squadron Leader at the time and I a Flying Officer, I didn't broach the subject!

**Sergeant Donald Witt later joined No. 7 Squadron and became an outstanding and highly decorated Stirling pilot, eventually rising to the rank of Group Captain.

The weather and visibility was good and the sight of the mountains in the moonlight was a never-to-be-forgotten sight. Once over the Alps GB had no trouble navigating, guiding us south of Lake Maggiore to Milan. We approached, descending to 8,000 feet from where he identified the target and prepared for the run-in. Because of the moonlight no flares were necessary, but I assumed my usual position by the flare chute - I was determined that the Italians were going to get their ration of my incendiaries! We carried out two bomb-runs against moderate opposition, with the bombs going down in the target area. I hoped that my contribution had done likewise.

After evading the defences we turned for home, climbing over the Alps without difficulty, and with the W/T working like a charm landed back at base at 04.50 hours. It had been an eight hour and fifty minute 'flog', but generally an easy ride; a case of 'third time lucky'.

While 'Shiny Ten' attacked Milan the other squadrons were facing tough opposition over Germany. The night's sole loss occurred over Holland where N1473 was shot down by Flak south-east of Haarlem. Pilot Officer C. J. D. Montague DFC perished with all of his crew.

During the night Driffield was again raided by the Luftwaffe in an attack that set No.1 hangar ablaze and severely damaged the Sergeant's Mess. Consequently the base was evacuated. No. 77 Squadron joined No. 58 Squadron at Linton-on-Ouse while No. 102 Squadron joined us at Leeming. Bombs fell on central London that night, thus Mr Churchill ordered a retaliation raid to be directed against Berlin by Wellingtons, Whitleys and Hampdens next night. On August 25th/26th the first raid on the German capital city during World War II took place.*

4 Group contributed nineteen aircraft, but not all got there. Pilot Officer N. O. Clements of No. 58 Squadron attacked Bremen docks from 2,000 feet against intense gunfire, causing fires. Despite the Flak he brought P5002 down to 100 feet to machine-gun searchlight

*Ironically, the bombing of London had been a mistake. German crews were under strict orders to avoid such actions, but at least one crew, hopelessly lost, dropped their load under the impression that the British capital was miles away. Thus Winston Churchill was given the heaven-sent opportunity to change the complexion of the war. The British retaliation so infuriated Adolf Hitler that he ordered Luftwaffe daylight attacks to be directed at London, commencing on September 7th and code-named 'Operation Loge'. At a stroke this single Bomber Command operation removed the pressure from the hard-pressed Fighter Command airfields - and the rest is history.

*The crew of P4957 of No.10 Squadron which crashed in the
Pennines returning from a raid on Magdeburg on 30th October,
1940. Sergeant George Dove is on the extreme right of this happy
group outside the cottage hospital at Alston. (George Dove)*

and Flak batteries and, amazingly, got away with it. All five aircraft
sent to the Ruhr aborted and brought their bombs home.

Attacks were again switched to Italian targets on August
26th/27th, when fifteen of the seventeen crews detailed   left their
forward bases to raid Milan and Turin. One of our No. 10 Squadron
aircraft, P4990 flown by Sergeant H. G. H. Howard, failed to return.
It fell to Flak at Valera, near Verese. Returning crews reported
considerable Luftwaffe activity over the Channel.

On August 27th/28th targets were selected in both Italy and
Germany. Sixteen aircraft were despatched and all returned claiming
moderate success. On the next night eleven Whitleys went to
Germany, attacking factories at Dortmund, Düsseldorf and Dessau.
Crews from our squadron, targetted to Dortmund and Düsseldorf,
reported heavy opposition and one fighter was seen. One crew made
three bomb-runs from nine, eight and seven thousand feet, reporting
fires and explosions. They also took the first night raid photographs
by a 4 Group aircraft.

Bad weather over the continent made target identification very
difficult on August 29th/30th, only three of the twelve Whitleys
bombing their primaries. On 30th/31st only No. 58 Squadron
operated, sending nine aircraft to Berlin. One crew, misinterpreting a

'Syko' received by W/T, jettisoned the bomb-load into the North Sea and abandoned the sortie. You can bet that the blame for that boob was passed around like a hot potato! Pilot Officer N. O. Clements' crew in P5002 abandoned the primary target after a fruitless search and bombed Nordhorn instead. The aircraft ran out of fuel on the return flight and Clements baled his crew out over Hornsea before ditching the aircraft offshore. Unfortunately one man drifted out to sea and was lost.

The last raid of the month was carried out by No. 10 Squadron, when six aircraft successfully attacked the synthetic oil plant at Wesseling on August 31st/September 1st.

After our raid on August 24th/25th, our skipper, Flying Officer Henry, left us in preparation for his eventual posting to No. 35 Squadron, the first Halifax squadron.* Having flown with him since the beginning of the war, during which time we had been on thirty raids together, I was naturally very sorry to see him go. The strict peacetime code of officer/airmen relationship which existed at the start of hostilities was now being relaxed slightly, especially as we had done more and more raids together. I like to think that by now a mutual respect had developed. Sergeant John 'GB' Shaw, our air-observer also left us. Thus Flying Officer Landale, George Dove and myself were left as the nucleus of a new crew. While it was being sorted out I managed to get away for a few days leave. Having now done thirty-three raids, seven in the past three weeks, I was glad to get away from an existence which now seemed to be made up of listening to interminable Morse Code and throbbing Merlins and being scared fartless when we were caught in the searchlights and Flak over Germany. During stand-downs I was spending more and more of my time in the locals, where I sometimes drank too much. Maybe the boys in the Section were right when they said I was getting 'Flak happy'.

So I went home, where I was able to get away from it all for a while and indulge in the luxury of going for leisurely walks on the nearby fells. However, even there you couldn't get away from it for long. There was always some noisy low-flying RAF so-and-so who screamed over your head at nought feet when you least expected it. Despite these minor irritations my leave, though too short, helped to re-charge my batteries and I returned to Leeming ready for the next round.

*He was killed on January 11th, 1941, in the squadron's first fatal Halifax accident.

It was late at night when I got back and groped my way through the blacked-out room past my sleeping comrades to find my bed. When I awoke next morning I discovered that while I'd been away some of my former room-mates had gone missing and had been replaced by new boys from the OTU. I recall that one of them asked me if I, like them, had just been posted in. I hope I resisted the temptation to pull the 'old sweat' routine on him, but I don't think I did.

When I reported to the section that morning I found that our new crew had been formed. Flying Officer P. W. F. Landale had been promoted to Captain, Pilot Officer W. D. Boxwell was our new second pilot, Pilot Officer R. J. Dickinson was air-observer and George Dove tail-gunner, with me as first WOP/AG. George and I were the only experienced members; Flying Officer Landale had done only eight trips as second pilot while Boxwell and Dickinson were complete beginners. I can't say I was enamoured with the set-up, but ours was not to reason why. I consoled myself with the thought that I might be 'screened' soon - courtesy of the Germans!

Summary of operations by 4 Group
1st - 31st August 1940

1st-2nd. Bombing - Oil Refinery at Düsseldorf.
58 Sqn. Seven a/c. One returned early, four bombed primary, one bombed an alternative targets.
102 Sqn. Eight a/c. Five bombed primary, three bombed alternatives.

2nd-3rd. Bombing - Oil Refinery at Salzbergen.
10 Sqn. Seven a/c. Two returned early, five bombed primary. Weather bad, opposition severe.
51 Sqn. Eight a/c. Seven bombed primary. Weather bad, opposition severe.

3rd-4th. Bombing - Oil Refineries at Mannheim and Düsseldorf.
77 Sqn. Eight a/c to Mannheim. All bombed primary.
78 Sqn. Three a/c to Düsseldorf. One bombed primary, two bombed Mannheim as alternative. Two force landed on return.

4th-5th. Bombing - Oil Plant at Sterkrade.
58 Sqn. Five a/c. All bombed primary. One fighter seen, but no attack.

5th-6th. Bombing - Oil Plant at Sterkrade and Dornier Aircraft Factory at Wismar.

10 Sqn. Seven a/c to Wismar. Six bombed primary. Two damaged by Flak.

51 Sqn. Eight a/c to Wismar. Six bombed primary. One damaged by Flak and force landed at Spurn Point on return.

102 Sqn. Six a/c to Sterkrade. Four bombed primary, one bombed an alternative target.

9th-10th. Bombing - Aluminium Works at Ludwigshaven.

77 Sqn. Nine a/c. Seven bombed primary.

78 Sqn. Five a/c. Four bombed primary, one bombed an alternative. One damaged by Flak. One fighter seen, but no attack.

10th-11th. Bombing - Industrial Targets at Frankfurt-am-Main.

58 Sqn. Ten a/c. Two returned early, four bombed primary, two bombed alternates. One crashed at Hemswell on return.

11th-12th. Bombing - Oil Refineries at Gelsenkirchen and Frankfurt - 'Razzling'.

10 Sqn. Eight a/c to Gelsenkirchen. All bombed primary and 'Razzled'. Four damaged by Flak, six damaged by burning 'Razzles'.

51 Sqn. Eight a/c. One returned early, six bombed primary and 'Razzled'. One fighter seen, but no attack, one FTR.

102 Sqn. Ten a/c to Frankfurt. One returned early, seven bombed primary.

12th-13th. Bombing - Industrial Targets at Heringen and the Ruhr.

77 Sqn. Ten a/c to Heringen. Bad weather, only five bombed.

78 Sqn. Five a/c to the Ruhr. Bad weather, only two bombed. Two damaged by Flak.

13th-14th. Bombing - Fiat Works at Turin and Caproni Aircraft Factory at Milan.

10 Sqn. Ten a/c to Turin. Two returned early, eight bombed primary. One damaged by fighter and ditched in Channel on return with two killed.

51 Sqn. Ten a/c to Turin. One damaged by Flak and returned early, nine bombed primary.

58 Sqn. Ten a/c to Milan. Three returned early, four bombed primary, three bombed alternatesive targets.

14th-15th. Bombing - Oil Targets at Bordeaux and St Nazaire - Caproni Aircraft Factory at Milan.

51 Sqn. Four a/c to Bordeaux. One returned early, three bombed primary. One hit balloon barrage on return, crew killed.

77 Sqn. Twelve a/c to St Nazaire. Two returned early, ten bombed primary. One hit balloon barrage on return, crew killed.

78 Sqn. Six a/c to Bordeaux. All bombed primary.

102 Sqn. Nine a/c to Milan. All bombed primary.

15th-16th. Bombing - Fiat Works at Turin and Caproni Aircraft Factory at Milan.

10 Sqn. Four a/c. Three bombed primary, one FTR.

16th-17th Bombing - Zeiss Works at Jena, Dornier Aircraft Factory at Augsburg and Power Station at Bohlen.

10 Sqn. Nine a/c to Jena. All bombed primary, one claimed a Bf110 destroyed and one FTR.

51 Sqn. Fourteen a/c to Bohlen. Two returned early, twelve bombed primary. One force landed at Nuneaton and one FTR.

58 Sqn. Eleven a/c to Jena and Augsburg. Two returned early (one hit by own AA), four bombed Jena and five bombed Augsburg.

77 Sqn. Five a/c to Augsburg. One bombed primary, three bombed alternative targets. Weather bad.

78 Sqn. Five a/c to Bohlen. Four bombed primary, one bombed an alternative target.

17th-18th. Bombing. Aircraft Factory at Augsburg.

102 Sqn. Five a/c. One returned early, three bombed primary and one FTR.

18th-19th. Bombing - Caproni Aircraft Factory at Milan and Aluminium Factory at Rheinfehlen.

10 Sqn. Ten a/c to Rheinfehlen. Very bad weather, eight bombed primary.

58 Sqn. Ten a/c to Rheinfehlen. Six bombed primary, one bombed an alternative target.

77 Sqn. Four a/c to Milan. Four bombed primary, one claimed a fighter destroyed.

19th-20th. Bombing - Power Station at Schornewitz.

51 Sqn. Ten a/c. One returned early, nine bombed primary, one FTR.*

78 Sqn. Six a/c. One returned early, four bombed primary.

24th-25th. Bombing - Electrical Factory at Milan - Aircraft Factory at Augsburg - Daimler-Benz Factory at Stuttgart.

10 Sqn. Ten a/c to Milan. Four returned early, six bombed primary.

77 Sqn. Ten a/c to Augsburg. Seven bombed primary, one FTR.

---

*Hitherto, it had not been possible to determine whether missing aircraft had actually reached a target and bombed, but the improvement in W/T procedure eliminated this.

102 Sqn. Nine a/c to Stuttgart. All bombed primary.

25th-26th. Bombing - Industrial targets at Berlin and The Ruhr.

51 Sqn. Nine a/c to Berlin. Weather atrocious, two bombed primary.

58 Sqn. Ten a/c. Three returned early, four bombed primary, three bombed alternative targets.

78 Sqn. Five a/c. None bombed due to adverse weather.

26th-27th. Bombing - Industrial targets at Turin and Milan.

10 Sqn. Six a/c to Milan. Five bombed primary, one FTR.

77 Sqn. Seven a/c to Turin. Five bombed primary.

27th-28th. Bombing - Industrial Targets at Turin and Milan - Aircraft Factory at Augsburg - Marshalling Yards at Mannheim.

51 Sqn. Five a/c to Augsburg. Three bombed primary.

58 Sqn. Six a/c to Turin and Milan. Three bombed primaries, two bombed alternative targets.

78 Sqn. Five a/c to Mannheim. Three bombed primary, two bombed alternative targets.

28th-29th. Bombing - Industrial Targets at Dortmund and Düsseldorf - Airframe Factory at Dessau.

10 sqn. Two a/c each to Dortmund and Düsseldorf. All bombed primaries.

102 Sqn. Seven a/c to Dessau. All bombed primary.

29th-30th. Bombing - Oil Plant at Wesseling - Petrol Store at Ludwigshaven.

51 Sqn. Seven a/c to Wesseling. Very bad weather. One bombed primary, two bombed alternative targets.

78 Sqn. Five a/c to Ludwigshaven. Two returned early, one bombed primary, two bombed alternative targets.

30th-31st. Bombing - Industrial targets at Berlin.

58 Sqn. Nine a/c. One returned early, seven bombed primary, one bombed an alternative target.

31st-1st. Bombing - Oil Plant at Wesseling.

10 Sqn. Six a/c. All bombed primary.

Chapter Nine

Operation 'Sea Lion' - Tamed

During the month of September, 1940, the Battle of Britain reached a crucial climax as Fighter Command emphatically denied the Germans the air superiority necessary to protect a successful invasion. While the fighter boys continued to hack down the Luftwaffe over southern England and the Channel, Bomber Command also played a decisive part. From early September to the end of the month, numerous sorties were flown by day and night against the fleets of barges and other shipping being assembled in the Channel ports of Ostend, Antwerp, Calais, Dunkirk and Boulogne. Even the Battles of 1 Group, the remnants of the ill-fated AASF, were thrown into the night war, their last operational sortie coming on 15th/16th September.*

It was subsequently revealed that our efforts weren't in vain. The losses inflicted on the German invasion fleet by the Blenheims by day, and the Wellingtons, Whitleys, Hampdens Blenheims and Battles by night, was a significant factor in the postponement and the eventual cancellation of 'Sea Lion'. On September 19th Hitler, postponing the operation 'indefinitely', ordered the dispersement of the invasion fleet to reduce the attrition caused by Bomber Command.

During one such attack on Antwerp on September 15th/16th, one of our 5 Group counterparts, Sergeant John Hannah, a member of a No. 83 Squadron Hampden crew, became the first WOP/AG to win the Victoria Cross during World War II.

Before this, however, No. 102 Squadron had been temporarily detached from 4 Group to Coastal Command, moving from Leeming

---

* The lack of recognition shown to Bomber Command aircrew for their work during the Battle of Britain, both from official sources and by post-war historians, has been a continuing source of bitterness to the survivors, and rightly so. The tactical and strategic work done by Bomber Command during the Battle of Britain was carried out at a high price and it is a fact that the number of aircrew killed, captured and missing during Bomber and Coastal Command operations considerably exceeded those sustained by Fighter Command during that time. While in no way denigrating the magnificent achievements of our fighter pilots, it should never be forgotten that others were there too. An admittedly extreme example occurred on August 13th, when twelve Blenheims of No. 82 Squadron attempted to raid Aalborg airfield in daylight without fighter escort. One returned early, the other eleven were massacred by the Luftwaffe....

to Prestwick on September 1st in order to carry out convoy and anti-submarine patrols over the Atlantic approaches.*

On the night of September 1st/2nd the weather was very bad over northern Germany. Thus eleven Whitleys were sent to attack Turin and Munich, some meeting heavy opposition. All returned, one No. 78 Squadron crew having attacked an airfield in France while enemy aircraft were in the circuit. Next night it was the turn of Genoa and Frankfurt. No. 58 Squadron lost two bombers; N1459, piloted by Flight Sergeant 'Dinty' Moore, ran out of fuel and was ditched fifteen miles north-north-east of Harwich, the crew being picked up unhurt by HMS *Pintail*. The second aircraft, N1427 also had fuel problems. They almost made it, but Squadron Leader G. A. Bartlett was eventually forced to ditch the aircraft just off Margate, where they evacuated the aircraft and paddled ashore in the dinghy. One No. 78 Squadron crew had a narrow escape after being 'coned' over Frankfurt for an agonising twenty minutes before getting away.

On September 3rd, the first anniversary of the outbreak of war, The British Prime Minister Mr Winston Churchill circulated to the Cabinet a document which, had we bomber crews been privileged to have seen it, would have done much to sustain our morale. It stated that our supreme effort must be to gain mastery of the air and, while the fighters were our salvation, the bombers alone provided the means of victory. The power to pulverise the entire industry and structure on which the war effort the enemy depended was to be our first priority. It was a doctrine that the future C-in-C, Bomber Command, Air Marshal Sir Arthur Harris, was to pursue vigorously.

That night, September 3rd/4th, it was our squadron versus Berlin! Our seven aircraft met severe opposition, one being damaged by Flak while Flight Lieutenant D. G. Tomlinson's P4967 was wrecked in a crash at Nether Stilton, near Northallerton, on return. There were no casualties. Berlin and Magdeburg were on the 'visiting list' for 4th/5th, when six aircraft were sent to each target. The returning No. 51 Squadron Berlin raiders also dropped 'RAZZLES', but lost Pilot Officer J. M. Taylor's P4973, which ditched off Holland after completing their attack and struggling to the North Sea.

On the next night, Regensburg and Turin were attacked, No. 77 Squadron crews reporting that a colossal explosion was seen at the

* No. 102 Squadron would return to 4 Group on October 10th, resuming bomber operations from Linton-on-Ouse.

190

Italian target sending up smoke to 5,000 feet. On 6th/7th when our squadron, the only Whitley force operating, sent five aircraft to Berlin, Pilot Officer R. H. Thomas and his crew didn't return. No German claims were made that night and it is believed that P4953 vanished into the North Sea on the return flight.

On September 7th/8th the targets were switched to the German invasion fleet assembling at Ostend and Boulogne but, because of the atrocious weather, not one of the six Whitleys were able to find their target. One crew in N1414 of No. 78 Squadron crash landed near Wells. The aircraft burnt out, but luckily Squadron Leader W. B. Tait and his crew escaped unharmed.

We were honoured next day when Leeming was visited by the 'Father' of the Royal Air Force, Marshal Lord Hugh 'Boom' Trenchard, who gave us a pep-talk and emphasised the morale-boosting effects our raids were having on the British civilians. Having just been on leave I could verify this, because everyone I'd met in our village had exhorted me in no uncertain terms to 'Give those Nazi so-and-sos a taste of their own medicine'*

That night (September 8th/9th) Bremen was raided by fifteen Whitleys, while another attempt was made to attack the concentrations of invasion barges at Ostend. Eleven aircraft were sent including ours, this trip to Ostend being a 'check-ride' for our newly formed crew. There were now very few of the original crews left of those who had commenced operations in September 1939, the wastage being due to both casualties and 'screening'. The Regulars were being replaced by the less experienced Volunteer Reservists. Some of the originals now found themselves having to fly with sprogs and I think I'd be correct in saying that they were doing so with reluctance. Still, 'If they couldn't take a joke, they shouldn't have joined'.

Our check that night was to be carried out by Flying Officer 'Pin-point' Prior, now one of the squadron's most experienced pilots. We got airborne in P4962 at 00.05 hours to discover that the weather was no better than it had been on the previous night. When we

---

* It was not only the British civilian moral that was boosted by Bomber Command. The noted Dutch aviation historian Gerrie Zwanenberg MBE, was a teenager in occupied Holland throughout the war, and observed: 'Although we knew that our friends were just across the North Sea and we knew that one day they'd return to liberate us, it was the sound of the engines of the British Bombers, going to Germany night after night, that gave us the courage to keep going. We will never forget them.'

arrived in the Ostend area the cloud was right down to the deck and, although we stooged about for some time, we were eventually forced to return, landing back at base fed-up and frustrated at 05.50 hours. One of our aircraft, P5094 flown by Pilot Officer J. C. Cairns, overshot on landing because of faulty hydraulics affecting the flaps. The aircraft ran across the Great North Road and crashed in the field beyond, injuring Pilot Officer Cairns when the instrument panel collapsed on his legs. Sergeant R. E. 'Blondie' Nicholson, the WOP/AG got him out through the top hatch just before the aircraft burst into flames. He was subsequently awarded a verbal pat on the back by our CO Wing Commander Bufton, but unfortunately nothing more.

Not one of the aircraft sent to Ostend managed to bomb, but although the Bremen attackers experienced heavy opposition, the weather was better and they achieved better results with all the aircraft returning safely. That night also, the Luftwaffe, badly mauled by Fighter in daylight, opened the London 'Blitz' by raiding the Surrey docks.

On the night of September 9th/10th, Berlin and Bremen were the targets for seventeen Whitleys. Opposition was severe - in the case of Berlin, vicious. Pilot Officer A. W. Millson of No. 51 Squadron attacked Bremen from 3,000 feet, claiming hits resulting in flames that reached 300 feet, but P5021 was badly damaged by Flak. Millson was forced to ditch 120 miles east of the Firth of Forth, where four of the crew were rescued by the Royal Navy, the fifth man being lost. The venue was unchanged on 10th/11th, when both Bremen and 'The Big City' were again attacked by eighteen aircraft, fires being noted in Berlin by returning No. 58 Squadron crews. Pilot Officer A. W. Dunn of No. 77 Squadron, also attacked Berlin. He dived his Whitley from 6,000 feet to release the bombs at 3,000, but P5046 was badly damaged and they were fortunate to get back. Not so lucky was another No. 77 Squadron aircraft, P5042 flown by Sergeant J. A. G. Deans. It was badly shot-up over the target and the crew were forced to abandon it over Hardenburg, Holland, at 04.00 hours. All the crew were captured. Severe opposition was again encountered over Bremen, one No. 77 Squadron aircraft being hit by Flak and another, T4134 from No. 58 Squadron flown by Pilot Officer J. E. Thompson, failing to return.

On September 11th/12th, the targets were unchanged; Berlin and Bremen. If at first you don't succeed, try, try, try again! Our crew was one of the twenty crews involved and we were briefed to bomb the Bremen dockyards and petrol storage sheds. Flying Officer N Prior was again riding as Captain to check out our crew because of the previous abortive trip to Ostend.

We took off at 19.35 hours in P4952. The outbound flight was without incident, but as we approached Bremen we could see that the fireworks had already started. There was a constant display of searchlights probing the darkness, while the coloured balls of light Flak hosed upwards and the heavy stuff exploded into dull red blossoms. Ever since that raid in May with my original crew, when we'd been clobbered but had got away with it, I'd had a healthy respect (fear!) of Bremen's defences. Fires were illuminating the target, so we commenced our attack, going in at 9,000 feet. There was no need for flares, so I stayed where I was to watch the proceedings. There was the usual gauntlet to run, but in spite of this we carried out three runs, dropping bombs in sticks (talk about 'ignorance being bliss'!). Beginner's luck must have been with our new skipper, because we got through without a scratch. George Dove called from the tail turret that we had stoked up the fires and indeed, when we were about sixty miles from the target he could still see them. On the way back the W/T was working well and we finally touched down at 02.35 hours. All in all it had been a successful sortie and our crew had passed the check-ride with flying colours. However I recall hoping that on subsequent raids our skipper and bomb-aimer would be a bit more economical with the bomb-runs; three times around a place like like Bremen was a bit much!

Our other six aircraft bombed successfully through the heavy gunfire, claiming fires in the target area. They all got back, although some were hit by Flak. P4961 was one of those hit and, after bombing and leaving the area, Flight Lieutenant D. G. Tomlinson carried out the usual 'body count' over the intercom. There was no reply from the rear turret and when Sergeant W. O. Walters, the air-observer, was sent to investigate he discovered that the tail turret had been turned to the beam position with the doors open and no sign of the of the gunner! Thus the aircraft returned with one crewman short and we subsequently ascertained that the missing man was a prisoner. For some time after that we wondered if we'd been nurturing a serpent in our bosoms, who was now giving the Germans all the 'gen about 'Shiny Ten'!

Since September 8th we had been at a state of alert, expecting the Germans to attempt their invasion. Consequently attacks on the assembling fleet in the Channel ports were stepped up. Eighteen aircraft operated against Dunkirk and Calais without loss on September 13th/14th, and next night it was our turn. Antwerp was our target and we climbed away at 19.40 hours. I was flying as tail-gunner to give George Dove an opportunity to keep his hand in at 'key bashing' and it was a welcome change to get my sticky fingers back on the four Brownings. In accordance with the now-routine practice, I tested the guns as soon as we'd crossed the coast and got the usual kick as the fiery stream arced down towards the sea.*

The weather was anything but good and we had to weave through numerous electrical storms, but fortunately it improved as we neared the target area and saw the searchlights and Flak. Our new bomb-aimer took us in for two runs at 12,000 feet and after the second I saw a big explosion in the dock area, followed by fires. Flak was moderate although none of it came close enough to cause any immediate panic, but I did see a Bf110 nightfighter above us. I kept him in my my sights, but thankfully he flew off without seeing us and we landed back at base at 01.50 hours. The rest of our ten aircraft attacked but one, P4966 flown by Squadron leader K. F. Ferguson, didn't come back. The tail-gunner, Sergeant Mark Niman, recalls:

"On the return flight one engine packed in and we were forced to ditch. Our position was approximately twenty miles off Spurn Head and the time was about 01.30 hours. The skipper carried out a remarkably fine ditching and the dinghy was launched successfully. However, in my haste to leave the rear turret, I went head-first into the huge metal tail-wheel spar which I had to climb over to reach the rear hatch, which raised an egg-shaped bump which I didn't feel until many hours later - I haven't been the same since!

---

*The gun-testing procedure was changed shortly afterwards. Instead of waiting until the aircraft was over the sea, it was decided that this could be done as we taxied out across the grass to the take-off point. Although the guns were fully depressed to fire down into the grass immediately behind the the aircraft, it didn't always happen that way and was fraught with danger. One night when one of our gunners carried out his check, the mechanism malfunctioned and the four guns 'ran away'. Before he could grab the ammunition belts and pulled them from the gun breeches, bullets were flying in all directions - some of them in the direction of the hangars and control tower. Fortunately on-one was hurt, but some laundry bills increased!

*Sergeant Mark Niman of
No. 10 Squadron. (M.
Niman)*

"We all got into the dinghy and cast off from the rapidly sinking aircraft, which took only a couple of minutes to disappear beneath the waves. The dinghy bounced around in a very rough North Sea for the next few hours before we were sighted and picked up by the crew of the Royal Navy minesweeper *Kurd*, a two hundred ton vessel which had just laid a minefield that we were shocked to learn we had alighted into! We also learned later that they had been very reluctant to pick us up until that had firmly established that we were British - one of them told us in no uncertain terms that had we been otherwise, we'd have ended up in the 'oggin.

"We remained their 'passengers' for the next two days while they completed their task, then they returned to Grimsby, where they took us on one helluva pub-crawl before we were taken back to Leeming."

A significant factor in their rescue was that their dinghy had been sighted and reported by another No. 10 Squadron crew, that of Willis in T4143.

The other squadrons, sending a further twenty aircraft to the same target, lost N1478 of No. 78 Squadron flown by Pilot Officer C. S. Robson.

Next night, September 15th/16th, we continued our attacks against the Channel ports by sending eleven aircraft to Ostend and Dunkirk and a further eight to Berlin and Hamburg. The weather was bad over Germany, but two No. 77 Squadron crews managed to attack Berlin through heavy opposition. While over Ostend Pilot Officer A. W. Dunn of the same squadron bombed from 6,700 feet, claiming direct hits, then took P5046 down to 100 feet from where his gunners raked the barges with machine-gun fire.

There were no 4 Group operations next night due to bad weather, so we took advantage of this bonus of a night off by indulging in our various social activities. As usual quite a few of us hied off to our local; the 'Green Dragon' at Bedale. By now enemy aircraft were flying over our area by night. No doubt our 4 Group airfields were their targets, thus decoy airfields were constructed to confuse the German aircrews. These were set up in remote uninhabited locations and one such 'dummy' was constructed in the hills west of Leeming. At night this site would be illuminated and sometimes, as we wended (staggered) our way back from Bedale, we had a grandstand view of the attacks. Their procedure was similar to ours; first the flares for identification, followed a few moments later by the flashes of bomb explosions. As the sounds reached us we were thankful that the decoys were working - it's much safer to give than to receive!

The weather improved on the night following (17th/18th) and in addition to attacks upon Zeebrugge and Ostend the battleship *Bismarck* berthed at Hamburg was selected for attack. Twenty-seven Whitleys set out, the target for our squadron being the *Bismarck* and one No. 10 Squadron aircraft turned back - ours. We were only thirty minutes out from from Leeming when the tail turret hydraulics packed in, forcing us to abandon the sortie.

No. 78 Squadron attacked Zeebrugge under intense Flak, one aircraft descending to 3,500 feet to machine-gun the defences while another, hit by Flak, suffered one man slightly wounded.

September 18th/19th proved to be a bad night for No. 58 and Squadrons who provided the twenty-seven aircraft detailed to raid Marshalling yards in Germany as well as the ports of Zeebrugge and Antwerp. No. 58 Squadron lost one aircraft when Pilot Officer E. Ford's P5008 was shot down by Flak at Groenlo, Holland. Two aircraft were reported missing from the (unlucky) thirteen sent by No. 77 Squadron. Pilot Officer R. P. Brayne's P4992 was shot down in flames over Antwerp, while N1425 flown by Pilot Officer P. E.

Eldridge is believed to be that which fell to Flak near Osnabruck. In all three cases there was not a single survivor.

Next night Mannheim was raided by eight of No. 78 Squadron and on the night following, 20th/21st, we joined twenty-two Whitleys attacking Flushing, Brussels and various targets in Germany. Our squadron, briefed to raid the marshalling yards at Hamm, mustered ten Whitleys and we got airborne in T4143 at 21.25 hours. After a smooth outward flight we approached the target finding it lit up by searchlights and Flak. Hamm was always a 'hot one' and it was obvious that it was living up to its reputation and giving some of the preceding aircraft a lively reception. The Germans were using the technique of putting curtains of Flak at various heights, so it made no difference what altitude you attacked from. The risk of being hit was ever present. We spent some time stooging around the outskirts until 'Tubby' (Pilot Officer Dickinson, our air-observer) had firmly identified the target, then we began to run-in. Our new skipper was learning fast.

I was in my usual position by the flare chute, dropping my loose incendiaries and preparing to drop flares if they were called for. During the final stages the Flak was bursting uncomfortably close and I could smell the acrid smoke as we flew through the bursts. The 'Bombs gone' came over the intercom and I was glad to leave my position, crawling through the tunnel leading to the cockpit to join the others at the sharp end. As I put my hand on the table in from of the W/T set to raise myself back into my seat I felt a sudden stab of pain in the fleshy part of my thumb, near my wrist. At this time my hand was on my open W/T log book and as I lifted it I saw blood on the pages. 'Tubby' also saw the blood and his eyes popped. This was only his fourth trip and from his expression he was obviously believing the hair-raising tales the old hands had been feeding him. I reassured him that I wasn't grievously wounded and removed my gauntlet. As I did so I saw that my white silk inner glove was now red and protruding from my hand was a sliver of metal, which I removed. I wrapped a handkerchief around my 'wound' which soon staunched the seeping blood and I was able to resume my 'key-bashing' without much discomfort.

After escaping the unwelcome attentions of the defences we set course for home, landing back at Leeming at 04.30 hours where during de-briefing and our after-flight bacon and eggs I had to put up with some leg-pulling concerning my wound! This was George Dove's last trip with us as tail-gunner. He left us to become first WOP/AG with another newly-formed crew to finish off his tour. He nearly didn't make it because on the night of October 29th, returning from a raid and flying in thick cloud, they flew into a hill three miles from Slaggyford, Northumberland. George's account shows how lucky they were to survive:

"My thirty-first and last scheduled trip of my first tour was nearly my last one, period! We had been to Wilhelmshaven. Pilot Officer W. E. Peers was the skipper and we'd had no problems to speak of, but when we arrived overhead Leeming on return we were instructed to leave the area as there were German intruders in the circuit. We set course in a north-westerly direction and after a whide the skipper decided we should return to base and asked me to get a QDM (homing bearing) which I did. A few minutes later I got another QDM but when I passed it to skipper he said he wasn't happy with the bearings and was going to turn onto the reciprocal. Just then there was a tremendous bang on the starboard wing and the cockpit began to fill with smoke.

"At that time we were flying at 2,000 feet and the skipper called out 'We've hit a balloon cable. Bale out!' I left the cockpit and put on my parachute as I made my way down the fuselage. 1 reached the door and grabbed the handle. A split second before 1 pulled it we hit again and I was thrown back to the main spar. 1 was being tossed around and, with the noise and confusion, 1 had no idea what was happening, except that the aircraft appeared to be breaking up. Then, after what seemed to me an interminable time, though it could only have been a few seconds, everything went silent.

"Dazed and confused 1 clambered out of the wreck into long grass in pouring rain and pitch black darkness. The 1 heard voices; someone said, 'Is everyone OK?', and one by one the rest of the crew appeared. My left arm was bleeding badly and giving me some pain, but otherwise I seemed to be all right.

"No-one knew at this time what had happened except we were on the deck with a smashed aircraft. The first thing we had to do was to get out of the rain and patch up those of us who were injured, so we got the first-aid kit from the aircraft and did what we could. Also we found some undamaged Thermos flasks still with coffee in them and some flying rations which we shared out. The time was just after midnight, so we settled down to spend the night in the aircraft. - fortunately there had been no fire.

"It started to get light at about six am so we emerged from the wreckage to look around, get our bearings and figure out what had happened. We found we were on top of the Pennines and had apparently flown between a double line of hills with no way out at the end. The first impact had been when the starboard wind had hit one of the hills, then the aircraft had carried on to hit the last hill, where it careered down the slope shedding wreckage before stopping on the brink of a fifty foot drop.

"As we were assessing the situation we saw a figure approaching, from where we couldn't guess as there was nothing to see for miles. It turned out that he was a hill shepherd who, by a stroke of good fortune, was carrying a flask of whisky which he passed around. He told us we had crashed approximately two miles from the nearest habitation - Alston on the Cumberland/Northumberland border. Itwas then that we saw a line of figures in the distance, walking on the sky-line. We searched around, found the Verey (flare) pistol and some cartridges in the grass and although they were wet, they worked.

"It was then that we saw a line of figures in the distance, walking on the sky-line. We searched around, found the Verey (flare) pistol and some cartridges in the grass and although they were wet, they worked.

"In the meantime our navigator, who had set off at first light to get help, was having a shotgun pushed into his ribs by the farmer of a nearby farm, who refused to believe he wasn't a German. Fortunately he eventually convinced him otherwise and he was able to return to us.

"The line of figures we'd seen on the sky-line was a police search party, who saw our Verey signals and, after reaching us, they took us down the from the hills in cars to Alston village hospital. There it was discovered that 1 had come off worst, with a broken wrist and a badly gashed left arm. The hospital staff ministered to our medical needs, then we were billeted in separate accommodation kindly provided by the local people. I stayed with a doctor and was looked after very well.

"Two days later we were transported back to Leeming. On return I was asked for my W/T log book which I had fortunately salvaged and retained. I think they'd had me set up for the 'high jump', suspecting I had made an operating error. However, when they compared it with the ground operator's log book for the period, it was discovered he had given me QDR's (reciprocal bearings) instead of QDM's (homing bearings). The unfortunate operator ended up by being put on a 'Fizzer' (RAF Form 252 - charge sheet). I was given a fortnight's sick leave after which I was posted to 19 OTU, to instruct."

The Battle of the Barges continued on the night of September 21st/22nd with twenty-two Whitleys raiding Boulogne, but on the next night the targets were further afield when our crew was one of twelve sent to Berlin and an aluminium factory at Lauta. Our particular target was Lauta and we got into the air at 19.10 hours with Sergeant 'Slim' Summerville replacing George Dove as our tail-gunner. When we crossed the enemy coast the weather deteriorated into numerous electrical storms which caused severe interference to W/T reception and indeed caused W/T failure for two of our returning crews. We eventually reached the designated area and spent time searching for the target, but as we made our run-in we were surprised at the opposition. This was supposed to be a 'virgin' target deep in the heart of Germany. We had been under the impression that it wouldn't be so well defended, but I suppose that the No. 77 Squadron boys had already stirred them up before we got there. Despite the really hostile Flak defences we made two runs at 11,000 feet, hoping that at that altitude we would be outside the range of the light stuff. As we high-tailed it away from the target area Slim reported fires burning. We set course for home and the electrical storms increased to such an extent that it became very difficult to read the Morse through the crackling interference. I eventually managed to get my 'Bombs gone' signal back to Group and obtained a couple of fixes from Butser Hill, but it was 'one of those nights'. Shortly afterwards we were hit by lightning, which burnt off the trailing aerial at the end of the fairlead (the tube leading from the W/T position to the bottom of the fuselage which carried the aerial), which damaged my transmitter and receiver, and then the engine-driven generator packed in. However we scrambled into Linton-on-Ouse at 05.40 hours, having been airborne for ten and a half hours. As we turned off the flarepath at end of the landing run, one of the engines cut out - we'd run out of 'gravy'! In order to 'blood' new crews - known as 'Freshmen' - it was becoming the practice to send them on their first one or two trips to short-range targets. So on the following night, while twenty-four Whitleys from the other squadrons set out for Berlin, three of ours went on a 'nursery trip' to attack Calais docks. One was damaged by Flak but there were no casualties. The Berlin attackers faced severe difficulties, ten having to bomb alternative targets and those of No. 51 Squadron having to 'RAZZLE' the Black Forest area. The only casualty of the night was P5046 of No. 77 Squadron, flown by Pilot Officer A. W. Dunn, whose eventful and courageous operational career was brought to a tragic end. After bombing the 'Big City' they were forced to ditch in the North Sea. Their last reported position was eighty miles out from the English coast and a search by flying boats on the morning of September 24th located the dinghy, but unfortunately contact was soon lost. The dinghy was not seen again until the 26th, when HMS *Bedouin* found it with only two crew members aboard. Sergeant Riley was taken to the Royal Navy hospital at Rosyth, but Sergeant Allen was unfortunately dead in the dinghy. Of the others, there was no sign, emphasising the added dangers that crews faced on every raid.

Berlin was again attacked the following night, September 24th/5th, but only two of the nine aircraft attacked the primary. One, N1470 of No. 58 Squadron, crashed shortly after take-off from Linton-on-Ouse, killing Sergeant H. Cornish and two of his crew when the bombload blew up. Our squadron was detailed to raid power stations at Finkenheerd, near Frankfurt-on-Oder and we left Leeming at 18.40 hours. The cloud began to build up as we reached Germany, but we ploughed on, weaving in and out of the cloud and taking evasive action to prevent the German defences from plotting our course. On our ETA at Finkenheerd we were still flying in cloud so, after stooging unsuccessfully looking for a break, the skipper decided to go for our alternative target; Tempelhof airfield at Berlin. As we set course for the 'Big City' I recalled that on my last visit we'd dropped them a load of paper. This time the load would be more lethal.

We reached Berlin to find broken cloud, but were unable to pin-point the aerodrome. However, through the breaks the air-observer spotted and identified the main railway station which, it was decided, would be our target. At this time 1 think we must have been the only aircraft over Berlin and had the defences all to ourselves!

As we started the run-in, the bomb-aimer complained that cloud was partially obscuring the target and he might have to take us around for another run. He was at once advised that if he couldn't see railway lines, tram-lines would do. By now the Flak was coming up thick and fast. I was down by the flare chute, off- loading my incendiaries as fast as possible and although I couldn't see the Flak I was getting the results as it burst nearby.

The good advice must have improved our bomb-aimer's eyesight because he got rid of our load on one run. Then we left the area fast, heading into what we deluded ourselves was the safety of the clouds. We had got away unscathed and our good fortune continued because we were able to proceed unhindered across Germany and the North Sea. Then, with the aid of a few fixes and QDMs, we were able to land at West Raynham, our planned diversion airfield, at 05.20 hours. We had been airborne for ten hours and forty minutes, my longest operational flight to date.

On September 25th/26th twenty-one Whitleys attacked Berlin, the battleship *Scharnhorst* at Kiel and Antwerp docks without loss, while on the next night barges and docks at Le Havre were attacked by fifteen more. The following night, 27th/28th, only our squadron operated by sending twelve aircraft to bomb the port of Lorient. We were detailed, leaving base at 19.45 hours and it was a pleasant change not having to cross the North Sea and then spend nail-biting hours over the heavily defended German mainland, as we had been doing recently against targets well over six hundred miles from our bases.

We flew to the south coast down the corridor allocated to us by the Air Defence organisation, then across the Channel to the north-west corner of occupied France. For a change the weather was good and we proceeded down the coast to Lorient, which was easily identified. We bombed against slight opposition and as we left Slim reported fires burning around the target. We landed back at Leeming at 04.35 hours. I suppose that if any operation could be classified as easy then this was it.

Berlin and the Fokker factory at Amsterdam were selected as targets on September 28th/29th, plus 'RAZZLING'. The operations were carried without loss by twenty-two aircraft and the next night the target was switched to oil, when installations at Magdeburg and Hanover were attacked, eighteen Whitleys being despatched. One No. 77 Squadron crew attacked Minden as an alternative then, because of the bad weather, became 'temporarily uncertain of their position. Passing over a stretch of water mistakenly identified as the Zuider Zee, they headed inland and attacked what they assumed was an airfield in northern Holland, but was actually RAF Marham! Fortunately their navigation was equalled only by their marksmanship and no damage or casualties resulted.

Another crew, also from No. 77 Squadron, carried out a successful raid on Amsterdam, again as an alternative, starting a large fire at a coal depot and another four blazes in nearby installations. After leaving the target one engine failed, but they managed to scramble back over the North Sea, landing safely at Bircham Newton.

On the morning of September 30th, Squadron Leader Evans-Evans the Group Signals Officer - known as 'Evans Squared' by the disrespectful 'key-bashers' throughout 4 Group - paid us a visit. During his stay he came to our W/Tsection to have a chat with the boys and during that conversation asked us in turn how many operations we had carried out. When I told him I'd chalked up my fortieth three nights previously, he did a double-take and told me I should have been screened before now. He then contacted our squadron commander and told him that he proposed to get the Group Admin wheels in motion to have me posted without delay to one of the Whitley OTUs as an instructor.

I offered no objection, having matured enough during the past year to realise that you can push your luck just so far. Besides, by now nearly all my old aircrew 'Oppos' with whom I had started operations had now left the squadron in one way or another! Also, according to the other WOP/AGs in the section, I was showing signs of becoming just a bit 'Flak happy'. However, any elation which the Squadron Leader's announcement might have caused was dampened later in the day when I was informed that I was required to fly on Ops. that night. I got the usual commiserations from my 'Oppos': 'If you can't take a joke etc.' and 'What's one more to an Ace like you?.

My morale dropped even further that night when our briefing revealed the target: The Reich Chancellery in Berlin! I tried to lift my flagging spirits by kidding myself that there's nothing like finishing on a high note, but I was then told that our skipper, Flying Officer Landale, had been injured. His place was to be taken by Flight Lieutenant D. G. Tomlinson, while Slim Summerville was being stood down and his place was to occupied by the Group Gunnery Officer Flight Lieutenant Clarke. All in all, it was a bit of a scratch crew, but at least I would be doing my last 'dice' with the 'higher paid help'.

I think I took a little longer with my preflight preparations, ensuring I missed nothing from the superstitious ritual - lucky coins, the lot. We took off in T4143 at 18.00 hours and by the time we reached the enemy coastline I'd regained some of my composure. However, as we passed to the south of Wilhelmshaven my complacency was disturbed when someone remarked 'They're knocking hell out of some poor so-and-so over there!' It did my confidence no good at all when I looked out my side window to see the aircraft in question held at the apex of a cone of searchlights, into which the Flak batteries were throwing everything they had. As I watched, I was sure I saw the stricken aircraft fall away in flames. My reaction was to turn up the volume of my '1082' and concentrate on my listening watch to take my mind off what I'd just seen.

Eventually we weaved our way to the 'Big City' where it was evident from the Searchlight and Flak activity that the reception committee was having a go at the early arrivals. By this time the bomb-aimer was map reading us to the target and preparing for the run-in. Meanwhile I was now back in the fuselage, ready to drop flares. After I'd dropped a couple, we began the run-in at 11,000 feet and I did my incendiary- dropping 'bit' to take my mind off the thuds and jolts of the exploding Flak. Eventually it was 'Bombs gone!' and we were away like Flynn, because by now the defences were really having a go at us - evident from the way Flight Lieutenant Clarke's voice rose in pitch as the Flak got close. All my lucky charms must have worked, because we got away without a scratch. Back at the W/T set, I sent the 'Bombs gone' signal and listened as the other WOP/AGs in our other aircraft did likewise. I was pleased to hear Blondie Nicholson's signal from T4130 at 23.00 hours, but my pleasure was short-lived because I was to learn later that shortly afterwards T4130 had been shot down. Sergeant V. Snell and his second pilot were killed when the Whitley fell to the guns of Oberleutnant Werner Streib of 2 *Staffel, Nachtjagdgeschwader* 1 over Badbergen, some twenty minutes later.

As can be imagined, the homeward flight seemed interminable, but I kept busy on the W/T as we headed back across the North Sea to our scheduled diversion airfield of Watton. When we arrived, the trailing aerial was never wound in faster or my X195 (landing signal) sent with greater pleasure! After de-briefing, a meal and a lapse of a few hours, we returned to Leeming where we learned that in addition to the loss of Sergeant Snell's aircraft, we had also lost N1483. This crew had navigation problems on return and Flying Officer L. D. Wood ditched in the Irish (yes, Irish) Sea. Fortunately the crew were rescued by a trawler and landed at Holyhead.

Squadron Leader Evans-Evans fulfilled his promise on October 3rd, when I was posted to Kinloss to instruct with 19 OTU.

So ended my first tour of forty-one operations, carried out during a period when the chances of surviving thirty were calculated as between forty and fifty per cent. I can only conclude that someone 'up there' was keeping watch and had decided that at nineteen I still had a lot more flying to do.

Summary of operations by 4 Group
lst - 31st September 1940

lst-2nd. Bombing - Industrial Targets at Milan, Turin, Munich and South-East Germany.

51 Sqn. Three a/c to Fiat works Turin. All bombed. Three a/c to Munich marshalling yards. All bombed.

78 Sqn. Three a/c to Milan. One bombed primary, one bombed French airfield. Two a/c to BMW works at Munich. One bombed primary, one bombed alternative.

2nd-3rd. Bombing - Industrial Targets at Genoa - Oil Plant at Frankfurt.

58 Sqn. Six a/c to Genoa. Five got off, three bombed primary, two bombed alternatives. Two ditched on return, crews safe.

77 Sqn. Six a/c to Frankfurt. Five got off, all bombed.

3th-4th. Bombing - Oil Plant at Berlin.

10 Sqn. Seven a/c. All bombed. One damaged by Flak and one crashed on return, crew safe.

4th-5th. Bombing - Power Station at Berlin - Oil Tanks at Magdeburg-'Razling'.

51 Sqn. Six a/c to Berlin. Five bombed and 'razzled', one FTR.

78 Sqn. Six a/c to Magdeburg. Five bombed primary, one bombed Bremen.

5th-6th. Bombing - Oil Target at Regensburg - Fiat Works at Turin - 'Razling'.

58 Sqn. Bombing - Nine a/c to Regensburg. Five bombed primary, four bombed alternatives and Razzling.

77 Sqn. Six a/c. Five got off and bombed, claiming good results.

6th-7th. Bombing - Oil Target at Berlin.

10 Sqn. Five a/c. All bombed. Opposition severe, one FTR.

7th-8th. Bombing - Invasion Fleet at Ostend and Boulogne.

51 Sqn. Four a/c. Three got off but none bombed due to adverse weather. One crashed on return, crew safe.

78 Sqn. Three a/c. None bombed due to weather.

8th-9th. Bombing - Dockyards at Bremen - Invasion Fleet at Ostend.
10 Sqn. Six a/c to Ostend. Filthy weather, only one bombed. One crashed on return, crew safe.
58 Sqn. Three a/c to Ostend. None bombed due to weather. Six a/c to Bremen. One returned early, four bombed primary, one bombed an alternative.
77 Sqn. Two a/c to Ostend. None bombed due to weather. Nine a/c to Bremen. One returned early, seven bombed primary, one failed to bomb.

9th-10th. Bombing - Bremen Shipyards - Industrial Targets at Berlin.
51 Sqn. Nine a/c to Bremen. One returned early, six bombed primary. One badly damaged and ditched on return, four rescued, one drowned.
58 Sqn. Four a/c. Three bombed primary, one bombed Wesermunde.
78 Sqn. Four a/c to Berlin. Two bombed primary, two bombed alternatives. Three a/c to Bremen, all bombed successfully.

10th-11th. Bombing - Bremen Shipyards - Industrial Targets at Berlin.
58 Sqn. Six a/c to Bremen. Weather bad, all bombed alternatives. One FTR Four a/c to Berlin. All bombed. Very successful attack.
77 Sqn. Four a/c to Bremen. Three bombed primary, one bombed alternative. One damaged by Flak. Four a/c to Berlin. Two got off, both bombed primary and both hit by Flak. One FTR.

11th-12th. Bombing - Shipyards and Fuel Stocks at Bremen - Industrial Targets at Berlin.
10 Sqn. Seven a/c to Bremen. All bombed. One tail-gunner 'lost' over target.
51 Sqn. Four a/c to Berlin. All bombed primary, one damaged by Flak. Four a/c to Bremen. All bombed.
78 Sqn. Five a/c to Berlin. One returned early, two bombed primary, two bombed alternatives.

13th-14th. Bombing - Invasion Fleet at Calais and Dunkirk.
58 Sqn. Nine a/c to Dunkirk. All bombed, causing large fires.
77 Sqn. Nine a/c to Calais and Dunkirk. All bombed with good results.

14th-15th. Bombing - Invasion Fleet at Antwerp.
10 Sqn. Ten a/c. All bombed causing fires. One fighter seen, but did not attack. One ditched, crew rescued.

51 Sqn. Twelve a/c. Only one bombed due to severe weather and electrical storms.

78 Sqn. Eight a/c. None bombed, one FTR

15th-16th. Bombing - Invasion Fleet at Ostend and Dunkirk - Hamburg Docks - Industrial Targets at Berlin.

58 Sqn. Three a/c to Berlin. All bombed alternatives. Three a/c to Hamburg. All bombed alternatives. Three a/c to Ostend. All bombed.

77 Sqn. Bombing - Eight a/c to Dunkirk and Ostend. One bombed and strafed Ostend docks. Two a/c to Berlin, both bombed.

17th-18th. Bombing - Bismarck at Hamburg - Invasion Fleet at Zeebrugge and Ostend.

10 Sqn. Ten a/c. Nine got off, one returned early, nine bombed. Severe opposition at Hamburg.

51 Sqn. Ten a/c. One returned early, nine attacked Zeebrugge successfully.

78 Sqn. Eight a/c. Seven bombed primary, one bombed alternative. One damaged by flak, one man wounded.

18th-19th. Bombing - Invasion Fleet at Zeebrugge and Antwerp - Marshalling yards at Krefeld, Mannheim, Soest and Hamm.

58 Sqn. Eight a/c to Zeebrugge. All bombed. Three a/c to Krefeld. Two bombed. Three a/c to Hamm. Two bombed, one FTR.

77 Sqn. Thirteen a/c to Antwerp, Mannheim and Soest. Eleven bombed successfully. One FTR from Antwerp and one FTR from Mannheim.

19th-20th. Bombing - Marshalling Yards at Mannheim.

78 Sqn. Eight a/c. Five bombed primary, three bombed alternatives.

20th-21st. Bombing - Marshalling Yards at Hamm - Flushing Docks - Industrial Targets at Brussels, Krefeld, Mannheim and Osnabruck.

10 Sqn. Ten a/c to Hamm. All bombed, four damaged by Flak.

58 Sqn. Three a/c to Osnabruck. All bombed. Two a/c to Mannheim, both bombed. One a/c to Flushing. Bombed.

77 Sqn. Seven a/c to Krefeld, Brussels and Flushing. All bombed.

21st-22nd. Bombing - Invasion Fleet at Boulogne.

51 Sqn. Twelve a/c. All bombed. Opposition severe.

78 Sqn. Ten a/c. All bombed. Opposition severe.

22nd-23rd. Bombing - Aluminium Works at Lauta - Industrial Targets at Berlin.

10 Sqn. Four a/c to Lauta. All bombed, causing fires.

58 Sqn. Five a/c to Berlin. One returned early, three bombed primary, one bombed an alternative. Two a/c to Lauta, but failed to bomb due to weather.

77 Sqn. Three a/c to Lauta. All bombed.

23rd-24th. Bombing - Calais Docks - Industrial Targets at Berlin - 'Razzling'.

10 Sqn. Three a/c to Calais. All bombed.

51 Sqn. Nine a/c to Berlin. Primary obscured, all bombed alternatives.

77 Sqn. Six a/c to Berlin. One returned early, rest bombed with good results. One ditched on return, one man rescued.

78 Sqn. Nine a/c to Berlin. Seven bombed primary, two bombed alternatives at Wismar and Hamburg.

24th-25th. Bombing. Industrial Targets at Berlin and Finkenheerd.

10 Sqn. Twelve a/c to Finkenheerd. Primary obscured, alternatives bombed. Two a/c damaged.

58 Sqn. Seven a/c to Berlin. One crashed on take-off with three killed. Primary obscured, alternatives bombed.

77 Sqn. Two a/c to Berlin. Both bombed with good results.

25th-26th. Bombing - Scharnhorst at Kiel - Antwerp Docks - Power Station at Berlin.

51 Sqn. Eleven a/c to Berlin and Kiel. Five bombed Scharnhorst, two bombed Berlin, two bombed alternatives.

78 Sqn. Ten a/c. Four bombed Scharnhorst, three bombed Antwerp, three did not bomb.

26th-27th. Bombing - Invasion Fleet at Le Havre.

58 Sqn. Seven a/c. All bombed.

77 Sqn. Eight a/c. All bombed.

27th-28th. Bombing - Installation at Lorient Naval base.

10 Sqn. Twelve a/c. All bombed.

28th-29th. Bombing - Industrial Targets at Berlin - Fokker Aircraft Factory at Amsterdam-'Razling'.

51 Sqn. Twelve a/c. Eleven got off, six bombed Berlin, four bombed alternatives.

78 Sqn. Eight a/c to Berlin. One aborted, three bombed primary, two bombed alternatives, two failed to bomb.

29th-30th. Bombing - Oil Plants at Magdeburg and Hanover.

58 Sqn. Ten a/c to Magdeburg. Nine got off, four bombed primary with good results, one bombed an alternative, five failed to bomb.

77 Sqn. Ten a/c to Magdeburg and Hanover. One returned early, remainder bombed primaries or alternatives. One returned on one engine from Amsterdam.

30th-lst. Bombing - Reich Chancellery in Berlin.

10 Sqn. Ten a/c. All bombed. Opposition severe. One FTR, one ditched in Irish sea, crew saved.

Epilogue

In his book 'Out of the Blue', Wing Commander Laddie Lucas DSO, DFC, aptly sums up the first year of air operations:

> "The opening act of 1939/40 was as different in character from the closing operations of 1944/45 as the theatres in which the dramas were played out. The actors who moved across the stage in the first sixteen months of the war were learning their parts as they went along. They had no prompters in the wings. They were in front of the footlights and expected to say their lines. In terms of operational experience, it was one of the roughest periods of the war. The hazards were very great because the odds were so poor and because of the pioneering nature of the work. The aircrews and with them, the ground crews, were chucked in 'at the deep end'. They had to swim for it - or sink."

And so it was for we crews of Bomber Command. The first few months of the war revealed many deficiencies in our equipment and training. When the bombing war started, targetting was haphazard; too many targets for too few aircraft without adequate navigational and bombing aids. It is not surprising that subsequent investigations revealed that many claims of successful attacks had been exaggerated. Senior officers, who could have gained first hand knowledge of conditions and deficiencies, were prevented from doing so due to the restrictions imposed by Air Ministry which prevented them from participating in air operations. Thus improvements were slow in coming. They were unfortunately put in the position of 'leading from the back'.

It was not until February 1942, when Air Marshal A. T. Harris was appointed Air Officer Commanding-in-Chief Bomber Command, and later, in August 1942 when an organised 'pathfinding' force was organised, that things changed for the better and the bomber force started to realise its full potential.

In the meantime, during the years following 1940, 4 Group increased in strength with the addition of new squadrons and the faithful old Whitley was replaced by the four-engined Halifax.

Whitleys continued to operate with Bomber Command until 1942, carrying out their last Main Force raid against Ostend on April 19th/20th. However they were recalled from retirement for the Thousand Bomber attacks against Cologne and Essen on May 30th/31st and June 1st/2nd respectively.

Besides operating in the bomber rôle, Whitleys were selected for the development of our airborne forces, resulting in another 'first' when, on February 10th/11th 1941, No. 78 Squadron dropped Special

Air Service troops to destroy an aqueduct at Tragino, Italy (Operation Colossus). A year later, Wing Commander 'Percy' Pickard led No. 51 Squadron Whitleys to Bruneval, dropping paratroops to capture vital components of German radar apparatus.

Whitleys were also used by Coastal Command in the anti-submarine war and chalked up another 'first' when an aircraft of No. 502 Squadron sank U-206 in the first successful U-boat sinking without naval assistance. In 1943 No.10 OTU was loaned to Coastal Command and their Whitleys flew many anti-sub operations over Biscay, losing several crews but attacking a number of U-boats. One was sunk and several others damaged.

They were also the first 'heavy' aircraft to be used in clandestine operations by dropping agents and equipment to resistance groups on the continent, and were also used for glider towing. All in all, a very creditable performance and it is a source of regret that none of these versatile aircraft have been preserved for posterity.

When my Whitley tour ended on October 1st, 1940, I went to Kinloss as a wireless operator instructor, training replacements for the 4 Group squadrons . Thus I continued to fly in Whitleys until I volunteered for a second bomber tour. In July 1941 I was posted to No. 76 Squadron, the second Halifax unit to be formed, which was based at Middleton-St-George. I rejoined my original No. 10 Squadron skipper, Squadron Leader R. Bickford DFC. Unfortunately he was killed shortly afterwards when returning from a raid on Frankfurt on August 30th. Two engines failed at 2,000 feet over Finningley and although the crew baled out, he and his tail-gunner both perished (I was not a member of his crew at that time).

My second tour, during which I was awarded the Distinguished Flying Medal after completing another six raids, was curtailed in April 1942, when I was sent to the Electrical and Wireless School at Cranwell, where I successfully re-mustered as WOM/AG (wireless operator mechanic/air gunner) and was posted to Coastal Command. I converted onto Sunderland flying-boats and then joined No. 461 (Royal Australian Air Force) Squadron to do a third tour. This time it was daylight operations over the Bay of Biscay and I completed another thirty-four operational sorties between November 1942 and August 1943. This included the time (May to August 1943) when more U-boats were attacked and more air combats took place in the Biscay area than at any other time during World War II.

It was during this third tour that I again applied for pilot training. Throughout my service it had been my ambition to become a pilot, having always wanted to experience the ultimate satisfaction of solo flight. Having also learned early on that it was a pilot-dominated air force, I worked on the premise that, 'if you can't beat 'em, join 'em'. I had submitted applications previously which had been rejected for a variety of reasons: 'Apply when you've finished your tour', 'You're needed as an instructor' and 'Apply when you've finished your second tour'. However, my persistence, aided by the support I received from my Aussie sponsors, eventually paid off and I was accepted. At the end of August 1943 I was posted for initial training, followed by flying in Canada, which I successfully completed at the beginning of 1945, when I was also commissioned. The war ended before I was able to get back on operations, but I was able to stay in the Royal Air Force, flying as a pilot until December 1966, when I was invalided out on medical grounds.

So ended an eventful flying career spanning twenty-eight years, during which time I progressed from 'Tail-end Charlie', then 'Key-Basher' to 'Driver - airframe', surviving the war and later experiencing the interesting transition from piston-engines to jets. However, in retrospect the time during 1939-40, when we carried 'Bumph' and bombs to Berlin in our Whitleys, will always be an unforgettable memory.

Pilot Officer Cairns. After recovering in hospital following his crash-landing on return from bombing the invasion barges at Ostend on the night of 8/9 September 1940, he was posted to instruct at the Wellington OTU at Wellesbourne Mountford. During his spell instructing he participated in the first two 'Thousand Bomber Raids' on Cologne and Essen in May and June 1942. He returned to operations for a second 'tour' in 1943, this time with No. 429 (RCAF) Squadron. He was shot down on the night of 26/27 April, 1943, by a Bf110 nightfighter and crash landed his aircraft on an aerodrome near Bergen-nord, Holland. He and his crew were taken prisoner and he spent the remainder of the war in the infamous Stalag IIIB at Sagan, (from where the 'Great Escape' took place on the 24/25 March 1944, resulting in the murder of fifty RAF officers by the Gestapo).

Squadron Leader Ray Chance. After his harrowing experience of ditching in the North Sea during a raid on the enemy held airfield at Trondheim, Norway, on the night of 18/19 April 1940, he spent a considerable time in hospital. When he recovered he returned to operations with No. 21 Squadron in 2 Group, during its most lethal period. He survived and spent a spell at the Air Ministry as a Staff Officer. This was followed by postings to Bengal and Burma. He left the RAF at the end od hostilities and joined the legal profession. He was called to the Bar in 1958.

Sergeant James Deans. 'Dixie' was to achieve fame for his exploits and leadership while a prisoner-of-war, gaining the highest respect from both his fellow inmates and the Germans. At first he was held in Stalag Luft III, then Stalag Luft IV, where he was elected official PoW leader. Repatriated in 1945, he was appointed Member of the Order of the British Empire in recognition of his sterling work as a prisoner. Sadly, he died in 1989.

Sergeant George Dove. George did a second tour of bomber operations in 1943 with No. 101 Lancaster Squadron, during which he survived another incident for which he was awarded the Conspicuous Gallantry Medal. After the war he returned to Alston in 1953 to attempt to locate the Whitley crash site, but was frustrated by bad weather. However, a former Royal Observer Corps member, who had been on duty that night and had plotted their course, told him that they had heard the crash and on informing the police, had been told that no search would be attempted in such bad weather as: 'There would be no survivors, anyway'.

Flying Officer Henry. 'Enery' was tragically killed on 11th January 1941, in No. 35 Squadron's first Halifax fatal accident.

Sergeant Malcolm Lucas. Malcolm baled-out on the night of 5/6 June 1940, when a flare went on fire in his aircraft after taking off to bomb troops and transport in France. Four nights later he had a miraculous escape when his aircraft pranged into the bomb-dump at RAF Abingdon, on return from a raid on road and rail communications in France. He was then taken off active flying operations and he resumed his career as Sergeant Armourer. He stayed in the Armament Branch as an instructor until he was selected to train as an Air Traffic Controller. He completed the course successfully, was commissioned in February 1943, and served in the Air Traffic Branch until the end of hostilities. On his discharge from the RAF in

*Sergeant Malcolm Lucas,
Observer with No. 77
Squadron.*

January 1946, he joined the CAA as a Civil Air Traffic Controller.
He retired in December 1976, as Chief Examiner, in charge of CAA
Air Traffic Licencing.

Sergeant Mark Niman. Mark was to suffer two more crashes.
Exactly a month after his first crash, on October 14th/15th they ran
out of fuel whilst returning from Stettin and abandoned the Whitley
over Billingham, Northumberland. The third time came in July 1941.
After he had finished his bomber tour and was part of the crew of a
Handley-Page Harrow transport aircraft. He endured another ditching
whilst en-route from the UK to the Middle East, coming down in the
sea some twelve miles from Gibralter. The aircraft remained afloat
due to the bouyancy afforded by the empty fuel tanks. Motor launch
121 was sent out to pick them up and its commander attempted to
tow them in, but succeeded only in pulling both engines from their
mountings. The Harrow crew, out on the wings watching, found it all
highly amusing - until they realised that the aircraft was now
sinking! They transferred to a launch and the aircraft duly sank. It
transpired that the weekly consignment of servicemen's mail had
been aboard the Harrow, thus they were given a less than
sympathetic reception when they arrived at Gib'.

Mark Niman survived the war, and although in poor health, still retains the cheerful sense of humour which stood him in good stead during his adventures.

Pilot Officer Jim Verran. Jim completed his tour in April 1941 then, after a spell instructing with No. 19 (Whitley) OTU at Wellesbourne Mountford, he joined No. 9 (Lancaster) Squadron for a second tour which terminated abruptly on March 1st/2nd, 1943, in a mid-air collision over base on return from Berlin. A year later and just four months after leaving hospital he joined No. 83 (Pathfinder) Squadron, flying Lancasters on his third tour: 'Once is enough, two is pushing, but three is bloody greedy!'. On his last scheduled sortie of this tour he was shot down over the Danish coast by a Bf110 and, terribly injured, was captured together with his bomb-aimer. After the war he pursued a career in civil aviation.

Sergeant Don Witt. Don later joined No. 7 Stirling Squadron and became an outstanding and highly decorated Stirling pilot, eventually rising to the rank of Group Captain.

Glossary of Terms

AC - Aircraftman.

ACH/GD - Aircraft hand, general duties 'Dogsbody'.

Ack-Ack - Anti-aircraft gunfire.

AOC - Air Officer Commanding.

AOC-in-C - Air Officer Commanding-in-Chief.

ASTRO - Navigation using sextant bearings on known stars.

Best Blue - Airmen's No.1 uniform.

Bind - Inconvenience.

Bint - Arabic for woman.

Boffin - The service nickname for scientists engaged in developing new weapons.

Bog Trotter - Irishman.

Boost - Engine power.

Brocks Benefit - Firework display; term used by airmen to describe Flak.

Bumph - Derogatory term for propaganda leaflets and other paperwork.

Chance Light - Mobile floodlight used during night flying.

Char and Wads - Tea and NAAFI cakes.

Charpoy - Urdu for bed.

Chiefy - Flight Sergeant.

Cpl - Corporal.

D/F - Direction Finding.

DI - Daily Inspection.

Ditch - Land an aircraft on the sea in an emergency.

DR - Dead Reckoning, the basic method of air navigation.

Erks - Aircraftmen of ground crew status.

Fatigues - Imposed menial tasks such as peeling potatoes in the cookhouse.

Flak - German anti-aircraft gunfire (Flieger Abwehr Kanone).

Flg Off - Flying Officer.

Flt Lt - Flight Lieutenamt.

Flt Sgt - Flight Sergeant.

GEE - Electronic navigational aid.

Gen - Information.

Goldfish Club - Club for airmen who survived a ditching. The insignia was a 'Goldfish' badge worn on the sleeve.

Goosenecks - Name given to paraffin flares used during night flying. The can containing the fuel had a gooseneck-shaped spout.

Gravy - Slang term for aviation fuel.

Grp Capt. - Group Captain.

H/F - High Frequency.

Housewife - Term given to the sewing kit issued to other ranks.

H2S - Electronic navigational aid.

Irons - Knife, fork and spoon issued to other ranks.

Jankers - Term given to 'CB' (imposed punishment of confinement to barracks).

Kcs - Kilocycles per second (radio frequencies).

Key Basher - wireless operator.
Kite - aircraft.
LAC - Leading Aircraftman.
Mahogany Bomber Pilot - Derogatory name for staff officers who 'flew desks' at Headquarters.
M/F - Medium Frequency.
NAAFI - Navy, Army and Air Forces Institute.
OBOE - Electronic bombing aid.
Oggin - Service term for the ocean.
Old Sweat - Long serving serviceman.
Oppos - Friends, comrades.
OR's - Ranks other than commissioned.
Plt Off - Pilot Officer.
Prang - Aircraft crash.
Rapide - Twin-engined De Havilland biplane courier aircraft.
Screening - Being rested from operations.
Sgt - Sergeant.
Skipper - Aircraft captain.
Sparks - Wireless operators.
SNCO - Senior non-commissioned officer; Sergeant, Flight Sergeant and Warrant Officer.
Sprog - Inexperienced 'new boys'.
Sqn Ldr - Squadron Leader.
Swede Basher - Country bumpkin.
SYKO - Special signalling code.
Wapiti - Single-engined Westland biplane.
Whitehall Warrior - Derisive nickname for members of the government.
WOP/AG - Wireless operator/Air gunner.
W/T - Wireless Telegraphy by Morse Code.
W/T Fix - Aircraft position ascertained by cross bearings from W/T ground stations.
Wt Off - Warrant Officer.

4 Group Order of Battle

September 3rd, 1939

Dishforth. No. 10 Squadron. Whitley IV.
     Wing Commander W. E. Staton, MC, DFC.
Linton-on-Ouse. No. 51 Squadron. Whitley III.
     Wing Commander J. Silvester.
Linton-on-Ouse. No. 58 Squadron. Whitley III.
     Wing Commander J. Potter.
Driffield. No. 77 Squadron. Whitley III.
     Wing Commander J. Bradbury DFC.
Dishforth. No. 78 Squadron. Whitley IV.
     Wing Commander R. Harrison DFC, AFC (Non-operational)
Driffield. No. 102 Squadron. Whitley III.
     Wing Commander C. F. Toogood.

Losses and Casualties to Whitley Squadrons

Taken from Squadron Operation Record Books (Forms 540/541) held at Public Record Office, Bomber Command Loss Cards at Ministry of Defence Air Historical Branch and Accident Cards microfilmed at the Royal Air Force Museum archives.

3.9.39 58 Sqn K8969 Damaged. No details available.

5.9.40 58 Sqn K8990 Tailplane damaged.
FltSgt G. J. Ford and crew unhurt.

8/9.9.39 77 Sqn K8961 Hit Dewoitine D520 landing.
Flg Off G. L. Raphael and crew unhurt.

8/9.9.39 102 Sqn K8950 Missing from the Ruhr.
Shot down by flak over Thuringia. Sqn Ldr S. S. Murray, Plt Off A. B. Thompson, Sgt C. A. Hill, ACs S. A. Burry and P. F. Pacey all PoW.

8/9.9.39 102 Sqn K8985 Missing from the Ruhr.
Interned in Belgium. Flt Lt W. B. Cognan, Plt Off. A. W. Mack, Sgt G. J. Henry, Cpl S. R. Wood and AC A. Steer all interned. Released 16.12.39.

8/9.9.39 102 Sqn K8951 Damaged by Belgian fighter.
Flt Lt Connell and crew unhurt.

9.9.39 77 Sqn K8961 Damaged. No details available.

16.9.39 10 Sqn K9030 Belly landed at Dishforth.
Sgt L. A. Keast and crew unhurt.

19.9.39 51 Sqn K9001 Took off with controls locked, stalled and crashed.
Sgts B. Mullin, F. H. Griffiths and three unnamed aircrew killed.

30/1.10.39 10 Sqn K9027 Crashed near Bolton on return from the ruhr.
Flt Sgt H. G. Cattell, Sqn Ldr F. A. J. Pollock-Gore, ACs W. R. Irving and J. C. Fahy and Cpl E. Saunders all unhurt. Aircraft damaged.

1/2.10.39 10 Sqn K9018 Missing.
Flt Lt J. W. Allsop, Plt Off A. G. Salmon, ACs J. R. Bell and A. F.

Hill, LAC F. Ellison all believed lost at sea.

4.10.39 77 Sqn N1352 Collided with K8953 at dispersal.
Flg Off J. A. Meade and crew unhurt.

4.10.39 77 Sqn K8953 Unoccupied, hit by N1352.

4.10.39 77 Sqn N1355 Undercarriage collapsed landing at Driffield at night.
Sgt R. A. Bigger and crew unhurt.

9/10.9.39 58 Sqn K8965 Crashed on take-off from Rheims.
Sgt A. G. E. Dixon, Flg Off B. W. Currie, Sgt J. S. Cameron, ACs R. D. Fowlie and J. Thomas all unhurt. Aircraft burnt.

11.10.39 166 Sqn K7185 Overshot Abingdon.
Flt Lt G. M. Lindeman and crew unhurt. (1)

15.10.39 102 Sqn K8958 Crashed near Driffield.
Plt Off R. C. Bisset and crew safe. (2)

15/16.10.39 10 Sqn K9023 Force landed due to oil on the windscreen.
AC Donnelly hurt due to ventral turret remaining extended when landing. Flg Off R. Bickford and remainder of crew unhurt.

15/16.10.39 77 Sqn K8947 Missing from Frankfurt.
Flg Off R. Williams killed, Flg Off J. Tilsley, Sgt J. W. Lambert, Cpl A. R. Gunton and LAC E. E. Fletcher captured.

16.10.39 102 Sqn K8943 Overshot Aston Down on delivery flight.
Plt Off A. H. Hewitt and crew safe.

18.10.39 102 Sqn K8996 Stalled at 100 feet over Catterick.
Sgt H. J. Gaut and crew believed all killed.

18/19.10.39 10 Sqn —— Force landed at Amiens, crew unhurt.
24/25.10.39 77 Sqn N1358 Missing from Wilhelmshaven.
Plt Off P. E. W. Walker, Sgts R. A. Bigger and G. A. Burrell, ACs J. A, Topham and A. B. MacDonald all killed.

27/28.10.39 51 Sqn K8984 Abandoned over France on return from Munich.
Sgts T. W. Bowles, A. A. Emery, E. J. Barber, A. Griffin and AC R. Jackson all safe. Aircraft wrecked.

27/28.10.39 51 Sqn K9008 Crashed in France on return from Frankfurt.
Flt Sgt J. H. P. Wynston. Sgts D. C. Hyde, W. Foster, Cpl E. Short

and AC A. J. Heller all safe.

27/28.10.39 102 Sqn N1377:P Badly damaged by Flak. Plt Off K. N. Gray and crew unhurt.

31.10.39 51 Sqn K8984 Damaged. No details available.

31.10.39 51 Sqn K9008 Damaged. No details available.

6.11.39 51 Sqn K8938 Overshot Linton-on-Ouse on training flight.
Flg Off B. W. Hayward and crew safe.

6.11.39 166 Sqn K7203 Undershot Abingdon.
Plt Off R. H. Kewish and crew safe.

8.11.39 51 Sqn K9021 Belly landed at Linton-on-Ouse on delivery flight.
Flt Lt P. A. Gilchrist and crew safe.

8.11.39 97 Sqn K7225 Undershot Abingdon and crashed into houses.
Plt I. St. J. Beere and crew believed killed.

10/11.11.39 77 Sqn N1364 Crashed in France returning from the Ruhr.
Sqn Ldr J. A. Begg, Sgts R. Walsh, C. Thomas, LACs H. Taylor and H. Laybourne all killed. Aircraft wrecked.

26/27.11.39 102 Sqn N1381:M Damaged by lightning strike.
Flt Lt D. H. W. Owen and crew unhurt.

29.11.39 78 Sqn K9054 Overshot Linton-on-Ouse at night.
Sgt R. N. Peace and crew safe.

9.12.39 51 Sqn K8980 Hit K9042, taxiing at night at Dishforth.
Sgt J. W. Murray and crew safe.

9.12.39 51 Sqn K9042 Unoccupied, hit by K8980 at Dishforth.

12.12.39 102 Sqn N1369 Damaged in night taxiing accident at Driffield.
Sqn Ldr J. C. MacDonald and crew safe.

12/13.12.39 77 Sqn N1373 Damaged by Flak.
Flg Off J. A. Meade and crew unhurt.

17.12.39 102 Sqn N1383 Undershot Driffield at night.
Sqn Ldr R. G. Harman and crew safe.

18.12.39 97 Sqn K7260 Crashed on training flight.
Flg Off J. G. Howard and crew killed.

19.12.39 78 Sqn K9055 Night landing accident at Linton-on-Ouse.
Flg Off H. M. Selwyn and crew safe.

29.12.39 77 Sqn N1350 Landing accident at Linton-on-Ouse.
Flg Off J. A. Piddington and crew safe.

3.1.40 77 Sqn N1367 Damaged force landing near Fecamp, France.
Sqn Ldr J. B. Tait and crew safe.

4/5.1.40 10 Sqn K9020 Crashed at Dishforth on return from Bremen.
Flg Off V. R. Patterson, Sgt W. S. Hillary, ACs W. R. Armstrong, B.
L. Henry and Sgt H. J. Davis all unhurt.

10.1.40 102 Sqn N1385 Damaged in heavy landing at Driffield.
Plt Off A. W. Mack and crew safe.

11/12.1.40 102 Sqn N1420 Damaged in heavy landing at Driffield.
Plt Off J. J. McKay and crew safe.

2.1.40 58 Sqn K8964 Crashed at night. No details available.

1/2.1.40 10 Sqn K9026 Crashed at Dishforth on return from Berlin.
Sgt A. S. Johnson, Flt Lt P. J. Harrington, Sgt W. B. Lyma, LAC F.
P. McQuade and AC G. A. Chalmers safe.

3/4.3.40 10 Sqn K9022 Overshot Dishforth.
Sgt L. A. Keast and crew safe.

12.3.40 166 Sqn K8960 Crashed near Abingdon.
Plt Off R. B. Vaux and crew killed.

15.3.40 78 Sqn N1350 Damaged taxiing at Linton-on-Ouse.
Flg Off F. Aikens and crew safe.

19/20.3.40 51 Sqn K9043 Damaged by Flak.
LAC Birch, rear gunner, wounded. Flg Off G. Birch and remainder
of crew unhurt.

19/20.3.40 51 Sqn N1405 Missing from Sylt.
Flt Lt J. E. Baskerville, Plt Off E. O. Fennell, Sgt B. D. Shepperson,
LAC L. Close and AC W. G. Newton all killed.

25/26.3.40 51 Sqn K9024 Undershot Dishforth.
Sgt D. C. Hide and crew safe.

25/26.3.40 102 Sqn —— Damaged by Flak.
Sgt L. T. Langton and crew unhurt. (3)

25/26.3.40 102 Sqn N1379 Overshot landing at Dishforth.

Sqn Ldr R. G. Harman and crew unhurt.

27/28.3.40 77 Sqn N1357:H Missing from the Ruhr. Shot down at Pernis, Holland, by Dutch fighter.
Flg Offs T. J. Geach and W. P. Coppinger interned, Sgt J. E. Miller killed, LAC S. H. E. Caplin and AC R. B. Barrie interned. Internees released 10.5.40.

27/28.3.40 77 Sqn N1351 Missing from the Ruhr.
Flg Off J. R. J. Boardman PoW, Plt Off G. L. Norman killed, Sgt W. R. Taylor, LAC J. Masters and AC W. Cowie PoWs.

2.4.40 166 Sqn K8993 Damaged taxiing at Jurby.
Flg Off Hannigan and crew safe.

2/3.4.40 102 Sqn N1368 Overshot Driffield. Plt Off K. N. Gray and crew safe.

5/6.4.40 51 Sqn K9040 Ditched ten miles from Miford Haven on cross-country training flight.
Flt Lt F. O. Dickson, Flg Off Gould, Sgt R. G. Bruce, LAC E. M. Beynon and AC J. Boyd believed safe.

6/7.4.40 10 Sqn K9032 Crashed near Grimsby on return from the Ruhr.
Flg Off G. W. Prior, Sgts D. W. Green and B. M. Mathers, ACs B. L. Henry and A. G. Miller unhurt.

11/12.4.40 77 Sqn N1347 Ditched sixty miles from English coast returning from Denmark.
Flg Off G. E. Saddington, Plt Off C. R. Kebeler, Sgt J. R. Ibbotson, Cpl O. Haine and AC P. W. S. Chalmers presumed lost after a long search.

16/17.4.40 77 Sqn N1387 Crash landed by Captain near Granton-on-Spey after remainder of crew abandoned aircraft following operations over Vaernes.
Sqn Ldr M. H. Hastings, Flg Off J. A. Piddington, Sgt R. H. Burr, Sgt Wright and AC Pacey all unhurt.

17/18.4.40 58 Sqn N1460 Damaged taxiing at Linton-on-Ouse.
Flt Lt K. B. F. Smith and crew safe.

18/19.4.40 77 Sqn N1352:B Crashed into North Sea returning from Trondheim.
Flt Lt R. Chance resceued, Plt Off R. Hall drowned, Sgt Tindall,

223

LAC O'Brien and AC Douglas rescued.

20/21.4.40 51 Sqn N1418 Damaged force landing in field due to engine failure.
Sqn Ldr G. P. Marvin and crew safe.

22/23.4.40 51 Sqn K9043 Missing from Aaborg.
Flg Off J. R. Birch, Sgts L. A. Compton, and H. Jackson, Cpl J. C. McIntyre and AC N. A. Young all killed.

23/24.4.40 51 Sqn K9049 Missing from Oslo.
Flg Offs T. K. Milne and B. W. Hayward, Sgt J. B. Ritchie, AC F. Hargreaves and LAC A. W. G. Lynne all PoW.

24/25.4.40 102 Sqn N1383 Missing from Aalborg.
Flt Off O. G. Horrigan killed, Sgt V. Barr PoW, Sgts J. F. Hayes and N. Haithwaite and AC C. C. Whitley killed.

25.4.40 78 Sqn K9050 Tyre burst on take-off from Brackley LG.
Sgt D. A. Rix and crew safe.

29/30.4.40 102 Sqn N1421 Missing from Fornebu.
Flg Off K. H. P. Murphy, Sgt B. G. Warner and J. F. Graham and Cpl D. McGee PoW, LAC J. Elwood killed.

30/1.5.40 58 Sqn N1465 Missing from Stavanger.
Sgts C. R. Heayes, B. Tomlinson, H. A. Peel, Cpl P. H. Ditmas and AC D. Robertson killed.

30/1.5.40 51 Sqn K9039 Crashed at Burnside Fell on return from Fornebu.
Plt Off E. Cotton injured, Plt Off E. Gilmour and Sgt W. R. Coveney died, ACs P. D. Salmon and H. Maylin injured.

1.5.40 102 Sqn N1500 Crashed near Inch on transit from Kinloss to Driffield.
Plt Off K. N. Gray, Sgt J. H. Hopper Sgt F. J. Bass, AC G. Main, AC H. Buttery, AC J. A. Hewitt, AC F. Wallwork, AC A. H. W. Hart; 5 killed, 2 died of injuries, 1 injured.

1/2.5.40 51 Sqn N1406 Abandoned over Easingwold on return from Fornebu.
Sqn Ldr G. P. Marvin, Plt Off A. J. Oettle, Sgt J. Brisbane, LAC Fisher safe. AC Hepburn died of injuries.

11/12.5.40 51 Sqn N1407 Damaged by Flak.
Sqn Ldr P. A. Gilchrist and crew unhurt.

11/12.5.40 77 Sqn N1366 Missing from Munchen-Gladbach.
Flg Off T. H. Parrott killed, Flg Off D. Blue PoW, Sgt T. T.
Aitchison, LAC T. Poad and AC T. Jones killed.

11/12.5.40 102 Sqn N1386: P Damaged by Flak.
Flt Lt D. W. H. Owen and crew unhurt.

11/12.5.40 102 Sqn N1375: N Damaged by Flak.
Flt Sgt E. L. G. Hall and crew unhurt.

11/12.5.40 102 Sqn N1381 Crashed landing at Driffield.
Plt Off J. J. McKay and crew safe.

15/16.5.40 58 Sqn N1470: J Damaged by Flak.
Sqn Ldr Hallam and crew unhurt.

17/18.5.40 10 Sqn P4957 Crashed on take-off from Dishforth on sortie to Bremen.
Sqn Ldr P. Hanafin, Sgt D. W. Green, Sgt J. Shaw, LAC J.
Thompson and AC S. Oldridge unhurt.

17/18.5.40 10 Sqn P4952 Damaged by Flak.
Wg Cdr W. E. Staton and crew unhurt.

17/18.5.40 10 Sqn P4956 Damaged by Flak.
Sgt A. S. Johnson and crew unhurt.

17/18.5.40 10 Sqn P4967: J Badly damaged by Flak.
Sqn Ldr R. Bickford and crew unhurt.

17/18.5.40 10 Sqn P4961 Damaged by Flak
Sgt McCoubrey and crew unhurt.

17/18.5.40 10 Sqn P4963 Damaged by Flak.
Flt Lt A. S. Phillips and crew unhurt.

17/18.5.40 10 Sqn —- Damaged by Flak, no casualties.(4)

17/18.5.40 51 Sqn N1414 Damaged by Flak.
Flt Lt J. B. Tait and crew unhurt.

18/19.5.40 77 Sqn N1388 Shot down by Bfl10 off Holland and ditched.
Flt Lt G. L. Raphael, Plt Off R. P. Brayne, Sgt Prescott, LAC Storey
and AC Parkes all rescued.

19.5.40 10 Sqn P4964 Undershot Dishforth.
Plt Off R. J. Warren and crew safe.

19.5.40 58 Sqn N1462 Heavy landing at Linton-on-Ouse.

Sgt J. B. Jones and crew safe.

19/20.5.40 77 Sqn N1348 Badly damaged by Flak.
Plt Off T. G. Mahaddie and crew unhurt.

19/20.5.40 102 Sqn N1417 Missing from Duisburg.
Flt Lt W. G. G. Cognan killed, Plt Off L. Miller PoW, Sgt K. V. Thrift killed, LAC J. R. Nicholson and AC E. H. Bros PoW.

19/20.5.40 102 Sqn N1376 Missing from Gelsenkirchen.
Flt Sgt E. L. G. Hall, Plt Off J. T. Glover Sgt D. L. Dick, LAC McCutcheon and AC Murray all PoW.

20/21.5.40 77 Sqn N1384 Missing from Catillon. Crew abandoned aircraft near Amiens.
Flg Off D. D. Pryde and Plt Off A. W. Dunn returned, Sgt A. C. Thompson PoW, ACs T. B. Kenny and F. Crawford returned.

20/21.5.40 10 Sqn N1380 Missing from Oise bridges.
Flt Lt D. H. W. Owen, Plt Off D. F. S. Holbrook, Sgt D. H. J. Barrett, LAC R. J. Newberry and AC M. D. Dolan all killed.

20/21.5.40 102 Sqn N1528 Crashed in France.
Plt Offs G. H. Womersley and R. F. Beauclair, Sgt J. Derbyshire and ACs H. F. Hurt and A. Sedgeley all returned.

21/22.5.40 51 Sqn P4980 Missing from Rheydt.
Sgt T. W. Bowles (died as PoW), Sgt G. Raper, Sgt F. C. Collard, LAC L, J. R. Barber and AC J. E. W. Stainer all PoW.

23/24.5.40 58 Sqn N1361 Missing from La Capelle.
Plt Off I. L. McLaren killed, Sgts J. R. Mirfin, J. Buckfield, LAC J. Spencer and AC H. Wilkinson PoW.

23/24.5.40 102 Sqn N1499 Damaged by Flak.
Sgt S. E. Masham and crew unhurt.

24/25.5.40 10 Sqn P4958 Damaged by Flak.
Flg Off Peterson and crew unhurt.

24/25.5.40 58 Sqn N1427 Damaged by Flak.
Sqn Ldr J. S. Bartlett and crew unhurt.

25/26.5.40 102 Sqn N1420: L Crashed on return.
Sgt J. J. Gale and crew safe.

25/26.5.40 102 Sqn N1524: O Damaged by Flak.
Plt Off W. C. McArthur and crew unhurt.

27/28.5.40 58 Sqn N1436: F Damaged by Flak.
Flt Sgt L. F. East and crew unhurt.

27/28.5.40 58 Sqn N1466: G Damaged by Flak.
Sgt A. G. E. Dixon and crew unhurt.

28/29.5.40 77 Sqn N1432 Missing from Hirson-Avesnes.
Plt Off T, J. Geach, Sgts L. J. Brookes and C. H. Butler, and ACs A. Fryer and K. C. Chatfield all killed.

2/3.6.40 10 Sqn P4962 Damaged by Flak.
AC Cornforth, gunner, wounded. Sqn Ldr R. Bickford and remainder of crew unhurt.

2/3.6.40 77 Sqn N1356 Damaged by Flak, two aircrew wounded.
Sqn Ldr Tomlin and rest of crew unhurt. (5)

3/4.6.40 10 Sqn P4963 Crashed at Battisford on return from Hamburg.
Flt Lt A. S. Phillips, Flg Off G. L. C, Bagshaw, Sgt D. Donald, Sgt J. B. Nicholson, Plt Off A. H. Fields killed.

3/4.6.40 77 Sqn N1410 Crashed landing at Driffield.
Flt Lt J. A. Crockett and crew safe.

4/5.6.40 77 Sqn N1522 Abandoned over Abbeville on sortie to Gelsenkirchen.
Plt Off A. C. Meigh, Sgts W. G. Best and M. A. Oliver, LAC V. G. Allen and AC D. V. Browne all PoW.

5/6.5.40 77 Sqn N1476 Abandoned by four crew when flare ignited in fuselage, landed by captain at Finningley.
Plt Off A. W. Dunn, Plt Off C. J. D. Montague, Sgts M. Lucas, Kennedy and Martin unhurt.

8.6.40 77 Sqn N1356 Crashed at Jurby due to burst tyre.
Sgt T. E. Coogan and crew safe.

8/9.6.40 10 Sqn P4962 Crashed on take-off from Dishforth on sortie to Essen.
Sqn Ldr R. Bickford, Sgt H. G. Howard, Sgt R. N. Lown, Sgt J. W. Stephenson, LAC H. V. Seed unhurt.

9/10.6.40 51 Sqn N1414 Damaged by Flak.
Sgt McNeill, tail gunner, wounded. Sqn Ldr J. B. Tait and remainder of crew unhurt.

9/10.6.40 77 Sqn N1372 Crashed at Abingdon on return from Somme area. Aircraft burnt.
Plt Off A. W.Dunn, Plt Off C. J. D. Montague, Sgt M. Lucas, Sgt Kennedy, Sgt Martin safe.

11/12.6.40 10 Sqn P4954 Missing from Abbeville.
Sgt L. A. Keast, Plt Off D. F. Braham. Sgts J. J. Myers and J. M. Black and LAC R. R. H. Nuttall all killed.

11/12.6.40 77 Sqn N1340 Missing from Turin.
Sgt N. M. Songest, Sgt D. H. J. Budden, Sgt A. Findlay, Sgt R. C. Astbury, Sgt E. Ombler.

12/13.6.40 58 Sqn N1427:K Damaged by Flak.
Sqn Ldr J. S. Bartlett and crew unhurt.

14/15.6.40 77 Sqn N1371 Damaged by Flak.
Wg Cdr J. C. MacDonald and crew unhurt.

17/18.6.40 58 Sqn N1463 Missing from Gelsenkirchen.
Flt Sgt G. Ford, killed, Sgt H. P. McGuire, Sgt E. Jones-Robertson, Sgt A. E. Furze, Sgt F. S. Stanley PoW.

18/19.6.40 58 Sqn N1460 Missing from Dusseldorf.
Plt Offs J. T. McInnes and C. N. Buist and Sgts M. L. Dent, L. Whittle and C. F. McKay all killed.

18/19.6.40 77 Sqn N1499 Missing from Bottrop.
Sgts S. E. Masham, C. M. Clayton, D. W. Dawson, H. A. F. Giblin and C. A. Hanlon all killed.

19/20.6.40 10 Sqn P4960 Crashed at Ampton Park on return from Ludwigshaven.
Flg Off H. V. Smith kulled. Plt Off R. H. Thomas, Sgt N. J. Godfrey, Sgt L. Roberts, LAC A.Cowie safe.

19/20.6.40 77 Sqn N1476 Ditched off Hastings on return from Wanne-Eickel.
Plt Offs A. W. Dunn and.C. J. D. Montague and Sgts B. L. Saville and J. M. Dawson and Plt Off Watt all safe, one wounded.

19/20.6.40 77 Sqn N1371 Damaged by Flak.
Flt Lt D. D. Pryde and crew unhurt.

20/21.6.40 58 Sqn N1442 Missing from Essen.
Flg Off G. E. Walker, Plt Off J. Plant and Sgrs R. R. Schofield, C. H. Neary and H. R. Holmes all PoW.

20/21.6.40 102 Sqn N1375:N Damaged by Flak and belly landed at Manston.
Plt Off W. C. McArthur and crew safe.

23.6.40 51 Sqn P4971 Belly landed at Shire Bridge, Newark due to engine failure.
Sgt H. J. Fitz and crew safe.

26/27.6.40 58 Sqn N1355 Force landed after three crew baled out.
Flt Sgt Trewin and crew unhurt.

27/28.6.40 51 Sqn P4934 Damaged by Flak.
Flt Sgt Deacon and crew unhurt.

28/29.6.40 10 Sqn P4965 Damaged by Flak.
Plt Off H. G. Cattell and crew unhurt.

28/29.6.40 10 Sqn P4955 Damaged by Flak.
Flg Off W. M. Nixon and crew unhurt.

28/29.6.40 58 Sqn P4951 Hit by own AA gunfire, then forced down by Spitfires.
Flt Lt F. Aikens and crew unhurt.

29/30.6.40 77 Sqn P4948 Missing from Essen.
Sqn Ldr M. Hastings, Plt Off P. J. Gard and Sgts A. J. Davison, H. A. Storey and Plt Off R. F. Lumb killed.

1/2.7.40 58 Sqn N1461 Missing from Kiel.
Plt Off C. J. Jones, Flg Off L. H. McFarlane, and Sgts D. Leishman and H. E. A. Craven PoW, Sgt Caldwell killed.

2/3.7.40 10 Sqn P4957 Damaged by Flak.
Sqn Ldr P. Hanafin and crew unhurt.

6/7.7.40 102 Sqn N1523 Missing from Kiel.
Plt Off J. M. Lewis (died as PoW), Plt Off D. F. M. McKarness, Sgts J. Fisk, L. Askam and S. Fieldhouse PoW.

7.7.40 77 Sqn N1390 Damaged in heavy landing at Driffield.
Sqn Ldr G. T. Jarman and crew safe.

8/9.7.40 10 Sqn N1496 Missing from Kiel.
Flt Lt D. A. Ffrench-Mullen, Plt Off W. A. K. Carr, Sgts P. R. Donaldson and J. P. Atkinson and AC A. G. W. Miller PoW.

8/9.7.40 10 Sqn P4955 Damaged by Flak.

7777

Plt Off W. M. Nixon and crew unhurt

8/9.7.40 51 Sqn P4958 Damaged by Flak over Eckernforde.
Sqn Ldr C. Whitworth wounded.

8/9.7.40 51 Sqn P4974 Damaged by Flak.
Flg Off A. J. Oettle and crew unhurt.

11/12.7.40 58 Sqn N1424 Missing from Leverkusen.
Sgts F. F. Young, D. B. Hopes, L. Isherwood, B. M. Bennett and N. Emerson killed.

12/13.7.40 102 Sqn N1502 Hit by Flak and ditched off Cromer returning from Emden.
Sgt L. T. Langton, S/L C.S.Byram, and Sgts C. P. Coad, G. Gibson and C. Wood rescued.

13/14.7.40 51 Sqn P4969 Damaged by Flak.
Flg Off Lane and crew unhurt.

13/14.7.40 77 Sqn N1365 Badly damaged by Flak and force landed at Martlesham after three crew abandoned aircraft.
Flg Off J. A. Piddington and crew safe.

13/14.7.40 77 Sqn N1521 Badly damaged by Flak and force landed at Duxford.
Plt Off McGregor and crew unhurt.

19/20.7.40 51 Sqn P5007 Missing from Gelsenkirchen.
FltLt S. E. F. Curry and Sgt A. J. Harris killed, Sgt G. R. Hunter PoW, Sgts J. Tansley and R. N. Lewis killed.

19/20.7.40 102 Sqn N1379 Damaged by Flak.
Sgt R. S. Williams and crew unhurt.

20/21.7.40 10 Sqn P4952 Damaged by Flak.
Flg Off G. W. Prior and crew unhurt.

20/21.7.40 10 Sqn N1497 Damaged by Flak.
Sgt D. W. Green and crew unhurt.

20/21.7.40 10 Sqn P4946 Damaged by Flak.
Plt Off A. W. Somerville and crew unhurt.

20/21.7.40 58 Sqn N1438 Damaged by Flak.
Plt Off L. Crooks and crew unhurt.

21/22.7.40 78 Sqn N1487 Missing from Hamm.

Sgts V. C. Monkhouse, C. G. Hill, N. H. Burton, L. McCrorie and J. Sulter all killed.

22/23.7.40 58 Sqn R1472 Missing from Paderborn.
Sgt J. B. Jones, Plt Off J. D. Smith, Sgts J. L. Candlish, J. K. Easton and E. Hill all killed.

23/24.7.40 77 Sqn N1371 Badly damaged by Flak and returned on one engine. Force-landed at Bircham Newton.
Flg Off J. A. Piddington and crew unhurt.

26/27.7.40 102 Sqn N1377 Missing from Manheim. Crashed in Holland.
Plt Offs R. F. Beauclair, J. C. W. Bushell, Sgts E. A. Galloway, G. Wood and K. J. Read all PoW.

27/28.7.40 10 OUT N1503 Damaged by Flak. Crew unhurt. (6)

30.7.40 77 Sqn N1367 Damaged taxiing at Bircham Newton.
Flg Off F. Burbridge and crew safe.

3/4.8.40 77 Sqn N1435 Force landed near Saxon Wold on operations.
Flg Off W. A. Sten and crew safe.

3/4.8.40 77 Sqn N1474 Force landed at Flamborough Head on operations.
Plt Off M. R. Brownlie and crew safe.

3/4.8.40 78 Sqn P4941 Force landed near Pickering, Yorks on return from Dusseldorf.
Flg Off D. S. Robertson, Plt Off Stedman, Sgts Collinge and Barton and Flt Lt McLeod unhurt. Aircraft severely damaged.

5.8.40 58 Sqn N1470 Damaged taxiing at Linton-on-Ouse on night operations.
Sqn Ldr Hallam and crew safe.

5/6.8.40 10 Sqn ---- Damaged by Flak.
Flg Off G. W. Prior and crew unhurt.

5/6.8.40 10 Sqn ---- Damaged by Flak, no casualties.

5/6.8.40 51 Sqn P4970 Force landed at Spurn Point.
Sgt J. M. Kearney and crew unhurt.

9/10.8.40 78 Sqn P4996 Damaged by Flak.
Flt Lt V. R. Paterson and crew unhurt.

10/11.8.40 58 Sqn N1436 Crashed landing at Hemswell on operations.
Plt Offs L. Crooks and O'Duffy, Sgts Parkes and Jesse and Plt Off
A. C. Fennell all unhurt.

11/12.8.40 10 Sqn P5018 Damaged by Flak.
Sgt Towell and crew unhurt.

11/12.8.40 10 Sqn P4961 Damaged by Flak.
Flg Off A. W. Somerville and crew unhurt.

11/12.8.40 10 Sqn —- Damaged by Flak.
Flt Lt G. L. Raphael and crew unhurt.

11/12,8.40 10 Sqn —- Damaged by Flak, no casualties.

11/12.8.40 51 Sqn P4983 Missing from Gelsenkirchen.
Sgts J. M. Kearney, A. E. Bowes, F. J. C. Brown, W. H. Mercer and
E. H. Platts all PoW.

12/13.8.40 78 Sqn N1485 Damaged by Flak.
Plt Off D. S. Robertson and crew unhurt.

12/13.8.40 78 Sqn P4950 Damaged by Flak
Flt Sgt L. F. East and crew unhurt.

13/14.8.40 10 Sqn P4965 Damaged by fighter over Turin and ditched off Lympne.
Plt Off E. I. Parsons DFC and Sgt A. N. Campion missing, Sgts W.
Chamberlain, J. R. Marshall M. M. Sharpe rescued.

13/14.8.40 51 Sqn P4987 Damaged by Flak.
Flt Lt Bradley and crew unhurt.

13/14.8.40 58 Sqn P5003 Force landed at Ifield, Sussex, on night operations.
Sgt C. D. Boothby and crew safe.

14/15.8.40 51 Sqn P4982 Hit balloon cable at Slough and crashed.
Flg Off S. P. Swenson and Sgts A. E. K. Dawson, J. B. O'Brien, R.
A. W. Tait and L. P. Stubberfield all killed.

14/15.8.40 77 Sqn P5044 Hit balloon cable near Eastleigh and crashed.
Flg Off W. A. Stenhouse, Plt Off R. B. MacGregor and Sgts C. L. G.
Hood, J. Burrows H. Davies all killed.

15/16.8.40 10 Sqn N1497 Missing from Turin. Hit by Flak in target area, Crew baled out over the Alps.

Sgt D. W. Green PoW, F/O K. H. Higson killed, Sgts H. J. Davis
and A. Millington and Flg Off A. E. V. Oliver PoW.

**16/17.8.40 10 Sqn P4955: G Missing from Jena, crashed near
Zeugenbergen.**
Plt Off W. M. Nixon, Flg Off P. G. Whitby and Sgts H. W. Bradley,
A. W. Somerville and E. R. Holmes PoW.

16/17.8.40 51 Sqn P4986 Missing from Bohlen.
Flt Lt J. S. Scott and Sgts F. A. Beale, R. W. P. Clarke, P. D.
Salmon and H. Haggett all killed.

16/17.8.40 102 Sqn N1382: A Missing from Augsburg.
Plt Off M. H. Rogers and Sgts M. W. T. Pollard, S. G. Jermond, J.
Patterson and W. F. Haywood all killed.

**19/20.8.40 51 Sqn P4968 Missing from Schornewitz, force-landed in
Holland.**
Flg Off P. G. Brodie, Plt Off T. F. S. Johnson and Sgts R. Entwistle,
T. P. White and W. A. Kelham PoW.

20.8.40 77 Sqn N1335 Undershot Cottam LG.
Sgt J. W. Ward and crew safe.

**24/25.8.40 77 Sqn N1473 Missing from Augsburg, crashed SE
Haarlem.**
Plt Off C. J. D. Montagu DFC, and Sgts J. W. Ward, R. T. Penny, A.
F. Webber and E. F. Clarke all killed.

26/27.8.40 10 Sqn P4990 Missing from Milan. Crashed in Italy.
Sgt H. G. H. Howard, Plt Off. J. H. K. Parvin and Sgts N. R.
Johnston, J. W. Stephenson and H. Carter lost, fates not known.

26/27.8.40 77 Sqn N1390 Damaged landing at Abingdon.
Plt Off A. W. Dunn and crew unhurt.

**28/29.8.40 102 Sqn N1489 Hit hill at Silsden Moor on cross-country
training flight.**
Sgt N. K. Bott, Plt Off A. W. Fletcher, Sgt G. W. Harrison and Sgt
A. Steele killed. Sgt L. G. Smalley severely injured.

**30/31.8.40 58 Sqn P5002 Abandoned over England, aircraft crashed
at sea.**
Plt Offs N. O. Clements and R. A. Hadley, Sgt I. A. Zamek and Plt
Off R. F. Williams rescued, Sgt M. Hill missing.

2/3.9.40 77 Sqn P5049 Belly landed near Finningley on operations.

Plt Off M. R. Brownlie and crew safe.

2/3.9.40 58 Sqn Nl459: A Ditched 15 rniles off Harwich out of fuel.
Flt Sgt D. H. A. Moore, Plt Off P. C. Elliott and Sgts J. F. Craig, M.
R. Harvey and R. E. Connor rescued by HMS Pintail.

2/3.9.40 58 Sqn Nl427: K Ditched off Margate.
Sqn Ldr J. S. Bartlett and Sgts F. M. Kerr, Coubrough, Plt Off J. L.
Mitchell and Sgt Caryll de Tilkin rowed ashore in dinghy.

3/4.9.40 10 Sqn P4967 Belly landed at Nether Stilton, near Northaller-ton on return from Berlin.
Flt Lt D. G. Tomlinson, Plt Off K. D. Brant and Sgts W. O. Walters
P. Hughes and A. McIntosh unhurt.

3/4.9.40 10 Sqn P4944 Damaged by Flak.
Wg Cdr S. Bufton and crew unhurt.

3/4.9.40 51 Sqn P5011 Crashed on take-off from Dishforth on operations.
Sgt J. P. Wilson and crew injured.

4/5.9.40 51 Sqn P4973 Missing from Berlin, ditched off Holland.
Plt Off J. M. Taylor PoW, Sgt M. H. Jones drowned, Sgts V. B.
Housego, H. Maylin and M. F. Johnson PoW.

6/7.9.40 10 Sqn P4935 Missing from Berlin.
Plt Offs R. H. Thomas and D. J. A. Stevens and Sgts R. Hilton, H.
V. Seed B. W. Neville killed.

7/8.9.40 51 Sqn Nl414 Crashed near Wells, Norfolk on return from Boulogne. Aircraft wrecked.
Sqn Ldr J. B. Tait, Plt Off Davies and Sgts Gray, Cresswell and
Short all unhurt.

8.9.40 51 Sqn P4981 Crashed on landing at Dishforth.
Sgt A. R. Camell and crew safe.

8/9.9.40 10 Sqn P5094 Overshot Leeming on return from Ostend. Aircraft burnt.
Plt Off J. C. Cairns injured, Sgt V. Snell, Plt Off F. R. Goddard and
Sgts R. E. Nicholson and A. S. Shand unhurt.

8/9.9.40 58 Sqn P4951 Undershot Linton-on-Ouse on operations.
Sgt W. T. Christie and crew safe.

9/10.9.40 51 Sqn P5021 Ditched 120 miles off Firth of Forth on return

from Bremen.
Plt Off Millsom and Sgt Brook rescued, Sgt W. G. McAllister killed,
Sgt Young and Plt Off Careless rescued.

9/10.9. 40 78 Sqn N1490 Crashed landing at Linton-on-Ouse on
operations.
Plt Off C. S. Robson and crew safe.

10/11.9. 40 77 Sqn P5042:K Missing from Berlin. Crashed at
Hardenburg, Holland.
Sgts J. A. G. Deans, J. B. Clarke, H. J. Agnew, H. Parkes and F. A.
Hill all PoW.

10/11.9. 40 77 Sqn N1431 Crashed landing at Linton-on-Ouse.
Plt Off P. E. Eldridge and crew safe.

10/11.9. 40 77 Sqn P5046:0 Damaged by Flak.
Plt Off A. W. Dunn and crew unhurt.

10/11.9. 40 77 Sqn N1420 Damaged in action, believed by Flak.
Sgt T. E. Coogan and crew safe.

10/11.9. 40 58 Sqn T4134:T Missing from Bremen.
Plt Offs J. E. Thompson, and T. H. Hadley and Sgts K. D. Hall, W.
Hughes and W. Bull all PoW.

11/12.9. 40 10 Sqn P4941 Rear gunner baled out over Germany on
night operations. Aircraft undamaged.
Flt Lt D. G. Tomlinson and rest of crew returned safely.

11/12.9. 40 51 Sqn P4974 Damaged by Flak.
Flt Lt Barclay and crew unhurt.

12/13.9. 40 10 OTU P4997 Abandoned by four of crew in bad weather.
Flt Sgt L. F. East landed undamaged aircraft near St Neotts and flew
out next day.

14/15.9. 40 10 Sqn P4966 Ditched off Spurn Head.
Sqn Ldr K. F. Ferguson and Sgts C. S. Rogers, W. Fraser, E.
Cummings and M. Niman all rescued by HMS Kurd.

14/15.9. 40 78 Sqn N1478 Missing from Antwerp.
Plt Off C. S. Robson and Sgts L. J. Furze, R. M. Heyworth, J. Ketly
and J. C. Grieg all killed.

15/16.9. 40 77 Sqn P4917 Crashed landing at Tholthorpe on night
operations.

Sgt E. E. Fenning and crew safe.

17/18.9.40 78 Sqn P4964 Damaged by Flak.
Sgt R. Graham, rear gunner, wounded. Sgt A. S. Ennis and remainder of crew unhurt.

18/19.9.40 58 Sqn P5008:M Missing from Hamm. Crashed at Groenio, Holland.
Plt Off E. Ford and Sgts A. E. E. Crossland, C. F. Marshall, R. E. Salebury and W. D. Austen killed.

18/19.9.40 77 Sqn P4992:T Missing from Antwerp.
Plt Offs R. P. Brayne and W. M. Douglas and Sgts J. A. Raper, J. Baguley and D. V. Hughes all killed.

18/19.9.40 77 Sqn N1425:E Missing from Soest.
Plt Off P. E. Eldridge, Sub Lt Williams and Sgts V. C. Cowley, F Crawford and R. C. Dawson all killed.

21/22.9.40 51 Sqn P5105 Overshot Dishforth on night operations.
Sgt V. W. Bruce and crew safe.

23/24.9.40 10 Sqn P4946 Damaged by Flak.
Plt Off Bridson and crew unhurt.

23/24.9.40 77 Sqn P5046:O Missing from Berlin and ditched in North Sea. Two men found in dinghy on 26th, one dead.
Plt Off A. W. Dunn and Sgts D. A. Gibbons and B. L. Saville missing. Sgt D. B. Allen dead. Sgt G. H. Riley rescued injured.

23/24.9.40 77 Sqn P4992:L Belly landed at Appleton, Yorks.
Plt Off A. C. Akroyd-Stuart and crew safe.

24/25.9.40 10 Sqn P5055 Damaged by Flak.
Plt Off Steyn and crew unhurt.

24/25.9.40 10 Sqn —- Damaged by Flak, no casualties.

24/25.9.40 10 Sqn T4130 Force landed out of fuel. Damaged attempting to take-off after refuelling.
Sgt V. Snell and crew unhurt.

24/25.9.40 58 Sqn N1470 Crashed on take-off. Aircraft burnt.
Sgt H. Cornish, Plt Off A. I. Waterson and Sgt L. H. Taylor killed, Sgts Fowlie and Chamberlain injured.

30/1.10.40 10 Sqn T4130 Missing from Berlin. Shot down near Badbergen.

Sgts V. Snell and G. L. Ismay killed, Sgts W. D. Chamberlain, R. E. Nicholson and A. S. Shand PoW.

30/1.10.40 10 Sqn N1483 Ditched off Eire.
Flg Off L. D. Wood, Plt Off K. Humby, and Sgts E. R. Mounsey, C. Douglas-Browne and R. H. Thomas all rescued.

Footnotes
(1) 166 and 97 Squadrons, although equipped with Whitleys at this time, were used solely in the training role, later merging to become No 10 (Whitley) OTU. The two units later operated as heavy bomber squadrons later in the war with 1 and 5 Groups respectively. The casualties are noted above only as a matter of historical completeness.
(2) Although notes of damage appear in the Form 540 of the unit ORB, quite often the details were omitted from the Form 541, thus it is not possible to determine which aircraft was damaged.
(3) Although aircraft serial numbers were supposed to be entered in the unit ORB, sometimes they were not.
(4) The term 'safe' is used in place of 'unhurt', since no fatalities were recorded in the accident card, but it is possible that men were hurt.
(5) Names of the casualties were not specified in the unit ORB.
(6) OTU aircraft, operating under Bomber Command, flew frequent leaflet operations over occupied France during this period. The Whitley casualties are therefore included.

Record of Raids carried out by the Author with No. 10 Squadron
1939 - 1940

Note: All bombing sorties unless otherwise indicated. For further details see text.

7.9.39. Whitley K9023. Target Kiel. Captain Flg Off R. Bickford. Leaflet dropping - Successful.

15.10.39. Whitley K9023. Target Hamburg. Captain Flg Off R. Bickford. Leaflet dropping - returned with U/S aircraft.

31.10.39. Whitley K9023. Target Hamburg. Captain Flg Off R. Bickford. Night reconnaissance.

6.12.39. Whitley K9035. Target Eckenforde. Captain Flg Off R. Bickford. Leaflets. Tail-gunner frost-bitten.

23.12.39. Whitley K9035. Target shipping off the German Coast. Captain Flg Off R. Bickford. No enemy ships sighted. Daylight operation.

31.12.39. Whitley K9035. Target Borkum and Hornum. Captain Flg Off R. Bickford. 'Security Patrol'.

5.1.40. Whitley K9035. Target Borkum and Hornum. Captain Flg Off R. Bickford. 'Security Patrol'.

1.3.40. Whitley K9023. Target Berlin. Captain. Flg Off R. Bickford. Leaflets and recce.

16.3.40. Whitley K9023. Target Dusseldorf. Captain Flg Off R. Bickford. Leaflets and recce. Landed in France.

19.3.40. Whitley K9023. Target Hornum. Catpain Flg Off R. Bickford. Successful.

11.4.40. Whitley K9023. Target shipping in the Kattegat. Captain. Flt Lt R. Bickford. Supply ship bombed without result. Aircraft damaged by Flak-ship.

18.4.40. Whitley K9029. Target Kjeller airfield. Captain Flt Lt R.Bickford. Aborted due to bad weather.

23.4.40. Whitley K9029. Target Fornebu airfield. Captain Flt Lt R. Bickford. Bombed alternative target due to bad weather.

1.5.40. Whitley K9029. Target Stavanger airfield. Captain Flt Lt R. Bickford. Successful.

12.5.40. Whitley P4953. Mönchen-Gladbach. Captain Flt Lt R. Bickford. Successful. One E/A seen.

15.5.40. Whitley P4953. Target Dinant. Captain Flt Lt R. Bickford. Successful. One 250lb bomb hung-up.

17.5.40. Whitley P4967. Target Bremen. Captain Flt Lt R. Bickford. Successful. A/c badly damaged by Flak.

21.5.40. Whitley P4953. Target Julich. Captain Flg Off Henry. Successful. A/c damaged by Flak.

22.5.40. Whitley P4953. Target Givet. Captain Flg Off Henry. Successful. One 250lb bomb hung-up.

24.5.40. Whitley P4953. Target Binche. Captain Flg Off Henry. Successful.

25.5.40. Whitley P4953. Target Reisholz. Captain Flg Off Henry. Successful. One E/A seen.
6.6.40. Whitley P4953. Target Rheydt. Captain Flg Off Henry. Successful.
8.6.40. Whitley P4953. Target Essen. Captain Flg Off Henry. Successful.
9.6.40. Whitley P4953. Target Neufchateau. Captain Flg Off Henry. Successful.
11.6.40. Whitley P4953. Target Turin. Captain Flg Off Henry. Hit by lightning and aborted.
17.6.40. Whitley P4953. Target River Rhine/Bingen. Captain Flg Off Henry. 'W' bombs. Did not bomb.
24.7.40. Whitley P4957. Target Hamburg. Captain Flg Off Henry. Failed to find target. Did not bomb.
2.8.40. Whitley P4953. Target Salzbergen. Captain Flg Off Henry. Successful.
5.8.40. Whitley P4953. Target Wismar. Captain Flg Off Henry. Successful. A/c hit by Flak.
11.8.40. Whitley P4953. Target Gelsenkirchen. Captain Flg Off Henry. Successful. A/c hit by Flak.
13.8.40. Whitley P4953. Target Turin. Captain Flg Off Henry. Aborted with U/S engine.
16.8.40. Whitley P4966. Target Jena. Captain Flg Off Henry. Successful.
18.8.40. Whitley P4967. Target Rheinfelden. Captain Flg Off Henry. A/c hit by lightning. Did not bomb.
24.8.40. Whitley P4966. Target Milan. Captain Flg Off Henry. Successful.
8.9.40. Whitley P4962. Target Ostend. Captain Flg Off Prior. Failed to find target. Did not bomb.
11.9.40. Whitley P4952. Target Bremen. Captain Flg Off Prior. Successful.
14.9.40. Whitley P4957. Target Antwerp. Captain Flg Off Landale. Successful. Bf110 seen.
17.9.40. Whitley P4957. Target Hamburg. Captain Flg Off Landale. Tail turret U/S. Aborted.
19.9.40. Whitley T4143. Target Hamm. Captain Flg Off Landale. Successful. A/c damaged.
22.9.40. Whitley T4143. Target Lauta. Captain Flg Off Landale. Successful.
24.9.40. Whitley T4143. Target Finkenheerd. Captain Flg Off Landale. Primary not found. Bombed Alternative target.
27.9.40. Whitley T4143. Target Lorient. Captain Flg Off Landale. Successful.
30.9.40. Whitley T4143. Target Berlin. Captain Flt Lt Tomlinson. Successful.

Index to RAF Personnel

241

Green.D.W. Sgt. 178.
Gudgeon.F. LAC. 33.
Hall. Plt.Off. 94, 95.
Hall.E.L.G. Flt.Sgt. 116.
Hanafin.D.P. Sqn.Ldr. 90, 98, 113, 124.
Hannah.J. Sgt. 189.
Harris. Sir A. Air Marshal. 190.
Hastings.M. Sqn.Ldr. 92, 147.
Heayes. R. Sgt. 99.
Heller.A.J. LAC. 130.
Henry.M.T.P. Plt.Off. 25, 33, 39, 40, 42, 57, 59, 65, 66.
Henry.M.T.P. Fg.Off. 116, 158, 184, 214.
Hepburn. AC. 101.
Higson. Fg.Off. 178.
Hill. AC. 49.
Hillary.W.S. Sgt. 161.
Horrigan.O.G. Fg.Off. 98.
Howard.H.G.H. Sgt. 183.
Hutton.R. LAC. 57.
Hooper.E.H. Wg.Cdr. 68.
Irving. LAC.44.
Ives. AC. 49.
Jackson.R. Cpl. 123.
Johnson.A.S. Sgt. 73, 74, 97, 113, 161.
Johnston.N.R. Sgt. 117.
Jones.J.C.T. Plt.Off. 153.
Jones.J.B. Sgt.159.
Kearney.J.M. Sgt. 173.
Keast.L.A. Sgt. 139.
Knapper.A. Sgt. 65, 66, 156.
Landale.P.W.F. Fg.Off. 158, 184, 185, 203.
Lane.G.A. Fg.Off. 157.
Langton. Sgt. 157.
Lewis.P.M. Plt.Off. 155.

Long. Plt.Off. 61.
Lucas.M. Sgt. 132, 135, 214.
Ludlow-Hewitt. Sir. E. Air Chief Marshal. 67.
MacDonald.J.C. Sqn.Ldr. 73, 80, 90.
MacIntyre.J.C. Cpl. 80.
Mahaddie.T.G. Sgt. 43.
Mahaddie.T.G. Plt.Off. 116.
Maclaren.I.L. Flt.Lt. 119.
Marshall.J.R. Sgt. 174.
Martin. Flt.Sgt. 23, 32.
Marvin.G.P. Sqn.Ldr. 101.
Masham.S.E. Sgt. 143.
Mathews.T. AC. 20.
Mc.Coubrey.J.G. Sgt. 161.
Mc.Gregor.R.B. Plt.Off. 157.
Mc.Innes.J.T. Fg.Off. 143.
Mc.Kay.J.J. Fg.Off. 73.
Mc.Neil. Sgt. 134, 135.
Meigh.A.C. Plt.Off. 131.
Miller.A.E. Sgt. 82.
Millington.A. LAC. 57, 90.
Millington.A. Sgt. 178.
Millson.A.W. Plt.Off. 192.
Milne.T.K. Fg.Off. 98.
Monkhouse.V.C. Sgt. 158.
Murphy.K.H.P. Fg.Off. 98.
Murray.S.S. Sqn.Ldr. 42, 45.
Nelson.W.H. Fg.Off. 130, 143.
Newall Sir C. Marshal of the RAF 68.
Nicholson.R.E. Sgt. 192, 204.
Niman.M. Sgt. 194, 195, 215.
Nixon.W.M. Fg.Off. 179.
O'Brien. LAC. 95.
Oldridge.S. AC. 98, 124.
Owen.D.H.W. Flt.Lt. 117.
Parkes. AC. 115, 116.

Parrott.T.H. Fg.Off. 109.
Parson.E.I. Plt.Off. 161, 174.
Patterson.N.V.R. Fg.Off. 69.
Peers.W.E. Plt.Off. 198.
Phillips.A.S. Flt.Lt. 113, 114, 131.
Pickard.P. Wg.Cdr. 212.
Piddington.J.A. Fg.Off. 157, 159, 179.
Pike.V.F. Plt.Off. 179.
Portal Sir C. Air Marshal 153.
Prescott. Sgt. 115.
Prior.G.W. Fg.Off. 89, 179, 191, 193.
Pryde.D.D. Flt.Lt. 116, 158, 160.
Raphael.G.L. Fg.Off. 74, 115.
Raphael.G.L. Flt.Lt. 179.
Riley. Sgt. 200.
Robertson.D.F. Fg.Off. 170.
Robson.C.S. Plt.Off. 195.
Saddington.G.E. Plt.Off. 70, 91.
Scott.J.S. Flt.Lt. 179.
Sharpe.M.L. Sgt. 143, 174.
Shaw.J. Sgt. 158, 184.
Smith.H.V. Fg.Off. 117, 143, 144.
Snell.V. Sgt. 204.
Songest. Sgt. 138.
Staton.W.E. Wg.Cdr. 38, 49, 58, 59, 72, 80, 113, 123, 137, 138.
Staton.W.E. Gp.Capt. 155.
Stenhouse.W.A. Fg.Off. 174.
Still.R. Cpl. 58.
Stokes.A. Sgt. 177.
Storey. LAC. 115, 116.
Summerville. Sgt. 199, 203.
Swensen.S.P. Fg.Off. 174.
Tait.W.B. Sqn.Ldr. 134, 191.
Taylor.J.M. Plt.Off. 190.

Thomas.R.H. Plt.Off. 191.
Thompson.A.B. Plt.Off. 45.
Thompson.J.E. Plt.Off. 192.
Thompson.A.G. Sgt. 117.
Tindall. Sgt. 95, 96.
Tomlin.B.A. Flt.Lt. 74, 75, 76.
Tomlin.B.A. Sqn.Ldr. 131.
Tomlinson.G.D. Flt.Lt. 190, 193, 203.
Trenchard Lord H. Marshal of the RAF 191.
Turner.P. LAC. 49.
Turner.W.H.N. Sqn.Ldr. 115, 130.
Verran.J. Plt.Off. 176, 215.
Wakefield.F.G.J. Fg.Off. 57, 117.
Walker.G.A. Fg.Off. 144.
Walters.W.O. Sgt. 193.
Welte.H. Plt.Off. 102, 103.
Whitby.P.G. Fg.Off. 143.
Whitworth.J.N.H. Sqn.Ldr. 112, 155.
Williams.R. Fg.Off. 52.
Willis. Plt.Off. 49, 60.
Willis. Sgt. 195.
Witt.D. Sgt. 181, 215.
Womersley.G.H. Plt.Off. 117.
Wood.L.D. Fg.Off. 204.
Wynton.J.W.P. Flt.Sgt. 156.
Young.H.M. Plt.Off. 176.
Young.F.F. Sgt. 156.

Aircraft Serial Numbers

AW23. K3585. 11.

Mk.l. Prototype. K4586. 11.

Mk.l. K7191. 11.

Mk.IIIs.
K8947. 52.
K8950. 42.
K8951. 43.
K8980. 54.
K8984. 56.
K8985. 42.
K8989. 53.
K9008. 54.

Mk. IVs.
K9018. 49.
K9020. 69.
K9023. 37, 65, 74, 77, 97, 99, 102.
K9026. 74.
K9029. 97, 99.
K9032. 89.
K9035. 66.
K9039. 99.
K9043. 80, 97.
K9048. 98.

Mk.Vs.
N1342. 125.
N1346. 59, 172.
N1347. 70, 91.
N1348. 70, 116.
N1352. 93, 94.
N1356. 131.
N1357. 70, 81.
N1361. 119.

N1362. 138.
N1365. 74, 157, 179.
N1366. 74, 109.
N1371. 159.
N1372. 135.
N1376. 116.
N1377. 61, 63, 160.
N1378. 73.
N1380. 117.
N1381. 73.
N1383. 98.
N1384. 116, 158.
N1387. 75, 92.
N1388. 115.
N1405. 80.
N1406. 101.
N1408. 115.
N1410. 116.
N1414. 134, 191.
N1417. 116.
N1420. 90, 122.
N1421. 98.
N1424. 156.
N1425. 196.
N1427. 190.
N1434. 179.
N1442. 144.
N1446. 174.
N1453. 174.
N1459. 190.
N1460. 143.
N1461. 153.
N1463. 141.
N1465. 99.
N1466. 179.
N1469. 146.
N1470. 201.
N1472. 159.
N1473. 182.